MODERN
HOMOSEXUALITIES

Fragments of lesbian and gay experience

Edited by Ken Plummer

London and New York

First published in 1992
by Routledge
11 New Fetter Lane, London EC4P 4EE

Simultaneously published in the USA and Canada
by Routledge
a division of Routledge, Chapman and Hall, Inc.
29 West 35th Street, New York, NY 10001

© 1992, selection and editorial matter, Ken Plummer; each individual chapter,
the contributor

Phototypeset in 10pt Baskerville by
Mews Photosetting, Beckenham, Kent
Printed and bound in Great Britain by
Mackays of Chatham PLC, Chatham, Kent

British Library Cataloguing in Publication Data
A catalogue record for this book is available from the British Library.

Library of Congress Cataloging in Publication Data
Modern homosexualities: fragments of lesbian and gay experience /
edited by Ken Plummer.
p.   cm.
Includes bibliographical references and index.
1. Homosexuality. 2. Lesbians. 3. Gays. I. Plummer, Kenneth.
HQ76.25.M63   1992
305.9′0664–dc20   92-6434
                                                                CIP
ISBN 0-415-06420-1
0-415-06421-X (pbk)

MODERN HOMOSEXUALITIES

Homosexuality is not what it used to be. When the modern lesbian and gay movements erupted on the world-wide cultural and political stage during the early 1970s, few could have seen the enormous ramifications. For although homosexuality still has its critics and its enemies, the modern lesbian and gay community has proliferated into distinctive ways of living together, of relating sexually, of responding to AIDS, of establishing identities and communities, and of being political. This book documents some of this rich and developing experience.

Modern Homosexualities presents 'fragments' of an experience that has become remarkably diverse. In nineteen original essays from activists and social scientists in eight countries, some of this diversity is charted. It is a unique collection, which draws together essays on a wide range of experience. The book explores the emergence of new communities and identities and the impact of AIDS on these communities. A major section examines the development and recognition of new patterns of 'families of choice' such as the Danish experiment in 'registered partnerships', the Australian immigration definition of lesbian and gay couples, the debate over lesbian motherhood, the issue of 'mixed marriages' where one partner is gay, and the new friendship networks among many lesbians and gay men which have themselves become 'new families'. There are discussions of the creation of new patterns of sexualities among lesbians, and the rise of renewed political campaigning in the face of a 'backlash'. While the focus of the book is the distinctive modern experiences found in Western countries such as Australia, Denmark, England, the Netherlands, Canada, and the USA, there are essays on Turkey and Mesoamerica which help create a baseline for comparative studies. Gay and lesbian studies is a vibrant new area of inquiry, and a major opening essay situates this development.

Modern Homosexualities will be required reading for lesbian and gay scholars, continuing as it does the task of developing a critical, interpretative and humanistic social studies around same-sex experience. It will be a landmark in consolidating past debates and suggesting pathways to the future.

Ken Plummer is Reader in Sociology at the University of Essex and Visiting Professor in Sociology at the University of California at Santa Barbara.

IN MEMORIAM

Philip Blumstein
Laud Humphreys
Levi G.W. Kamel
Richard Troiden

CONTENTS

CONTENTS

Part VI Shifting sexualities: the lesbian case

Part VII Making the future: radicalism, rights, and citizenship in the UK

CONTRIBUTORS

Barry D. Adam is Professor of Sociology at the University of Windsor (Ontario, Canada) and author of *The Survival of Domination* (New York: Elsevier/Greenwood) and *The Rise of a Gay and Lesbian Movement*. He is currently doing research in new social movement theory and on 'Impacts of HIV on personal, family and work relationships'. He has published on AIDS in *Contemporary Crises* and in *The Social Context of AIDS* (edited by Joan Huber and Beth Schneider).

Jason Annetts is a postgraduate student-teacher at the University of Reading, UK, where he specializes in media and sexual politics courses. He has co-authored *Soft-Core* and 'Snuff sex and Satan: contemporary legends and moral politics'; and he is currently researching male prostitution for a PhD. He is an equal rights activist in the Thames Valley area.

Henning Bech is presently engaged in a research project at the Institute of Cultural Sociology, University of Copenhagen, on various aspects of modernity. He has written a number of books and articles on homosexuality. He has conducted research for the Danish Parliament and Government; is an adviser to the Swedish social authorities on questions concerning research into homosexuality; and is a member of the editorial board of the *Journal of the History of Sexuality* and the *Zeitschrift für Sexualforschung*.

Vicki Carter was born in Bristol in 1962, escaping finally to London through a career in theatre and working for many small political theatre companies including Gay Sweatshop. She then did a BA in Women's Studies and Drama at Middlesex Polytechnic in London, spending a semester at Sacramento State University in California. She was involved in the Stop Clause 28 campaign, regrettably not as an abseiler. She is now a volunteer for London Lesbian and Gay Switchboard and working in broadcasting. This piece originated as her thesis.

Peter Davies underwent education in Llanelli, Oxford, and Cardiff where he did his PhD on disclosure networks of gay men and was active – in a fairly laid-back sort of way – in gay politics. He has lectured at South Bank Polytechnic and is currently a lecturer in sociology at the University of Essex. Since 1987 he has been Director of Project Sigma, the largest empirical investigation of the sexual behaviour of gay and bisexual men ever undertaken in the UK.

Tim Edwards completed his PhD 'The AIDS dialectics' at Essex University in 1990 and previous publications include 'Beyond sex and gender: masculinity, homosexuality and social theory' in Hearn and Morgan (eds) *Men, Masculinities and Social Theory* (1990). He is currently lecturing at Oxford Polytechnic and completing *Erotic Politics*, a work on contemporary sexual political history.

Maggie French gained her BA and MPhil from the University of Essex. She is currently teaching at Essex and has for several years been teaching for the University of Maryland. She has recently held ESRC and Essex County Council funded posts at Essex, investigating transport policy and elderly people, and has published several articles including 'Becoming a lone parent', in G. Crowe and M. Hardey (eds) *Lone Parenthood* (1991) and 'An ethnographic study of transport and elderly people', *BASAPP* Spring 1991.

John Hart left school at 15 and later went to the London School of Economics. After working as a probation officer and psychiatric social worker he taught in universities and polytechnics before migrating to Australia. He has written four books on sexuality, obtained his PhD in 1991, and is currently a Lecturer in the Department of Social Work and Social Policy, University of Sydney, Australia.

Valerie Jenness is an Assistant Professor of Sociology at Washington State University and gained her doctorate from the University of California at Santa Barbara. In addition to her work on lesbian identities, she has published work on the contemporary prostitutes' rights movement and is currently working in the area of hate crimes.

Stephen O. Murray is a sociologist working in public health in San Francisco. An activist and a prolific writer, he is the author of *Social Theory, Homosexual Realities* (1984). His most recent book is *Oceanic Homosexualities*.

Peter M. Nardi is Professor of Sociology at Pitzer College, one of the Claremont Colleges located near Los Angeles, California. He has published articles on AIDS, anti-gay hate crimes and violence, magic and magicians, and alcoholism and families. He has recently edited a book on *Men's Friendships* for Sage Publications. He has also served as co-president of the Los Angeles chapter of the Gay and Lesbian Alliance Against Defamation.

Ken Plummer lectures in sociology at Essex University and has been a frequent visiting Professor at the University of California at Santa Barbara. He is the author of *Sexual Stigma* (1975) and *Documents of Life* (1983) and has edited *The Making of the Modern Homosexual* (1981) and *Symbolic Interaction* (Vols 1 and 2, 1991). He was an original member of the London GLF.

Diane Richardson currently lectures in the Department of Sociological Studies at the University of Sheffield and has been a visiting professor at San Francisco State University and at Murdoch University, Perth, Western Australia, where she was Visiting Scholar in Women's Studies. She has written extensively about the social construction of sexuality and lesbianism and is well known for her work on safer sex and how AIDS affects women. Her books include *The Theory and Practice of Homosexuality* (1981), *Women and the AIDS Crisis* (2nd edition, 1989), *Safer Sex* (1990), *Women, Motherhood and Childrearing* (1992), and *Introducing Women's Studies* (1992).

Pat Romans undertook her doctoral research into lesbian motherhood at the University of Essex. With her lesbian partner she has also managed, fairly successfully, to foster over fifty children – despite her sexual orientation! She seems to be spending a lot of her time lately talking to the media about this.

Beth E. Schneider is Associate Professor of Sociology at the University of California, Santa Barbara. She has written extensively on the sexualization of the workplace, lesbians at work, the contemporary women's movement, and women and AIDS. Forthcoming is her book with Joan Huber, *The Social Context of AIDS*. She currently serves as the President of the Board of Directors of the Gay and Lesbian Resource Center/AIDS Counseling and Assistance Program of Santa Barbara.

Judith Schuyf (1951) studied history and archaeology at Leiden University (the Netherlands). She spent six years in the Geography Department of Utrecht University researching small landscape features. While doing this, she became active in the lesbian and gay movement. Lesbian/gay media have held her interest: she wrote for *Homologie* and *Homojaarboek* and chaired a group that connected with lesbians/gays on radio and television. She is one of the founder-members of the Department of Lesbian/Gay Studies at Utrecht University where she is currently a lecturer in gay and lesbian history. She is a member of a government committee on violence against homosexuals and is writing a book on lesbian life-styles in the Netherlands prior to 1970.

Anna Marie Smith completed her doctoral dissertation on British New Right discourses on race, nation, and sexuality at Essex University and has published many articles on topics such as Section 28 (in *New Formations*,

Summer 1990), lesbian representation (in Boffin and Fraser (eds) *Stolen Glances*, 1991), and feminism and censorship (in McIntosh and Segal (eds) *Sex Exposed: Sexuality and the Pornography Debate*, 1991). She has also contributed to *Feminist Review*, *Square Peg*, *On Our Backs*, *Marxism Today* and *The Body Politic*. A revised version of her doctoral dissertation will be published as a book entitled *The Difference in Identity: British New Right Discourse on Race and Sexuality* (London: Verso, 1992). She currently holds a Canada Council post-doctoral fellowship and is engaged in research at the Centre for Theoretical Studies at the University of Essex. She is the co-founder of PUSSY (Perverts Undermining State Scrutiny), an affinity group in OutRage. PUSSY brings lesbians and gay men together in the fight against censorship from outside and within the community, and aims to put sex back into sexual politics.

Huseyin Tapinc gained an MA from Essex University in 1990, and has published articles on masculinity and homosexuality in Turkey. He is currently writing a book on arabesque music in Turkish society.

Peter Tatchell is an author, journalist, and activist. An adviser to MPs on AIDS and lesbian and gay issues, he is involved with the campaigning groups ACT UP and OutRage, and is the author of *The Battle for Bermondsey* (1983), *Democratic Defence – A Non-Nuclear Alternative* (1985), *AIDS: A Guide to Survival* (1990), and *Europe in the Pink: Lesbian and Gay Equality in the New Europe* (1992).

Bill Thompson, having completed a PhD at Essex University on contemporary moral crusades and British fundamentalist religion, now teaches at Reading University, where he established the Human Sexuality and Gender Course. He co-authored *Soft-Core* with Jason Annetts, is completing a study of antipornography crusades, and is a well-known public advocate of civil rights for sexual minorities.

PREFACE

Homosexuality is not what it used to be. In scarcely a quarter of a century, same-sex experiences in the Western world have been ruptured from the simplified, unified, distorting, often medical, frequently criminal, always devalued categories of the past. Instead, they have increasingly become a diverse array of relational, gendered, erotic, political, social, and spiritual experiences, difficult to tame and capture with restrictive and divisive labels. Criss-crossing their way through class, gender, and ethnicity, a stream of emerging identities, new experiences, political practices, and ways of living together have been firmly placed on the political agendas of the future. In just two decades – symbolically since Stonewall and the rise of the second wave women's movement – the loves that once dared not speak their name, that were hidden from history, that were shrouded in stigma have emerged as a visible and vocal force. This book is an attempt to capture a little of this new understanding of *Modern Homosexualities*.

One sign of these enormous changes has been the growth of a rich, diverse, and literate new area of interdisciplinary, intellectual inquiry: lesbian and gay studies, the topic of Chapter 1. In reading lesbian and gay biographies before the 1970s it is a commonplace to hear how, in the search for self-understanding, little helpful literature could be found: most of what existed then was clinical, destructive, life-negating. It led people to believe they were freaks, alone in the world. This is certainly not the case today. Not only has the sheer volume of writing multiplied – one study compares 500 books listed in print in 1969 with 9,000 by 1989 (Gough and Greenblatt, 1990: xxi) – but so too has its range of questions, disciplines, readers. Writings on homosexualities have been largely rescued from the voices of the scientific 'experts' questing for the 'truth' of the homosexual person and have instead become the voices of the people with these experiences. Voices now speak publicly that were hardly capable of being imagined even two decades ago: film-makers, poets, artists, musicians, priests and priestesses, nuns, dramatists, novelists, politicians, librarians, educationalists, researchers. This is the new world where children and youth can write books telling their parents they are gay, while parents can write books telling their children they are gay! A radically new dialogue is emerging. Of course there are many enemies angered at the emergence of so many wide-ranging voices testifying to same-sex experiences. But it will be hard for them to stop their proliferation.

Modern Homosexualities brings together a range of voices concerned with documenting further the new range of experiences on the agenda. My introductory chapter provides a brief overview of lesbian and gay studies, telling the story of an important new area of inquiry: its pasts, presents, and futures. The significance of this area of inquiry should not be seen simply as reflecting changes in the lesbian and gay experience, as merely descriptive. For such writings never simply reflect the world: they also actively assemble it, setting languages, images, metaphors, discourses which enable a re-visioning and a re-creating. It enables us to move beyond the given worlds into newer, and hopefully more emancipating ones. The chapter describes how the various disciplines have each in turn made their contributions and established their relevance; how various conflicts have pushed the field ahead; and it suggests a series of key themes for the future.

The next section of the book could look a little out of place in a book on modern homosexualities, for the two chapters document experiences – here, of men – in Turkey and Mesoamerica that may partly be outside the routine understandings of the 'modern' West. Importantly, though, they further illustrate the power of social constructionist analysis by signposting the wide-ranging diversities of lesbian and gay experiences across the world. They hence serve as a baseline to see how socially variable and shifting same-sex experiences are. The two articles here present 'fragments' of male experience for cultures where the family is central and the meanings given to same-sex experience highlight the distinction between masculine and feminine ways of men being with men, meanings which dominated the Western model until very recently. Both essays seem to connect to the earlier, pre-Stonewall, Western model of lesbian and gay experience where polarized gender played a stronger role than it does today. Both essays present valuable models for thinking about different patterns of same-sex experience, and suggest how crucial roles are assigned in these societies to religion and the family in socially organizing same-sex experience.

The next section points to concerns which have been central to lesbian and gay research over the past two decades: identity and community. Knowing oneself to be gay and living in a gay community are the hallmarks of the modern gay and lesbian. While this may in fact neglect many same-sex experiences which are not organized this way, few would deny the centrality of both identity and community as crucial pivots of what may be termed the modern experience. These are issues returned to regularly throughout the book in other contributions. But here the authors spell out some central issues in the formation of communities and the construction of identities. Each author comes from a different country – the Netherlands,

England, and North America; two deal with lesbianism and one with male gays. Yet, across country and gender, I sense a commonality of concern. Judith Schuyf may speak of lesbian communities in the 1950s in the Netherlands, but shades of these are still identifiably around in the 1990s. The earlier communities keep their lingering traces but are being supplemented with an ever-growing range of possibilities, and this is as true of the male gay world as of the lesbian one. Val Jenness may speak of the lesbian categorization problem, but it is surely equally applicable to men, as Peter Davies' article makes clear. 'Coming out' is the momentous moment of the modern homosexual experience: the moment of entering the personhood of gay and lesbian publicly and of exiting from the closet, at least in part. Implicitly, the themes of these discussions inform much of the remainder of the book.

Five key essays on 'pretending to be families' follow. 'The family' has taken on a new centrality in gay and lesbian debates (cf. Weston 1991). For sure, one of the most recurrent of grounds for modern attacks on homosexuality declares that it is a threat to the traditional family, and it it most surely is. Gays and lesbians show that it is possible to live outside the blood-linked nuclear family. But the debate on the family goes much further than this, for gays and lesbians have become one of a number of groups actively involved in the redefining of the basis of family life, of ways of living together, of loving and of supporting each other. Modern homosexualities may, most ironically, be signs of the family to come. Gays and lesbians, far from being pretend families, show the shapes of future, even postmodern, families. At the very least, we can see now so clearly that gay and lesbian lives touch upon existing families in numerous ways – as sons and daughters, aunts and uncles, mums and dads, brothers and sisters, grandparents, step-parents and stepchildren. But we can see more: new families may be increasingly matters of conscious choice and less of congealed blood.

The article by Maggie French discusses her English research on one of these family relationships: the situation where one partner of a marriage decides he or she is gay or lesbian, and she traces the stages of such relationships. For Pat Romans, the theme is lesbian motherhood – women loving women who raise children. Another sign for the future? For Peter Nardi, the theme is 'friends as family': how the lesbian and gay communities provide opportunities for love and care that are as strong as any traditional family, and which may indeed provide blueprints for future relationships. Legal recognition of gay or lesbian marriage is happening in quite a few countries, and these are among the themes pursued by John Hart and Henning Bech.

It is clear then that at the turn of the twentieth century family experiences mean something very different from those at the turn of the nineteenth century. 'Families' are everywhere, but they are different. Their dark side is now clearly seen; but so too is their diversity and range across the life cycle. Such diversities are surely a threat to the family as traditionally conceived, but they are not in its newer, richer, and more complex forms. Here they are very much part of the new 'families'. The five articles in this section make us aware of these newly emerging forms, giving us a glimpse of the future. Although all the articles highlight oppression as a backdrop to the modern lesbian and gay experience, they also signpost how new worlds are being made: vibrant, positive, and curiously familial. Is this the shape of things to come?

No late twentieth-century writing on same-sex experience can neglect AIDS and HIV. Both as disease and and as symbol it has played a powerful part in the reshaping of gay and lesbian communities throughout the 1980s. The articles in the next section are clearly concerned with the tragic nature of the diease: with the death and the grief that has touched so many lives. But they go well beyond this. For predictions of 'holocausts' and the 'end of the homosexual' have been transcended. Instead, these articles demonstrate the growth of new communities of support, care, and activism. Taken together, these three articles depict a range of new ways of living in the future. One contribution by Tim Edwards talks to gay men about their experiences around HIV and AIDS, tracing their awareness of it, how it influenced their identities and sexualities, and most intriguingly how it shaped their view of death. The two other articles – by Beth Schneider and Barry Adam, established commentators in this field – discuss the broad impact of AIDS on the lesbian and gay communities. Once again, the recurrent themes of family, identity, support, care, and community surface.

The next section turns to the issue of sexualities and focuses upon the lesbian experience. Just as there is nothing fixed about 'the homosexual', so there is nothing fixed about 'the sexual'. All that is solid melts into air. The sexuality of modern gay men in the 1970s was often 'fast', but during the 1980s – with AIDS education playing a major role – it often shifted gears into a more affectionate, even romantic, mode. Certainly, 'non-penetrative' sex became a part of safer sex. But for women the story shifts in a slightly different direction. Deprived in the past of a sexual language by a predominantly male culture, lesbianism was largely constructed as either romantic or a male 'turn on'. The two articles presented here take us into the reformulation of lesbian desire. Diane Richardson argues for the inscription of a new lesbian language of sexuality, for new ways of talking about sexuality, enhancing and facilitating a lesbian sex. Anna Marie Smith argues for the need to place this language in a public and political context, to challenge and overthrow the hegemony of traditional politics and their discourses.

The final essays of the book turn more explicitly to aspects of campaigning. The history of the 'homophile movement' might stretch back a hundred years, but the gay and lesbian movement really comes into its own from the early 1970s onwards as one of the new social movements shaping new communities, identities, and politics. From its inception, and like other movements, it has been riddled with internal schisms and conflicts as to appropriate strategies of change. Some recent commentators have suggested that we should smarten up our act and behave more like 'normals'. At the other extreme, some have grown so weary of so little progress within a generation that they have returned to a confrontational, aggressive campaigning which is exactly what others have condemned. Thus, OutRage in London employs direct action techniques such as kiss-ins, while in New York both 'outing' and Queer Nation have been established as new confrontational methods. In between, though not mutually exclusive from either of these positions, are those campaigning for a systematic charter of gay and lesbian rights within a model of citizenship. The three articles presented here are concerned with the political situation in the UK, but they have wider implications for the continuing issue of how to move ahead.

All the articles in this book have signposted changes in lesbian and gay experiences: they all move us beyond traditional notions of homosexuality, describing experiences already with us while anticipating trends to come. As such they are not only sociological descriptions but essays on political possibilities, fragments of futures. While the book aims to document experiences, in the very act of documentation it renders itself a text, and like all texts must come to have a life of its own. Of course, no text such as this can have a deep coherence: the offerings are only 'fragments' which provide certain voices on key aspects of lesbian and gay experiences. Many voices still remain absent, and their fragments must be found elsewhere. But crucial themes for the future are lodged in this book: the essays will be of direct, practical, and continuing relevance to the lesbian, gay, and bisexual communities over the next few years. Concerns that were established in the earlier days of lesbian and gay studies – such as questions of identity and community – lie side by side with current concerns over the family, internationalization (or globalization), politically correct sex, campaigning strategies and the new activism, and the continuing impact of AIDS on both the lesbian and gay communities. Taken as a whole they tell a positive and encouraging story of change.

At the same time, we are still left with fragments, and I hope the essays in this book can be approached this way. Gone are the days when the full truth of homosexuality could ever hope to be revealed, and here instead are partial perspectives on current experiences that can in no way be taken to signpost any massive truth or trend. Gay and lesbian experiences are, quite simply, too diffuse, too variable, too historically changing, too ambiguous to be captured by our neater and tidier story-telling about them. Hopefully such stories as are found here will jostle the imagination of the reader. They will succeed if they can provide some more metaphors for living life, some more complexities to disturb old routines, some more politics to disrupt the factions of the past, some more views to puncture the now crumbling view of a unified social order. Largely small-scale studies informed by politics, social science, or both, vast portions of lesbian and gay experience still remain missing from these tales. What we need are more and more fragments to guide us into the future: this book is one more step in the accumulation of them.

Santa Barbara
November 1991

Part I

INTRODUCTION
Gay and lesbian world making

The past twenty years have seen the growth of an enormous literature on gay and lesbian experience. This introductory article reviews its past, locates some of the controversies of the present, and anticipates a future. It tells the story of an important new area of inquiry.

A literature such as this never simply reflects the world it describes: it also actively assembles it. Lesbian and gay writing is engaged in the process described by the philosopher Nelson Goodman as 'world making'. It sets languages, images, metaphors, discourses which enable a re-visioning and a re-creating. It enables us to move beyond the given worlds into newer, and hopefully more emancipating, ones.

1

SPEAKING ITS NAME

Inventing a lesbian and gay studies

Ken Plummer

Solidarity is not discovered by reflection but created. It is created by increasing our sensitivity to the particular details of the pain and humiliation of other, unfamiliar sorts of people. Such increased sensitivity makes it more difficult to marginalise people different from ourselves by thinking 'They do not feel as *we* would', or 'There must always be suffering, so why not let *them* suffer?'. This process of coming to see other human beings as 'one of us' rather than as 'them' is a matter of detailed description of what unfamiliar people are like and of redescription of what we ourselves are like.

(Rorty 1989: xvi)

In the past, people have invented for themselves many forms of expression, forms of language, writing, mathematics, forms of art, forms of war, forms of family and community organisation; in short, they have invented for themselves 'forms of life'. And there is no reason to suppose that the process by which we transformed ourselves from cave dwellers in the past to what we are now is at an end. Cultural progress is surely still possible.

(Shotter 1984: 49)

A century ago, homosexuality was the love that dared not speak its name; now it has become a veritable Tower of Babel. For this is the Golden Age of gay and lesbian studies. Walk into a major city in the Western world, find the local lesbian and gay bookstore, and browse. An enormous, diverse, and rich literature has been produced on every conceivable aspect of gay life: from scientific studies to great literary experiences; from tour guides of the international gay world to lesbian sex manuals; from medical, legal, and self-help handbooks to lesbian detective stories, gay science fiction, and AIDS comic strips. It is still under siege from many political forces, but the sheer quantity and variety make this a New Time.

Gay and lesbian studies has become a major area of scholarship, smaller but comparable to black studies and women's studies. In universities and

INTRODUCTION

colleges around the Western world, courses have been offered. Some of the most prestigous universities in the USA – Harvard, Princeton, Yale, Berkeley, New York City, MIT, Duke, Santa Cruz, San Francisco – have hosted conferences or established courses. In Europe, the Gay and Lesbian Studies Centre at the University of Utrecht has employed a staff of thirty working in this field. Erasmus, the educational wing of the European Community, has funded several 'lesbian and gay studies' conferences for European students. And Toronto, Denmark, London, New York, and Amsterdam have all been the sites of international conferences. The *Journal of Homosexuality* was first published in 1974 and has become distinctive for its 'special issues' on topics as diverse as sodomy and history, gay youth, elderly gays and lesbians, alcoholism, and 'the family', and it has spawned several others such as the *Journal of Gay and Lesbian Psychotherapy* and the *Journal of the History of Sexuality*. There is the *European Gay Review*. Lesbian studies has produced several autonomous journals including *Sinister Wisdom*, *Hypatia – A Journal of Feminist Philosophy*, *Lesbian Ethics*, and *TRIVIA: A Journal of Ideas*. *Feminism and Psychology* and other feminist journals like *Signs* and *Feminist Review* incorporate many articles on lesbianism. Although homosexualities may still be stigmatized in many ways, it is clear that some real gains are being made in the areas of research, teaching, and scholarship. There is now, as Jeffrey Escoffier (1990) has nicely put it, an 'ivory closet', with several generations of scholars, the most recent of whom have grown up in a world where many of the assumptions of both feminist and anti-heterosexist inquiry have been routinely taken as baseline. This book is a product of this time.

BACK TO THE FUTURE:
A SHORT HISTORY OF LESBIAN AND GAY STUDIES

A first wave?

Gay and lesbian writing does not start in the 1970s, but seeps back into history. I am not suggesting returning to some notion of a universal lesbian and gay literature found in Socrates, Sappho, or Shakespeare. Instead, I am talking about a much more self-conscious and self-identified 'gay and lesbian literature' – sometimes disguised, but certainly informed by a sense of the modern *identity* of being gay in a context of *oppression*. This – the modern, Western homosexual – I take to be a unique, historically distinct experience and one which is the focus of this book.

The earliest self-conscious accounts start to arrive in the late nineteenth century. They emerge at the very moment when the homosexual category was being established alongside the hetero/homo binary split that has organized much of Western twentieth-century thinking (Sedgwick 1991). It was a time when the homophile rights movement was creating the first wave of 'gay liberation' alongside its frequent ally, the women's movement.

4

Ironically, it has now become increasingly clear that some of these earlier studies of the causes and classifications of 'the homosexual' – to be denounced by the 1970s – were in fact done by men (qua men) who would, these days, almost certainly be gay identified (but could not then because the very idea hardly existed). I am thinking of K.M. Kertbeny, the Hungarian doctor who coined the term 'homosexual' in 1869; of Karl Heinrich Ulrichs, whose term 'uranian' embraced the mistaken idea of a third sex with a woman's mind in a man's body, and vice versa – an idea which misleadingly pervades much contemporary sexology; of Magnus Hirschfeld, whose Scientific Humanitarian Committee and Institute for Sex Research inspected the lives of thousands of 'homosexuals' (Lauritsen and Thorstad 1974; Weeks, 1977). For lesbians the literature was different: mainly lodged in the Victorian male discourses of law, medicine, and pornography, it was murkier, more hidden, and more stigmatized. Women did not have much of their own discourse on sexuality outside that imposed by men, one that was usually very negative, rendering the lesbian into a morbid pathology directly linked to the diseased male homosexual (Faderman 1981; Jeffreys 1989). Nevertheless, several patterns of lesbianism become consolidated in this period: those of the Bohemian such as George Sand and of the middle-class cross-dresser such as Rosa Bonheur, and 'Romantic Friendships' (Faderman 1981; Vicinus 1989). It is in literature however that the new lesbian started to emerge, as part of the construction of the new woman (Smith-Rosenberg 1985), canonically and controversially as the 'mythic mannish lesbian' of *The Well of Loneliness* (Newton 1984; Showalter 1991).

For all their now much-considered flaws, these early writings of the modern period start providing an articulation and a coherence to 'the homosexual' as a distinctly modern idea. A lot of this writing, already underground, becomes more or less obliterated during the 1930s and the 1940s, only to resurface again – with ever-increasing clarity and confidence – from the 1950s onwards. And with it comes a shifting understanding of homosexuality, shifts that take it from being a largely medical and pathological condition to those that increasingly see it as social and political. Rose Weitz (1984), in her analysis of *The Ladder*, the first significant lesbian periodical in America, published between 1956 and 1972, dramatically details such a change and the growth of a politicized, radical approach.

A second wave

A much more explicit and articulate literature starts to emerge however with the advent of the homophile movement trickling into existence throughout the 1950s and the 1960s, and symbolically arriving through the new women's liberation movement and the Stonewall riots of the late 1960s (D'Emilio 1983). This is a literature written primarily by *male gays and lesbians about the male gay and lesbian experience: explicit, open, out.* Most of

5

these earlier writings occurred outside universities, published as articles in short-lived gay and lesbian newspapers or as campaigning pamphlets (becoming more widely accessible through anthologies such as *The Homosexual Dialectic, The Gay Liberation Book, The Lesbian Reader,* or *A Lesbian Feminist Anthology* (e.g. Covina and Galana 1975; Richmond and Noguera 1973).

In this early period, it was lesbian feminist theory which produced the most developed theoretical analysis of homosexuality, centrally as a critique of heterosexual relations (later to be called 'compulsory heterosexuality' (Rich 1980)). Although from the outset there were many feminists who rejected both sexuality in general and lesbianism in particular, a strong tendency was to argue for lesbianism as a revolutionary act: 'a lesbian is the rage of all women condensed to the point of explosion' (Radicalesbians, 1973); 'feminism is the theory, lesbianism the practice' (Ti-Grace Atkinson, cited in Echols 1989: 238); 'Feminism is the complaint, lesbianism the solution' (Johnston 1973). Some of the most influential ideas grew out of the Lavender Menace in May 1970 (Echols 1989: 214) and the Radicalesbian position paper on the 'Woman-identified woman' in which they argued:

> Only women can give to each other a new sense of self. That identity we have to develop with reference to ourselves, and not in relation to men. . . . Our energies must flow toward our sisters, not backward toward our oppressors. As long as women's liberation tries to free women without facing the basic heterosexual structure that binds us in one to one relationships with our oppressors, tremendous energies will continue to flow into trying to straighten up each particular relationship with a man . . . this obviously splits our energies and commitments.
>
> (Echols 1989: 216)

The analysis of political lesbianism extends the meaning of lesbianism beyond physical sex, progressively to capture an extensive world of womanly feeling, ritual, spirituality, culture. It weaves out into Jill Johnston's *Lesbian Nation*, Mary Daly's gynocentric universe, or Adrienne Rich's lesbian continuum: 'a range – through each woman's life and throughout history – of woman-identified experience'. This position has gained strength since this time (as lesbian separatism), but it has not been without its critics from both women of colour and women of desire (Moraga *et al.* 1983; Vance 1984).

The most prominent early text of gay male theory was Dennis Altman's (1971) *Homosexual: Liberation/Oppression*, which set up a range of debates to be constantly refined over the next twenty years. He highlighted the creation of a new identity with the rise of the lesbian and gay movement, distinctive from the past and hinting at 'identity politics' (cf. Phelan 1989). He provided one of the earliest analyses of 'persecution, discrimination, tolerance', then not a commonplace. Subsequent writers have developed this idea, such as

6

the French liberationist Guy Hocquenghem who began his book in 1972 by declaring 'The problem is not so much homosexual desire as the fear of homosexuality: why does the mere mention of the word trigger off reactions of recoil and hate?' (Hocquenghem 1978: 35). Altman's work, like so much of this time, was informed partly by a Marxist Freudianism and partly by the countercultures of the late 1960s, bringing a certain optimism about the possibilities of liberation. A curious recognition, present at the outset in Altman's book and a recurrent theme, is the idea that a true liberation would also dissolve the very object of liberation, the homosexual, since the idea itself is predicated upon the very distinctions to be attacked. As Beshtain remarked a decade later, 'A politics that would culminate in the withering away of the group on whose behalf its efforts are being mounted is a strange politics indeed' (Beshtain 1982/3: 253). It is the paradox of gay liberation. Here also in this modern text of gay liberation the issue of race is raised, an issue which anticipates an array of splits to follow in the 1970s and 1980s.

Altman has continued to be at the forefront of gay analysis, but it is interesting to reread this early classic to see just how far he anticipated most of the major debates (cf. Altman 1982a; Altman 1986). There are relatively few who follow in his wake: Guy Hocquenghem's *Homosexual Desire* (1978) and Mario Mieli's *Homosexuality and Liberation* (1980) from continental Europe, collections edited by Gay Left in 1980, David Fernbach's *The Spiral Path* (1981), and the writings of Jeffrey Weeks (1977, 1981a, 1981b, 1985, 1991) signpost the main UK work; while in the United States radical theory is largely ignored: Michael Bronski's much later *Culture Clash* (1984) stands out as a contribution. Only very recently with the growth of 'queer theory' has a more sophisticated theoretical turn been taken (see De Lauretis 1991; Fuss 1991; Warner 1991).

At the same time as these early radical publications were appearing, an important development was under way: the institutionalization of gay and lesbian 'studies' as a field of academic professionalized 'scholarship', complete with its own PhDs, reading lists, professors, centres, conferences, and courses. This was less than new. In some countries there had been earlier attempts to establish such work: Hirschfeld's Institute in Germany in the 1920s, various comparable centres in the Netherlands (Tielman 1988), and in North America the Institute for Homophile Studies, an alternative university, which enrolled over 1,000 students in the academic year 1957–8. Nevertheless, there was a definite take-off point during the 1970s, making this area of study internationally recognizable and comparable to developments in women's studies or ethnic studies (though much smaller, because so much more stigmatized). Such developments should not however be overstated: they were thin on the ground; in some countries, like the UK, negligible, and they were always conducted against a barrage of abuse and hostility. Below I will attempt briefly to survey some of these developments.

7

An interdisciplinary project: a brief review of trends

Gay and lesbian scholarship has embraced many disciplines – disciplines which sometimes speak past each other. In the 1970s, psychology, sociology, and history were particularly influential, while throughout the 1980s versions of cultural studies/literary theory and postmodern feminism became increasingly prominent. AIDS, as an area of research and theory, also came to play a central role during this latter period.

Psychology critiqued the sickness model, argued that homosexuals were really normal, just like everybody else, and maybe even 'healthier than straights' (Freedman 1975); introduced 'homophobia' as a major new concept; and analysed life-style differences – a crucial concern that continues today in such volumes as *Lesbian Psychologies* (Boston Lesbian Psychologies Collective 1987) and *Lesbianism: Affirming Nontraditional Roles* (Rothblum and Cole 1989; see also Gonsiorek and Weinrich 1991). Sociology studied subcultures (cf. Humphreys 1971; Ettore 1980; Risman and Schwartz 1988; Herdt 1992), but its key achievement was to shift focus from 'the homosexual' as a type of person to a concern with social responses to homosexuality which lead to radically different social constructions of same-sex experiences (McIntosh 1968; Gagnon and Simon 1973; Plummer 1975, 1981; Greenberg 1988; Stein 1990). This perspective accelerated into the 'constructionist/essentialist' controversy with the publication of Foucault's influential *History of Sexuality*: a new position and approach had been sketched out (Foucault 1979). History was also part of this, providing a very different conception of history from that of the past. No longer was it the 'famous kings and queens' that were paraded before our eyes: instead, slowly and carefully, there was a complete reworking of historical understanding from below. Initially, as in the influential account by Jeffrey Weeks (1977) of the creation of the modern gay movement and identity in England, it was a 'modern history'. But, subsequently, researchers have gone further and further back: to antiquity where sexuality was often the right of the free male over women, slaves, and youths and where the division into hetero-sexual and homosexual was scarcely noticed; through the creation of distinctive sodomite cultures from the fourteenth century on; to the homosexual peccadilloes of the sophisticated Italian élite of the sixteenth century. In all this, a vibrant new field of scholarship has emerged (e.g. Halperin 1990). Anthropology, too, has been affected (Herdt 1984; Blackwood 1986). Most of this work refuses to impose contemporary ethnocentric meanings around 'the homosexual' on to the past or other cultures; instead, there is an attempt to understand the dynamics of each time and place, to see how same-sex experiences emerge, are responded to, and hence socially shaped. Some of this writing is really dazzling in its scholarship and its findings; its contribution goes way beyond gay and lesbian studies to help in the rethinking of history and anthropology themselves. Throughout most of the 1980s the cutting edge stayed with socio-historical work, but there was a notable trend towards two other concerns: cultural studies and AIDS research.

The 1970s and 1980s have seen a steady proliferation of gay culture in all its forms: film, television, fiction, biography, music, art. It is symbolized, for example, by international gay and lesbian film festivals. Overlayered on all this has been a heightened self-conscious analysis of such works. Bonnie Zimmerman's (1990) study *The Safe Sea of Women*, for example, analyses some 200 instances of lesbian fiction published between 1969 and 1989, while Richard Dyer's *Now You See It* (1991) traces the development of genres of lesbian and gay film. Much of this newer critical writing draws from feminist postmodernism. It examines 'the complex entanglements of identity, voice, intersubjectivity, textualities, and sexualities'. It sees 'writing as re-vision', as 'the act of looking back, of seeing with fresh eyes, of entering an old text from a new critical direction'. It is an 'act of survival'. Just as 'every text is written from a gendered consciousness, just as every reading is a gendered experience', so is every text open to a gay or lesbian reading (cf. Jay and Glasgow 1990: 1).

These ideas have been taken furthest in the work of Eve Kosofsky Sedgwick. In two major books, *Between Men* (1985) and *Epistemology of the Closet* (1991), she has developed an account of feminist gay male theory, or anti-homophobic inquiry, in the most dazzling fashion. Seeing the homo/hetero distinction as a key classifier emerging in the late nineteenth century, she challenges all reading to become inscribed with an awareness of this distinction which can ultimately rupture it and move beyond it.

> What *was* new from the turn of the century was the world mapping by which every given person, just as he or she was necessarily assignable to a male or a female gender, was now considered necessarily assignable to a homo- or a hetero-sexuality ... [these] relations of the closet ... have the potential for being peculiarly revealing, in fact, about speech acts more generally.
>
> (Sedgwick 1991: 2–3)

It is not just so-called gay or lesbian texts (which include film, art, music) which can hence be read through this new perspective, but *all* texts. Underpinning twentieth-century discourse in all its variety in this binary opposition – the heterosexual presumption always implying the homosexual fear. A number of scholars are taking these ideas further, rereading a wide range of texts (Butters *et al.* 1990; Butler 1990; Dollimore 1991; Fuss 1991). Towards the end of the 1980s it was the stance that increasingly came to dominate lesbian and gay studies conferences, often leaving the earlier challenges of the social sciences looking quaintly old fashioned!

Along with this development, the 1980s saw another striking new area of study: AIDS. Indeed, for a while a new generation of scholars actually seemed to desert gay and lesbian research, with the dire needs of AIDS activism taking precedence over all concerns. Every aspect of the AIDS crisis developed its own literature. From behavioural studies of sex to psychological studies of 'coping with AIDS'; from media analyses to discourse tracts; from histories and politics to poetry and biography: an enormous culture of AIDS research and writing was generated (e.g. Altman 1986; Crimp 1988; Patton 1985; Watney and Carter 1989).

Schism and solidarity

By the end of the 1980s, the field of lesbian and gay studies had firmly established itself. What characterizes it now is a significant diversity. While 'queer theory' has sustained the cultural analysis of the homo/hetero divide as a text, and while this tradition has seemingly become hegemonic, a stroll around any lesbian and gay bookstore would soon show the wide range of work now being produced. There has been an increasing proliferation of concerns; spatial studies of where lesbian and gay communities are most likely to appear (Castells 1983); the beginnings of economic studies of the 'pink economy' and the household division of labour among gay and lesbian couples; oral histories which detail the lives and experiences of gays and lesbians in the recent past (e.g. Lesbian History Group 1989; Hall Carpenter Archives 1989a, 1989b; Bech 1989b; Lützen 1988; Porter and Weeks 1990). Few areas of academic inquiry remain untouched and the 1990s now seem set to see a new maturity and consolidation in lesbian and gay studies.

At the same time, conflicts and differences remain. The past twenty years could easily be documented as a history of perpetual schismatic conflict. Ideas develop through controversies, and lesbian and gay studies has certainly had its share of these. There has been a concern over whether such an area of study is in effect too narrow, reinforcing a separatist, ghetto mentality (Roscoe 1988). There has been the classic split between lesbians and gays, whereby many lesbians find their interests better served by the more fully developed women's studies while gay men remain largely aloof, patronizing, naive, or simply threatened (Stanley 1982; Frye 1983; Jeffreys 1990; Hanmer 1990). There have been splits between those who work inside the academy and hence are more formally sponsored, and those who work outside it – for their community and with much less support (Escoffier 1990). There have been the researchers working in the field of AIDS, where funding is more available, deserting the more orthodox concerns of lesbian and gay studies, and developing their own internal schisms. There have been apparent diagreements in disciplines: psychology comes under attack for effectively being just another mechanism for controlling and regulating our lives (Kitzinger 1987), while some of the newer developments in literary theory are branded as intellectual elitism. There have been the seemingly endless disputes over essentialism and constructionism, an argument that

10

has centre staged at least three international conferences (cf. Altman *et al.* 1989). There have been traumas enacted on an international scale between conflicting personalities (about which I will not speak here). There are emerging signs of intergenerational splits with younger lesbians and gays growing up, radically but unappreciatively, in a different climate of work to that of their 'pioneering' elders. And, of course, some of the most time-consuming controversies have been the attacks made on such studies from outside: a press waiting to pounce, a university administration too scared to champion such work, students worried about careers and tenure, colleagues who are homophobically entrenched. In thè midst of all this controversy it is surprising that a lesbian and gay studies has come to exist at all.

Compared to women's studies or black studies, with which strong parallels may be drawn, there are indeed relatively few institutionalized bases for gay and lesbian studies. Both women's studies and black studies have had their difficulties and their enemies, but they have not had the same sense of stigma attached to them. Lesbian scholars have frequently found their strongest affiliations to be with women's studies programmes, and the gay male academic has either also moved towards these or else, and most commonly, remained in relative isolation.

Both women's studies and black studies have long recognized the advantages and weakness of developing such programmes, and a lesbian and gay studies programme has a lot to learn from such debates. The case against such a study is quite strong. Along with arguments against the dilution of disciplinary studies, there is the real danger that we get hived off into a marginalized, minor academic ghetto where the malestream academic world can simply forget, ignore, or ridicule us. At the same time, by hanging around together in our little corners, we can easily lose contact with wider intellectual debates which could push the understanding of gay and lesbian lives into new and unexplored areas. At its very worst, we develop huge blind spots and enter a world where gay and lesbian concerns are the only things that matter, losing sight of wider differences, conflicts, struggles, and theoretical developments. (The women's movement, for example, was constantly accused of ignoring matters of race in its earliest years – and black studies was accused of ignoring gender.) Further, there is a problem of intellectual coherence; there is no essential object of study, for to take the constructionist arguments seriously is to see that gay and lesbian studies 'construct' an object for analysis that is itself much more diffuse, fragmented, overlapping, and multiple: it forces a unity that does not exist.

There are dangers then to creating a lesbian and gay studies. But at this stage, I cannot help feeling the merits outweigh these objections. For without a coherent programme of studies, we become dissipated, drained into other areas, lose ourselves with too much else to do. We can create a supportive

11

academic community, network more easily, know who is researching and studying in different disciplines, build our own journals. Crucial too is the political symbolism of such studies: a unified front is needed both for the gay and lesbian movement's own inside community and coherence – every social movement needs its intellectuals – and also for a demonstration to the outside world of our intellectual seriousness and our political strength. Our enemies are everywhere – it is hard to get funding, people would like to stop us doing our work, we may not get tenure, people look with suspicion on gay and lesbian causes, there is employment discrimination, and so on. A clear identity is needed to help foster a public recognition of the value of such work and to counterbalance objections.

There are distinct parallels in all this with debates that have gone on for a long time within women's/gender/feminist studies (e.g. Bowles and Klein 1983), within black/ethnic studies (e.g. Moraga *et al.* 1983), within feminist epistemology (e.g. Harding 1986), in the debate over men's studies (e.g. Hanmer 1990), or indeed quite simply within feminist and gay politics with the twenty-year-old (at least) distinctions between the radical and separatist politics, the more integrationist and liberal politics, and the radical, non-separatist, and usually socialist politics (e.g. Douglas 1990; Marotta 1981; Echols 1989). It is also to be found in the (hopefully now defunct) debate over essentialism and constructionism (Fuss 1990). Of course each debate is more complex and there have been 'sides' drawn up along these divisions for a long time.

My own position remains a contradictory one. It wants to go beyond the straitjacketing of the categories I have spent most of my academic life attacking. To have a lesbian and gay studies is to reinforce the very artificial divisions the dominant culture uses in the regulation of our lives. It is also intellectually naive – such a simple unitary object of study; and politically conservative – we can be hived off eventually into an academic ghetto and ignored. It can readily co-opt us into the dangerous fashionability of 'political correctness'. And yet, that said, we also desperately need a gay and lesbian studies. We need such a studies to advance *intellectually*, to open areas of study we haven't even dreamt of yet, but which simply need gay and lesbian imaginations to provide ideas and languages which will feed into the wider social world and shift intellectual stances – much as the new history and the new literary theory has done. We need such studies *organizationally*, because many of us work in conditions of isolation and sometimes hostility. And we need such studies *politically*, to demonstrate to the academy that we are here, we have important things to say, and we are not going away.

BEYOND THE HOMOSEXUAL?
FRAGMENTS OF A FUTURE

With all this, what might a lesbian and gay studies look like in the future?

Maybe, in the long run, it will cease to exist. Certainly strands of modernist thought take us this way. Although predicting the future is a fool's game, in what follows I will pick up on some recent discussions and ponder their relevance both for the future of homosexualities and for lesbian and gay studies.

The (post)modernization of (homo)sexualities

In 1981 I edited a volume entitled *The Making of the Modern Homosexual* (Plummer 1981a). Its contributors all debated the ways in which the modern idea of the homosexual had been invented and transformed. In the early 1990s this is now not so much a debate as a vast arena of historical, sociological, and literary research, depicting different historical periods, different pathways of growth, different features of the experience. Both for 'lesbians' and for 'male gays' the idea that 'the modern homosexual' comes with modernity is not really in dispute any longer: same-sex sexualities certainly exist across histories and cultures, but modernity brought with it distinctively new forms.

What got lost a little in this earlier 'constructionist debate', however, was the very notion of *The Modern*, usually equated with capitalism and the 'Western world'. This is no place to get into the many and complex debates about the nature of modernity; it is an era shaped by a contradictory twin process which also characterizes the emergence of homosexualization (the process by which 'the homosexual' gets socially organized in the Western world). One process is the *rationality project*: the spreading belief in science, experts, rules, bureaucracy, technological problem solving, and classification that characterizes much of Western thinking, making it logical, linear, and rational. This manifests itself in the creation of 'the homosexual' as a scientific category, as a field of surveillance and control, as an object of research, as a personage to be processed by bureaucracies. Here, the homosexual is allied to lots of other modern 'rational' inventions; no more, no less. At the same time, however, modernity brings in its wake the seeds of its own destructions: 'To Make it New' (cf. Bradbury 1988). Processes are at work which recognize difference, relativities, changes: potential chaos yet enormous possibility. With these come the radical options for diverse and diffuse sexualities – the divorce from traditional religions, traditional family structures, traditional communities, traditional politics, traditional limited and restricted communication channels. The workings of modern homosexualities seem largely congruent with the contradictions of modernist culture, on the one hand displaying an obsessive uniformity in its organization and on the other displaying in its flux that 'all that is solid melts into air' (Berman 1982). The homosexual is both rigid scientific discovery and diverse signifier of potential, plurality, polymorphousness.

13

The debate currently being staged around the emergence of a new 'postmodernist' culture may be seen as little more than the latest stage of this contradiction. Few would suggest that this is the dominant culture of our time; indeed at present it affects only small élite groups. Cultures today are composed of many strands. Nevertheless, there seems to be a heightening of these distinctions that may best be characterized as the late, the high, or the post-modern. What is this latest phase, and how does it relate to homosexualities?

The high modern era has been endlessly described. For Giddens, it is a time when we become increasingly cut off from local social relations and become 'disembedded'; a period of increasing 'risk' for all society's members, largely because all the old verities have ceased to be; and a time of growing self-reflexivity – when the very knowledge produced in the world helps shape the emergence of that world (Giddens 1990). For others it is 'the time of the sign', a time when media images, modes of information, 'regimes of signification' and the 'aesetheticization of everyday life' have become the engulfing feature of modern experience: we live in and through the media which become experiences in themselves (Poster 1990). It is the time of consumer culture (Featherstone 1991). It is a time when the grand narratives have come to an end; a period of fragmentation, de-differentation, indeterminacies, immanences, de-structurings, de-unification, de-centering. The quest for the grand truth, the scientific solution, the correct political position, the linear progression, and the theoretical purity are now all seen as flawed. Indeed, such pursuits have been used in the past as a means of coercion and tyranny; the need now is to recognize the fragments, the bits, the pastiches, the movements to and fro, the immanent divisions, ubiquitous and fluctual.

Such characterizations have profound implications for our homosexualities. The search for the truth of a unitary phenomenon designated 'homosexual' is discredited precisely because there is no such unitary phenomenon. The most astute observers of homosexuality have known this for a long time – from Freud through Kinsey to Foucault. What we have are a multiplicity of feelings, genders, behaviours, identities, relationships, locales, religions, work experiences, reproductive capacities, child-rearing practices, political disagreements, and so forth, that have been appropriated by a few rough categories like 'homosexual', 'lesbian', 'gay'. They may have served the dual functions of control and support in the early modern period, but they certainly don't cohere around a fixed or given phenomenon. In the late modern world, the very idea of 'being gay' will get transformed into the idea of a multiplicity of sexual/gendered/relational/emotional, etc., beings in the world. Henning Bech puts this very forcefully in his intriguing article. Enter the time of the post-gay and the post-lesbian? And, as importantly, the awareness of a dispersal of homosexualities must also mean the awareness of a dispersal of heterosexualities. Indeed, the late modernist project dissolves such a distinction at base. The separate genders and their separate sexualities cannot so clearly be sustained (cf. Katz 1990). Further, since the idea of a fixed meaning is dissolved, new readings of all manner of cultural phenomena become possible. Lesbianism, for example, may be seen as a complex metaphor: not a simple sex act, nor a simple way of being, but a profoundly complex symbol anchoring a range of concerns, pleasures, and anxieties. It feeds into a radical re-visioning, a task already started by the new Queer Theorists (De Lauretis 1991).

At the same time, some of the dangers of all this must be noted. Postmodernism can become massively self-contradictory – there are no grand narratives except, presumably, the one of postmodernism. It can be politically paralysing – since there is no grand goal and no chance of progress, what's the point of a political struggle? But to recognize the furthest excesses of postmodernist indulgence is not to fail to recognize that we are on the verge of a rapidly shifting social order: one in which the search for any grand truth – essences, universals, foundational philosophies, master narratives, dominant ideologies (call them what you will) – must give way to radical doubt; to contingency and irony; to fragments, multiplicities, diversities, complexities.

In gay and lesbian studies this will mean a lot. For instance, it certainly means we have yet another ground for rejecting all those so-called scientific studies made upon us in the past. The old quest for the cause of homosexuality is profoundly misguided: there might be a multiplicity of potential pushes into a plurality of experiences, but that is a decidedly different way of stating the issue. Likewise, the more recent work, including some of my own, which suggests that the process of acquiring a gay and lesbian identity inevitably moves through certain key stages must be open to radical doubt, a point taken up by both Val Jenness and Peter Davies in their articles. We need more and more ways of thinking about same-sex sexualities and relationships that do not lock us up in controlling categories, but which instead empower us towards difference and diversity.

The localization/globalization of homosexualities

We need to see homosexuality as an international phenomenon. Recently, two ideas have been favoured. For some, homosexuality is a universal – a gay and lesbian people exist across time and space. For others, homosexuality is an evolution: the experience of homosexuality is slowly unfolding into a true gay form. The first view – the universalization argument – reasserts essentialism and suggests that:

> Gay culture ... is old, extremely old, and it is continuous. The
> continuity is a result of characteristics that members teach each other
> so that the characteristics repeat era after era. I have found that Gay

15

culture has its traditionalists, its core group, that it is worldwide, and that it has its tribal and spiritual roots. Gay culture is sometimes underground, sometimes overground, and often both.

(Grahn 1984: xiv)

Such a view is found in many forms. For men, Bronski (1984) and Kleinberg (1980) suggest that its elemental feature is an obsession with sex, while Thompson (1987) and Roscoe (1988) hint at its more spiritual features. For women, there emerges a lesbian nation (Johnston 1973) and a strong identification with spirituality (Daly 1978). In varying degrees, all these arguments suggest a homosexual people, gay, lesbian or both, that are universal. The task in the modern world is to uncover the roots of the oppression of these people, and to search out the signs of our togetherness. It powerfully identifies a strong and continuous cultural tradition as an organizing focus of life and its politics.

The second position – neo-evolutionism – does not highlight such a universal entity as gayness, but sees something unfolding in a quasi-evolutionary fashion. It is hinted at by Stephen Murray in his article on Mesoamerica, and, in its boldest mode, it sees a universal trend towards ever more egalitarian relations: from unequal relations based on age (as in Ancient Greece) or gender roles (as in modern Mesoamerica), through those based on class (as in early capitalism), to those based increasingly on equal relations. It often traces the recent history of shifts in homosexuality through a series of stages. Thus, the politicization of homosexuality may be seen to start in Germany with the Magnus Hirschfeld Institute and the early gay rights movement, spread to various key locales in Europe (notably the Scandinavian countries and the Netherlands), diffusing to the United States before a radical world-wide symbolism (typical of USA imperialism) erupts through the Stonewall imagery of 1969, ultimately with Castro Street, West Hollywood, and Greenwich Village as the prototype of the future! This politicization leads to an increasing strengthening of gay and lesbian culture, gay and lesbian identity, and gay and lesbian politics – which has bit by bit diffused further and further throughout the Western world. For some it has been the Americanization of homosexuality (cf. Altman 1982). Ultimately, this model is projected as a global trend on to the future: the evolution of homosexuality in the white Western world is seen as a blueprint for other countries and races/cultures to follow. With the break-up of the Soviet Union, for instance, there might now be a convergence of Western homosexualities with those from Eastern Europe.

Neither of these two world views sits easily with my understanding of the global developments in the modern world. Rather than seeing homo-sexuality as a tribal and universal group or seeing it as evolving to a more advanced state of being gay, same-sex experience moves in fits and starts along diverse paths to disparate becomings. It is, as Ann Ferguson (1990)

16

has so clearly argued, part of a historical dialectic. And, in the 1990s, this must in part mean that same-sex experiences have become increasingly fashioned through the interconnectedness of the world.

Certainly the late modern world cannot be understood without seeing the interpenetrations of countries: of their economies, their cultures, their technologies. There is a world-wide process in which modern technologies have quite simply made the global world a local one: one in which news can be simultaneously consumed in many countries across the world at the same time, whereas it once took hours, days, weeks, or even years. It is a world where political changes, cultural changes, and endless diversities can be faxed or electronically mailed within seconds to any part of the globe (Gergen 1991). And homosexuality is part of this. Superficially, it would be easy to see, for instance, a mass homogenization of the male gay world through the development of such things as gay tourism, the gay disco, the gay bar, the women's bookstore, the lesbian community. There is a political literature and a cultural literature which certainly makes ties across countries. And there are organizations – like ILGA (the International Lesbian and Gay Association) – and conferences – like *Which Homosexuality?* (Altman 1988) – which bridge international differences and create a strong sense of an international community and culture. Indeed, the gay and lesbian movements house identities, politics, cultures, markets, intellectual programmes which nowadays quite simply know no national boundaries. Homosexualities have become globalized. The very movement itself appeared in a series of quick shudders as the ripples from Stonewall and the women's movement were heard around the world, and the pace has simply accelerated since that time in the late 1960s. Magazines circulate freely in the Western world and filter through elsewhere, sending out messages of what it is like to be gay and lesbian. Organizations grow, fostering international alliances. And the disco – that archetypal modernist institution of gay male desire – gets bigger and bigger as its sounds and lights flash from Brixton to Berlin to Boston. Costumes (e.g. the macho gay man and the dungaree-ed lesbian of the seventies) are not just national costumes but international ones.

But the globalization case must never be overstated. There are many countries – particularly in the African, Arabian, and Asian continents – where the globalization of homosexuality has hardly moved. And, although barriers are breaking down between East and West as I write, there are still many questions to be posed about homosexuality in the former Soviet Union. It would be dangerous to suggest a convergence in homosexual lifestyles across the world – into one true universal gayness. Further, each national and local culture brings its own richness, its own political strategies, its own uniqueness. Along with globalization comes an intensification of the local. Indeed, with the process of globalization comes a tendency towards tribalism: a fundamentalism winning over difference, a politics that separates rather than unites.

17

Ann Ferguson (1990, 1991) has discussed all these issues very succinctly in relationship to lesbian cultures. Arguing against universalist views, she suggests the need for a 'dialectical approach to lesbian cultures', one which remains sensitive to the self-determination of local and national lesbian cultures while trying to create an international lesbian movement. In a sense this echoes the wider concerns of many new movements: think globally, act locally. Yet this is a political prescription, and what I am trying to suggest is a description: this is how the gay and lesbian experiences are unfolding. From within these diverse cultural positions it may well seem like a struggle for uniformity; each wing of the movement, each disco corner, each co-option of political strategy may appear to be an homogenization. But in each case it takes on a different mode. Lesbian and gay studies needs to be clear about this international connectedness yet local uniqueness, neither trapping the unique in a global claim nor ignoring the global interconnections of the local.

The displacing of heterosexisms

Much of the last generation of writing on homosexuality firmly acknowledges that the foundation of the problem of homosexuality lies in the responses of others to human difference: Weinberg's statement, when first introducing the term 'homophobia', that 'The homosexual problem . . . is the problem of condemning variety in human existence' (Weinberg 1973: 139) remains a central idea. Much of the recent gay and lesbian studies addresses this crucial problem of why both societies and individuals become so hostile towards variety in human sexualities, and especially towards those which involve the same sex and gender (e.g. Greenberg 1988; Dollimore 1991).

A host of reasons for homophobia have been suggested in these writings. It is variously seen as a product of the Judeao-Christian religion; as a product of the need to have children to reproduce the species – non-procreative sex has to be repressed; as a Freudian reaction formation; as 'repressed envy'; as a threat to the idea of a natural order, and linked to ideas of ritual purity; as a threat to masculinity; as emerging from disturbed, authoritarian, restrictive personalities; as a threat to the values of the family under capitalism; as a 'fear of being homosexual oneself'; and as a continuing response to dissidence and the disturbing. The list now is really rather long. Yet it seems improbable, to me, that any one of these explanations succeeds on a general level. The reasons behind hostility to homosexuality are likely to change within and across societies and within and across individuals. Any attempt to champion one position is likely to collapse into a naive essentialism. Just as there is no one fixed reason for a presumed homosexual type there is no one fixed reason for a presumed response to it. There must of course be continuing detailed research and analysis of this central problem. Many times over the past two decades I have been asked to explain just why so many people get so upset about homosexuality, why governments keep trying to outlaw it, and why some people are literally driven to murder others because of it. I cannot see a general explanation, either for people or for societies. Clearly there are enormous differences. The Netherlands and the Scandinavian countries have a fairly high level of both legal and personal acceptance of homosexuality compared to most of North America and Britain; but these latter countries are astonishingly liberal when compared to the violent executions of homosexuals in some countries. Likewise, I have personally rarely directly experienced the hostilities and hatreds that I can so easily write about as befalling others.

What is demanded here is a sensitivity to the full range of possibilities: the varieties that anti-homosexual hostilities may take, and an awareness of the multiple roots out of which these hostilities are fashioned. The grander the claim, the more suspicious I would be of it. And simple terms, like homophobia, will no longer really sustain us because they render the opposition as simply too uniform, too directed, too personally individual, too pathological, and too fixed. Homophobia is a very specific and narrow concept targeting a very precise, personal fear. The future problem to consider is not so much homophobia, which will continue to exist in pockets, but heterosexism. I think feminists have been much clearer about this than gay men in the past. For them, the problem of 'compulsory heterosexuality' (Rich 1980) has always been to the fore, and there are many linked concepts being developed by other researchers: hierarchic heterosexuality (Hearn 1987), the sexual hierarchy (Rubin 1984), and the 'terrain of heterosexualism' (Brittan 1989).

Heterosexism may be defined as a *diverse set of social practices* – from the linguistic to the physical, in the public sphere and the private sphere, covert and overt – *in an array of social arenas* (e.g. work, home, school, media, church, courts, streets, etc.), *in which the homo/hetero binary distinction is at work whereby heterosexuality is privileged*. It is not a universal but is pervasive in this culture; it needs to be linked to other strategies of subordination, such as class, gender, generation, and race; and it is probably best analysed as a series of concrete moments – for instance, how it works directly in the school situation (cf. Plummer 1989) or in marriage relations (French this volume). Heterosexist practices are accompanied by a whole conglomerate of linked institutions: gender, families, procreation, penetrative sexuality, even 'love', which are usually hurled together into one major form of being, the married heterosexual family.

The 'family problem'

During the 1980s critics of homosexuality have seen homosexuality as an attack on the 'ideal' model of the heterosexual nuclear family. Jerry Falwell, for instance, declared in 1980 that 'homosexuals are antifamily', and, in

19

the UK, Section 28 makes it quite clear that 'a local authority shall not promote the teaching in any maintained school of the acceptability of homosexuality as a pretended family relationship'. Since this conventional family is usually the embodiment of heterosexist practices our enemies have a point.

But, and this is crucial, the ideology of *the* ideal nuclear heterosexual family is not the same as the myriad of ways of living together that are an increasing feature of late modern societies. The happy little nuclear family – of Judy Garland in *Meet Me in St Louis* – is largely a myth of the past. Today the stories are different. Not only do very few people indeed live the full cycle of their lives inside such families, there is mounting evidence that life within families may bring much unhappiness: spouse battering, child abuse, marital rape, and breakdown are simply signs that the family is often not 'the haven in a heartless world' it was once thought to be: it may indeed be quite the opposite. An idealized family may be just that: an idealization.

Yet homosexualities reach out and touch family life in a myriad of forms (Weston 1991). Gays and lesbians grow up inside families, usually having to keep their emerging sexuality a secret and often facing abuse once it is discovered, a form of sexual abuse never mentioned by the 'child sex abuse lobby'. Gays and lesbians often get married to heterosexual spouses and raise families, only to decide later that a gay or lesbian relationship is preferable, as Maggie French so clearly shows in her article. Gays and lesbians may be uncles and aunts, brothers and sisters, sons and daughters, or grandparents. Gays and lesbians may foster children – as Pat Romans discusses in this volume. Gays and lesbians may embark upon relationships that are as enduring and fulfilling as any heterosexual one, and in some countries such relationships have become legitimated by religion, or law, or both,. And gays and lesbians may provide mutual networks of support, care, and friendship that are as strong as any family, and maybe stronger because they are chosen rather than simply given (see the articles by Peter Nardi, Barry Adam and Beth Schneider in this volume). The lives of lesbians and gays touch upon 'family', as many of the articles in this volume show (cf. Bozett 1987; 1989). The ideology of *the* family engulfs too many people and provides a distorted mirror; but the realities of diverse fami*lies* are very different. Here gay and lesbian experiences must be increasingly recognized in all their rich and diverse forms. Gayness is not a simple threat to the family, but a sign of the increasingly rich and diverse ways in which late modern societies are coming to organize ways of living together, often in mutual support.

Indeed, this is also a sign that the deep heterosexist practices of the past have been somewhat modified over the past generation: while there remain massively homophobic newspapers and spokespersons, there has also been the growth of many agencies which are either more supportive or at least less negative than those of the past. Much of the liberal press, some television programmers, and certain so-called 'agents of control' including some police forces, courts, doctors, and social workers have all made statements to this effect; for some, the old heterosexism has been displaced. Likewise in some countries, Scandinavia and the Netherlands in particular, legislation on the age of consent, discrimination, and partnerships has almost reached a stage of complete equality between homosexuality and heterosexuality. These are, I think, significant changes which hopefully signpost the future: a point taken up by a number of contributors to this volume but most notably Henning Bech.

The construction of a culture of sexual citizenship

The end of the twentieth century has ushered in a great uncertainty over politics. The rise and decline of Reagan and Thatcher, the dissolution of the Cold War and the realignment of East/West relations, the failures of both socialism and the New Right, the rise of the new social movements around utopian politics, the reassertions of national tribalisms and religious fundamentalisms – all this is forcing a new thinking over political matters. New times, new world orders and new alignments have brought a new age of politics. Although, annoyingly, sexuality is usually ignored or relegated in such debates when staged by political scientists, it seems crucial for lesbian and gay studies to assert this question: where does the lesbian and gay politics which flourishes in the latter part of the twentieth century in the Western world sit in all this end of century change (cf. Showalter 1991)?

There is both a dark and a more hopeful answer to this question. The dark answer can look at most of the continents across the world – the Africas, the Arabias, the Asias – and find little evidence in the recent past of a benign attitude to women or same-gender experience. Frequently, indeed, these diverse cultures have looked to the West as 'the other' and have seen homosexuality as a sign of its decay and decadence. And indeed, in the face of famine, disease, and death, talk of lesbian and gay rights in some of these countries does indeed seem a rather indulgent luxury. Nearer home too the record has not been that good: there are constant signs of a backlash. New restrictive legislation like Section 28 in England gets introduced. AIDS brings a partial remedicalizing of homosexuality. More people get sucked into the criminalization process as gay offence statistics rise through increased police activity. Queer bashing and gay/lesbian homicides continue to make streets in many locales unsafe. Bigots can make defamatory remarks in the media which would long be regarded as indefensible by most if made about blacks, Jews, or straight women. There is no tolerance by heterosexuals for homosexuals simply to behave in equal ways in public. Gays and lesbians can still lose their jobs once their identity is known. Public opinion changes only in patches. No wonder that many gay and lesbian campaigners scream and grow angry, or tire and grow weary.

Yet, at the same time, there is surely a positive face to lesbian and gay 'rights' over the last quarter century. The 'rights' campaigns around *'being* gay' and 'lesbian' have had some remarkable pay-offs in the Western world. However bad things may sometimes seem now, they were surely worse in the recent past? Indeed, for some of us *being* gay and lesbian in the Western world has become a positive experience bringing no more problems than any other way of living and loving, and often some advantages. Most of the contributors to this book sense this too. Indeed, a few years back a book like this would have been inconceivable, as would so much of recent writing. We have gone beyond the old homosexuality. Gone are the old tragic stories of pathology so beloved of doctors and clinicians in the recent past. Instead, each essay in this book shows how the new 'modern lesbian and gay' of the Western world actively works to create a new social order. The essays show gays and lesbians making their own literature, philosophies, and politics; creating new ways of living together – with lovers, with children, with friends, and with heterosexual partners; building new communities, identities, sexualities, and politics; creatively responding to a major health crisis with passion, concern, and love. And doing all this on both a local and global scale. Gays and lesbians have become 'world makers' (Goodman 1978). These essays are only fragments of what is happening. But when we start to see how much has been achieved in such a short time, there are grounds for optimism. At the same time, we can begin to see why strands of a backlash should have happened: we *have* created new orders, and some of them *are* threats.

At the core of understanding the changes of the past two decades must be a heightened awareness of the role of the new social movements in shaping new identities, new programmes, new cultures, of political action. I stressed *being* gay or lesbian earlier, not because I believe that gays or lesbians really are forms of being, but simply that I believe we have made ourselves so in the modern period. We have invented a way of being, a sense of identity, and a way of speaking about ourselves that has made it possible to claim 'rights'. Part of the new political landscape has been the decline of traditional, exclusively class-based politics and the rise of new social movements, often based around Utopian images of the future, which create identities, rights, and an awareness of difference (Cohen 1985; Connolly 1991; Ferguson *et al.* 1990; Fraser 1990; Hall 1991; Young 1990). The gay and lesbian movement is a key part of this change, even though it is curiously ignored in some of the many discussions of these changes (e.g. Touraine 1988). Probably the central achievement of the lesbian and gay movement has been the creation of a strong, public identity around which political communities and programmes of change have evolved (cf. Adam 1987). The schisms and conflicts within these communities and politics have been enormous, but out of these very schisms has developed a vibrant politics. Many of the essays in this book – and some very explicitly – are testaments to this.

For a culture of sexual citizenship

One of the strongest claims made by the lesbian and gay movements has been the claim for equal rights (although some more radical wings have always rejected this). Rights are not 'natural' or 'inalienable' but have to be invented through human activities, and they are built in to the notions of communities, citizenship, and identities (Andrews 1991; Turner 1990). Rights and responsibilities depend upon a community of discourse which makes those same rights plausible and possible. They accrue to people whose identities flow out of the self-same communities. Thus it is only as lesbian and gay communities started to develop and gather strength that talk of a gay and lesbian citizenship became more and more plausible. The nature of our communities – the languages they use, the stories they harbour, the identities they construct, the moral/political codes they champion – moves to the centre stage of political thinking. Michael Sandel writes:

> Open ended though it may be the story of my life is always embedded in the story of those communities from which I derive my identity – whether family or city, tribe or nation, party or cause. On the communitarian view, these stories make a moral difference not a psychological one. They situate us in the world, and give our lives their moral particularity.
>
> (Sandel 1984: 6)

What has become both visible and practical over the past two decades (although the roots go further back) is the creation of new communities of discourse and dialogue championing rival languages, stories, and identities which harbour the rights and responsibilities of being sexual, pursuing pleasures, possessing bodies, claiming visibility, and creating new kinds of relationships. The old communities of rights spoke of political rights, legal rights, or welfare rights of citizenship; the language of lesbian and gay communities certainly draws upon this – such gains should not be lightly lost – but takes it further. A new set of claims around the body, the relationship, and sexuality are in the making. It is part of a new life politics (cf. Giddens 1991), a new politics of difference (Young 1990), and a new politics of discourse (Fraser 1990).

23

There is, of course, absolutely no agreement on what these new politics will be. It is, and will remain, a contested domain. The gay conservatives seem to want to enforce a code of limits: in *After the Ball* Kirk and Madsen claim that 'Gay liberation has failed', proceed to suggest that this is entirely due to the liberation movement being too flamboyant and outrageous, and end with a code of gay ethics which would make a Sunday School teacher happy. In a list of twenty-three ways to self-police, they suggest such things as: 'I won't talk gay sex in public', 'I won't cheat on my lover', 'I won't have more than two alcoholic drinks a day', 'I won't have sex in public places'. It is a code which completely denies the transgressive nature of queerness championed by others. Indeed, so weary of so little progress within a generation, some have returned to a confrontational, aggressive campaigning which is exactly what Kirk and Masden have condemned. Thus, OutRage in London and New York employs direct action and confrontation: outing, kiss-ins, queer politics – issues raised in the contributions by Anna Marie Smith and Vicki Carter to this volume. For them talk of 'rights' is supplanted by talk of dissidence and transgression.

There are many other attempts to create new discourses for the future. Some feminist writers have come up with lists of 'safe, forbidden and risky sex practices', not in terms of HIV risk but in terms of politically correct sexuality (e.g. Ferguson 1989). Others have returned to classic liberalism (Mohr 1988). Others, such as Peter Tatchell in this book, are attempting to develop a broad coalitionist strategy based upon principles of diverse equalities for many groups. The past twenty years have produced a miracle of diverse campaigns that have shifted the languages and identities through which we understand the complexities of our sexualities and politics. In a further proliferation of new languages and stories, claims and counterclaims, lies the future.

CONCLUSION: OPTIMISTIC INVENTIONS

This has been a somewhat optimistic introduction to lesbian and gay studies, and it remains to be seen if such optimism is justified. I am only too aware of the continuing discriminations, violences, and hostilities heaped on millions of lesbian and gay lives, and of the continuing need for militancy against such attacks. At the same time, as I look back on what has been achieved over the past two decades, a cautious optimism seems warranted. Socially, politically, and intellectually there have been significant contributions. As this article has attempted to show, a strong if schismatic lesbian and gay studies has been established across a range of academic disciplines and many nationalities, and its imminent growth seems assured. In a very real sense, the love that once dared not speak its name has now become a major public discourse. A space has been created for many and diverse voices to make claims and counter-claims as to what the lesbian, gay, and bisexual experiences were, are, and will become in the future.

Part II

ESTABLISHING THE MALE HOMOSEXUAL
The Turkish and Mesoamerican experience

If gay and lesbian studies have established anything over the past twenty years it is that same-sex experience is far from a unitary phenomenon. All the articles in this book display a range of diverse experiences, beings, and existences. Cumulatively, research has shown an array of men being with men and women being with women that defies the simple category of 'homosexual' given to the Western world in the late nineteenth century.

The two articles here present 'fragments' of male experience from cultures where the meanings given to same-sex experience highlight the distinction between perceiving masculine and feminine ways of men being with men, meanings which dominated the Western model until very recently. Without being evolutionist, both seem to suggest a tottering towards the Western model. Models for thinking about different patterns of same-sex experience are presented, and crucial roles are assigned to religion and the family in the ways in which homosexualities get socially organized.

2

THE 'UNDERDEVELOPMENT' OF MODERN/GAY HOMOSEXUALITY IN MESOAMERICA[1]

Stephen O. Murray

In what has been written about male homosexuality in the world's cultures, three basic social organizations recur. In so far as changes over history are visible, the types occur in the order (1) age-stratified, (2) gender-stratified, (3) gay. When and where homosexuality is age-stratified, for instance in ancient Greece, medieval Japan, or the New Guinea highlands until recently, the 'boy' is sexually receptive to an older boy or man who takes responsibility for helping the boy to become a man. In societies with gender-stratified homosexuality, as in the recent past in Northern Europe and North America, contemporary Latin America, and indigenous Polynesia, one partner acts the role of a woman, generally specializing in what is considered 'women's work' in a society, frequently stereotyping women's dress and behaviour. The 'gay' or 'modern' organization of homosexuality breaks from assigning one partner to the inferior role of 'boy' or 'wife', and – without regard to their sexual behaviour – insists that both are men who should have equivalent privileges, not the least of which is autonomy. Because the historical succession has been age to gender to gay, it is tempting to consider this a necessary, evolutionary order.[2] In this chapter, I will argue that such an 'evolution' is not inevitable, and discuss some of the obstacles to the globalization of an egalitarian (gay) organization of homosexuality even in the relatively industrialized and 'modern' capitals of 'developing' countries.[3]

The modern Western model of egalitarian homosexual relations without socially inferior gender (or age) roles is known to men participating in homosexuality in many places, and the term 'gay' has been borrowed into Japanese, Portuguese, Spanish, Thai, and other languages to label a way of being openly, exclusively homosexual without the flamboyant effeminacy traditionally signalling sexual availability in many cultures.[4] The prestige of gay homosexuality is also indicated by the application of such terms as *moderno* (in Peru), *internacional* (in México and Guatemala), *kwing* (in Thailand, a combination of the English words king and queen) to those who are neither *activos* (tops) nor *pasivos* (bottoms), kings or queens in Thai parlance.

29

What is not modern and international, what is old-fashioned and unsophisticated in these societies is the distinction between masculine inserters not considered homosexuals from feminine insertees who are. The sexually passive, effeminate *gatuhy* role in Thailand is more or less equivalent to the Latin American *maricón* role. A *gatuhy* is involved in what we might call gender exogamy with '100 per cent males' (*pô-chai dhem-dua*), just as the *maricón* is sexually involved with real *hombres*. In their widely-recognized womanly inferiority, the *maricón* and *gatuhy* visibly reinforce gender stratification and perpetuate men's fear of seeming effeminate. Those who are privately involved in receptive homosexuality, but who maintain a masculine public appearance, are obviously unwilling to forgo male privileges, and have a vested interest in maintaining stigma on effeminacy rather than on homosexuality. As in Latin America, the homosexuality of effeminate Thai men is taken for granted, and men who fuck them are not stigmatized as 'homosexual'. Young and poor men who consider themselves '100 per cent male' generally lack wives. In Bangkok, as in Latin American capitals, men tend to marry a decade or more after puberty. Increasingly, for urban Thais (with no farm to inherit), marriage in the mid-20s 'if I can accumulate some money' is a hope of men. The possibilities of sexual contact with 'good girls' who are the only candidates for future wives are virtually nil, so 'bad girls', prostitutes, or effeminate men provide culturally expected, quasi-legitimate sexual outlets, again as in Latin America.

In Thailand, as in Latin America, the typological system is very simple, with gender roles and sexual behaviour in neat conformity with each other. But in messy reality, sexual behaviour, gender appearance, and sexual identity are more complex. In private, over time (in a 'sexual career') or with different partners, a man's behavioural repertoire may diverge from the clear-cut dichotomy. In all places, most homosexual behaviour does not involve someone labelled (by himself or by others) a *maricón* or *gatuhy*. In a 1986 sample of 2400 men tested for HIV antibodies in Guadalajara, México, 74 per cent reported engaging in *both* insertive and receptive anal intercourse (Carrier 1989a: 132), although many of these men would not generally acknowledge their penetrability in public. That is, they say they are *activos*, regardless of what they do sexually with other men. Publicly masculine, married men may be insertees in homosexual behaviour in private in Thailand, also, while considering themselves 'straight' or as 'gay kings'. Although not at all comparably drawn, and probably even less representative a sample, those providing homosexual services in Bangkok bars reported that 50 per cent of their customers were kings, 30 per cent queens, and 20 per cent both (Allyn and Collins 1988: 3–4).

Homosexual behaviour is an insufficient basis of gay identity in Anglo-American societies, and, in my observations in Latin America, *pasivo* behaviour is even more disconnected from *pasivo* identity than homosexual behaviour is from gay identity in Anglo-America. The perplexity expressed in letters to a widely syndicated advice columnist in Thailand (some of which are translated and interpreted by Jackson 1989) exemplifies the reluctance and delay in applying stigmatizing labels to oneself. Masculinity is a fragile essence, more easily spoiled than maintained. In no culture that I know of do men want to question or analyse dispassionately their masculinity.[5] In Thailand 'everyone is responsible for maintaining face. Each person shows consideration by not allowing another to lose face' (Allyn and Collins 1988: 4–13). People are accepted 'at face value' and smooth interaction is highly valued. Introspection (self-scrutiny) and, still more, public discussion and criticism of stigmatizing information (public scrutiny) are avoided. Early in life Thais learn to keep their feelings to themselves, and to hide behind the impersonal, unemotional presentation called *cajjen* ('cool heart'). 'Whatever is to be found deep down in the self is a Thai secret about which one often knows little oneself', but, as long as people do not challenge the rules in public, 'there is room for some tolerated individual deviation' from the rules (Mulder 1985: 64, 82, 71).

Any variation from norms of masculinity risks loss of face, even though direct public criticism is exceedingly rare. In Latin America, as in other Mediterranean-influenced cultures, one's 'reputation' is important, but it is difficult to be sure how one is regarded:

> To be a man in a society where sanctions are discreetly expressed, if at all, and everyone is provided with a 'public' that in a sense 'honours' him, does not make life all that easy. The man must steer a deft and elegant course with very few signals from that public who are his judges. He can never be sure that his value is what he thinks it is, as he observes his bland reflection in his polite spectators.
>
> (Wikan 1984: 646)

Whether what is called machismo in Spanish and *citcajnahleeng* in Thai is inner-directed, or other-directed, approval-seeking performance, there may be elaborate collusions to avoid questioning appearances that could easily be challenged, and not to see deviance (gender, sex, or other). None the less, gossip is pervasive and, therefore, a predominant concern in urban Latin America and Thailand, as well as in the countryside – the stereotypical homeland of minding others' business. Moreover, the family's reputation may be compromised by that of any family member, and especially by those living with their natal family.

THE CENTRALITY OF THE FAMILY

Whatever the attractiveness to some individuals of role flexibility with respites from male posturing, and whatever interest there is in exclusively homosexual relationships, major structural obstacles to gay community formation and to public self-identification as both masculine and homosexual exist

31

in developing semi-peripheral countries and underdeveloped peripheries of the world system.[6] In much of the world the family retains economic functions. The family as a production unit exists to a considerable extent in African, Asian, Latin American, and Pacific societies, especially in rural areas. Even urban families that are not production units provide social security in countries far from being welfare states. In societies experienced by most of their inhabitants as capricious and heartless, the family provides more than merely psychological shelter. One struck down by illness or injury with no family to support him or her will be reduced to begging in the streets. Examples of this horrific danger are readily visible, so individuals cannot, and had better not, take for granted minimum security being supplied against disability, as citizens of welfare states can.

Because revelation of homosexuality is a basis for expulsion from the home and the economic as well as psychological security provided by the family, Latin Americans involved in homosexual liaisons cultivate family relations to a greater extent than do those who can take it for granted. In some cases, they exercise the right of males who have reached sexual maturity to come and go from home at will (literally 'without question') less than do their brothers. Within the home, their behaviour must be particularly circumspect in the presence of siblings, and particularly on the subject of sex. Reticence is expected for many people to live in a small space *juntos pero no revueltos* (together, but not scrambled) as Mexicans describe their households.

The men recurrently engaging in homosexuality, who neither migrate nor build their own families, live at home longer than do those who start families of their own. Unmarried men also show somewhat greater concern for – and make greater economic contributions to – their natal family. It bears stressing that, regardless of sexual orientation, persons continue to live at home, not just 'mother-fixated' homosexual men.

Taking prospective sexual partners to where one lives is rarely possible for people who live in extended-family households, especially when the whole family sleeps in one room. For the affluent, there are visits to resorts, repair to hotels in their own city, automobiles, and trysting apartments (called *puterias* in México). For those who are not affluent, there is the dark, especially of public parks. In both Latin America and Thailand, there are also public baths, varying in how predominantly they are patronized by those in search of homosexual encounters. In Thailand there are also rooms and 'off-boys' (*àwf dèk* or *dèk-käi' dhua*) available for a short time to patrons of bars and coffee houses. Although Thailand became internationally known as a destination for sex tourism during the 1980s, many facilities primarily patronized by locals exist (Allyn and Collins 1988). Even in the commercial institutions not catering to international sex tourists, however, the prices are prohibitive to many. Most men who would like to go regularly to these places must save money for the special occasion of a visit (cf. Whitam on São Paulo in Murray 1987: 29).

In most of the world, secure privacy for lovemaking is a luxury. The pattern of residence pushes pre- and extra-marital intercourse (heterosexual as well as homosexual) into the streets. This does not prevent quick sexual encounters, but is a major obstacle to ongoing relationships. Those who wish 'to walk in the plan of love' (*amblar en al plan del amor*) do not have the easy path – moving in together – open to Western Europeans and North Americans. Even families who accept a relationship within the family circle often do not want outsiders to know that they have produced a homosexual child and are harbouring a homosexual relationship. In gratitude for this (infrequently granted) minimum of acceptance, few couples are willing to demand more, such as the chance to be alone together sometimes. Some couples do manage to carry on long-term relationships without any place to which they can be together in private, but this is quite a difficult achievement.

Aside from the lack of a place to live with a lover, there is pervasive familial pressure to reproduce. Emotional relationships with women are not demanded – nor even expected – but heirs should be produced, and this is a significant bar against exclusive homosexuality, especially in Asian cultures. As Jackson (1989: 229–30) explained, 'Male homosexual relations must remain secondary to the primary marital relationship. That is, the homosexual lover or partner of a complete man should play a role equivalent to that of a concubine or prostitute.' The tolerance for homosexual behaviour so long as it does not become too consuming an interest or passion, and so long as it does not involve public gender deviance (as in *gatuhy* or *joto* behaviour/appearance) is far from acceptance of homosexual relations as being equal to or as important as procreative/familial relationships. There is no attempt in Thai law or in less formal means of social control to extirpate homosexual behaviour, but to some extent this is because homosexuality is not taken seriously as a way of life. Similarly, in regard to the tolerance for discreet homosexuality (or other forms of sexual pleasure) as long as family obligations (of which reproduction is the paramount one) are fulfilled, Khan wrote of the impossibility of gay life in Pakistan:

> Families are like organisms that extend themselves by absorbing their young, and grow stronger or weaker based on the contributions of the new entrants. This is not just one model of life in Pakistan; it is not a choice; it is the *only* way of life. . . . If a husband takes care of his family's security needs and produces many children, what he does for personal sexual satisfaciotn is quite irrelevant – and so long as it is kept a private matter – tolerated. . . . The most successful gay relationships in Karachi are quiet and heavily compromised. They are almost never the most important relationship for either partner; the family occupies that position.
>
> (Khan 1990: 12)

With only a sketchy identity as a person distinct from the identity as a member of a family, having a 'sexual identity' and/or building an 'alternative life-style' are literally inconceivable to many, even in urban centres.[7]

Patron–client relationships are very important in Latin America, and sexually complaisant youth are sometimes sponsored by contented patrons there. It is my impression that homosexuality is more common in patron-client relationships in Thailand (and in Islamic societies, including Indonesia) than in Latin America, and also that much younger Thai boys are involved. Adults 'nourish little ones' (*líeng dhâwy*) in sexual relationships in which the quasi-parent is the insertor. Impecunious youths are obliged to provide sexual access, deference, and gratitude to their patron.[8] Parents may encourage liaisons of their sons or daughters with affluent men hoping for family advancement and/or a share of whatever gifts the patron bestows upon dependants whose sexual services please him. In such instances, the existence of patron–client ties augments rather than challenges the family. For some youth without parents, a *líeng dhâwy* or an employer providing some kind of accommodation must suffice as a family. In Thailand, 'offboys' who have migrated to the cities and do not have local relatives often sleep in the rooms rented out for sexual liaisons during the hours the establishments are closed. The employees of bars form quasi-families, quite unlike the solitary hustlers in Northern Europe and North American cities.

COLLECTIVE CONSCIOUSNESS

Gay consciousness is no more automatic a product of homosexual behaviour than class consciousness is of 'objective class position' or ethnic consciousness of genealogy. As we know from our own society, not all the persons with a characteristic, consider themselves defined in any way by it, and some deny it altogether. The existence and importance of a characteristic must be realized if there is to be a consciousness of kind: characteristics are only potential bases and, if they are not publicly affirmed, tenuous bases. The public conflation of homosexuality with gender deviance makes it difficult and unpleasant to develop any consciousness of 'that kind'.

In Anglo-North America such a realization was facilitated by the congregation into 'gay ghettos' after World War II (Murray 1984: 17). Such residential concentration of homosexually inclined men is precluded where the unmarried continue to live at home. The specific pattern of historical development of gay communities in Anglo-North America need not be assumed to constitute the only possible route to gay solidarity. On the other hand, sex does not automatically produce a sense of peoplehood. Cruising areas and social networks of homosexually inclined men partying together exist and have existed with varying degrees of visibility in cities everywhere, while a sense of belonging to a community of those whose identity is based

34

on shared sexual preferences has not. Something more than sexual acts in 'the city of night' is needed to provide a conception of a shared fate. Where individual sexual acts are ignored and discretion is the rule of social life, homosexuality may not constitute a shared fate – not a fate in Thailand, and not shared in Latin America.

A Latin American cannot easily learn about the common experiences of those with homosexual desires from print media, any more than he can discuss homosexuality with his family. In Latin America police and judges exercise wide discretion to interpret what is immoral and to declare publications as 'apologies for vice', although there are now gay magazines with nude centrefolds and gay commercial assumptions openly sold in México.

The ready availabilty of sex in Thailand is not accompanied by openness in publications. Political and sexual censorship prevailed through most of the 1980s.[9] Over time, the popular press in Thailand has moved from lurid representations of tragic drag queens to sympathetic accounts of lobbying for social acceptance and organizing against AIDS. Thai readers of the popular press can read about their countrymen puzzling out homosexual desires and experiences in the popular advice columns of 'Uncle Go' (see Jackson 1989; Allyn 1990). Gay magazines, though expensive (about £1), are available at many of the myriad news-stands and small shops, though not displayed in some places where they are for sale to those who ask for them.

Sociation with like others is also limited – and not just by economics and lack of a place of one's own. For fear of having their reputation 'singed' (*quemada*) and their security thereby endangered, many Latin Americans involved in homosexual behaviour avoid being seen with or being acknowledged by males who might be judged effeminate, and also avoid places where homosexuals are known to congregate. The same pattern existed (indeed, exists!) among homosexual Americans, although more as fear of losing jobs than fear of the family learning of stigmatizing association as in Latin America.

Thai gay institutions cluster together with non-gay ones, so that being in, say, the Patpong district of Bangkok doesn't indicate anything about sexual orientation. Moreover, except perhaps among some Chinese Thais, homosexuality is not taken seriously enough to lead to throwing children out of their family.

Lack of positive literature and fear of guilt by association were obstacles overcome by gay liberation movements in Western Eurpe and North America, so there is evidence that such obstacles are surmountable. Indeed, the demonstration that change is possible is an advantage that gay movements in their early development today have. In post-war North America, without any known historical precedent, the possibility of change was difficult to conceive. On the other hand, in a welfare state in which there is not the economic necessity of staying with one's family, a critical

35

mass more easily developed in a visible territory. The growth and meta-morphosis of recreational facilities within an area of increasing residential concentration of homosexuals facilitated the sense of shared experience that led gay North Americans to reject stereotypes of homosexuality and to demand full acceptance. Whether there are functional alternatives to residen-tial concentration is at this point open to question.[10]

Although a sense of community is easier to instil if there is a visible territory, distinct gay facilities and services might develop without a residen-tial concentration. Continued residence with families scattered throughout cities is a considerable obstacle to the formation of gay consciousness, culture, and community as these have developed in Anglo-North America. Only time will tell if there are other routes to similar – or to other – developments. The 'four little dragons' (Hong Kong, Singapore, South Korea, Taiwan) have shown that economic modernization (i.e., industrial production that is competitive in the world market) may occur without modernization theory's vaunted values, so sociologists are quieter about proclaiming a singular, universal path to any sort of development. Perhaps a form of homosexuality not defined by age or by gender variance can also emerge where the importance of the family remains and even increases – based on the developing economy of Thailand, but not, I think, on the basis of the downwardly mobile economies of Peru and Mesoamerica.

And AIDS? Where is it in all this? Despite the devastation visited on gay lives, and the promotion of medical concerns to the centre of gay political agendas, the major effect on the conception of 'gay community' by gay North Americans has been to widen the circle considered part of that com-munity (Murray 1988). It seems possible that AIDS will be used to repress increasingly public homosexuality in Thailand and Latin America, although to date it has provided a basis for increasingly visible gay organization, as in North America (see Lumsden 1991).

Globalization of 'safe sex' campaigns (pushing condoms manufactured in the US) may further disseminate 'modern' homosexuality. The diffu-sion of an alternative model of homosexuality facilitates change. However, I think that the impersonal (bureaucratic) provision of economic oppor-tunity and security permitted the emergence of 'modern' homosexuality in Europe and North America. The continuing dependence for these on family and other personal ties in Thailand and Latin America has so far limited similar emergence there, and is likely to continue to do so.

NOTES

1 The social construction of lesbianism as similar to male homosexuality and/or as part of a single entity in European and North American discourses deserves study. The 'natives' with whom I have conversed in the cultures considered here do not see much commonality, and the entity 'lesbian/gay' is conceived

only by those who have travelled to Europe and/or North America. The centrality of the family in these societies restricts the possibilities of association by unmarried women even more than for unmarried men, so I think my analysis of obstacles to gay identification and institution building also applies to lesbian identification and institution building, although there are additional barriers for women (notably family 'honour' depending on their sexual behaviour). I have done some systematic data collection in México City and Guatemala City. My more limited participation in the homosexual subcultures of Bangkok, Chîeng Mi, Guadalajara, Arequippa, and Lima has been supplemented by guidance from Eric Allyn and Manuel Arboleda G., for which I wish to express my gratitude. They, Fred Whitam, Ken Plummer, and Joseph Carrier have also offered useful comments on an earlier draft of this chapter.

2 This typology and its history are detailed in Murray (1984: 45–53). Societies with age-structured homosexuality such as classical Greek states and Tokugawa Japan were not more 'primitive' in scale or technology than the Native North American or Polynesian societies. The change from age to gender seems to be related to warrior élites losing prestige after conquest or in extended periods of peace. It, and the gender to gay change, may be related to urbanization.

3 I should note that all four countries discussed here have substantial indigenous ethnic populations marginally integrated in the society and economy. The capitals are primate cities with many times the population of any other city in each country. Great numbers of people from the hinterlands continue to pour into these cities. However great the congestion, crime, and pollution in these cities, life there continues to attract peasants and rural workers who cannot make ends meet in the countryside, along with less impoverished immigrants drawn to the glamour and/or perceived economic opportunities in the capitals.

4 The new word tends to be fitted into the old *pasivo/gatuhy* model it is supposed to transcend, however (see Murray 1987: 129–38; Allyn and Collins 1988: Ch 5: p. 3; Jackson 1989: 22). At least in Thailand, 'gay' has become a fairly derogatory term. The decorous term there is *'mâi 'bhà dio gan'* literally 'the same trees in the same forest'.

5 Melanesian cultures with ritualized homosexuality in initiation rites (see Herdt 1984) provide the starkest cases of the view that masculinity is an achieved status – with relatively clear stages through which every boy proceeds.

6 Thailand appears to be rising to the semi-periphery as the economies of Guatemala, México, and (especially) Peru slide further into marginality.

7 Religion reinforces familial values, although to some degree providing socially acceptable alternative same-sex grouping. Buddhist monks are a visible and important force in Thailand, although of rapidly declining salience in cities (Komin 1988: 171). In Latin America, less than robustly masculine boys are channelled towards the priesthood. Family interests are also pursued within religious orders, and not just in the abstract sense of evidencing merit.

8 Komin (1988: 160) found gratitude to be the highest instrument value among rural Thais, surpassing even independence, the highest urban one. It bears noting that sometimes the sexual services of the young man are commercialized to produce profits for the patron in addition to or instead of having sex with him.

9   Enforcement of prohibitions against picturing pubic hair lapsed in 1990. Underground pornography, much of it Western, is relatively available in Thailand, particularly in roadside stands late at night. The representations of masculine Westerners getting fucked is an impetus to diffusing non-role-structured gay homosexuality. However, those without homosexual experience are unlikely to know how to find such videotapes, and also may lack any place to view them, despite the profusion of VCRs in recent years.

10 At least to the extent that sex workers who have migrated to Bankok from the north live on the premises, there is some residential concentration, and development of gay quasi-family. Whether Thais or Latinos want separate gay institutions and 'sexual identities' is open to question. Although some envy North American 'gay ghettos', others reject such a model and/or see no need for segregating themselves from the rest of society.

3

MASCULINITY, FEMININITY, AND TURKISH MALE HOMOSEXUALITY

Huseyin Tapinc

Turkey. A country geographically located in both Europe and Asia, where the Occident and the Orient meet. A country which has adopted Western-ization policies since the early 1920s – politically, legally, and culturally – yet where Islam is the dominant religion. A country where mainstream culture is formed with the fusion of European, Mediterranean, and Middle Eastern cultures. For some Westerners, as part of the mythology of Ottoman Turks, it is a country where strong, dark, and brutal macho men live with veiled women. For others, it is a country as modern as any in the West. Yet for many Easterners, especially Muslims, it is the only secular, modern, Westernized country where the dominant religion is Islam. For many gay Westerners, Turkey is the 'land of opportunity' with its Oriental offerings buried in its history, whilst for most gay Turks, it is the West which is the 'gay paradise'. So many contrasting myths and stereotypes abound in looking at Turkey.

This article aims to provide an introduction to the features of male Turkish homosexualities, found in a complex culture moulded by Occident and Orient. It is an experience ignored by Turkish scholars, and yet one that will become increasingly important as both feminist and gay politics become more crucial in Turkish life.[1]

I will look mainly at the *meanings* attached to homosexual behaviours so as to show the social organization of homosexuality in Turkish society. For, although homosexual behaviours may well be universally observed, the meanings given to them remain culturally specific (Gagnon and Simon 1973). It is through meaning attached to sexual behaviour that the links between society and sexuality may be seen. I am not suggesting any idea of a 'unitary society' which simply shapes sexuality. Rather, I see a fragmented portrait in which diverse sets of relationships, institutions, and practices play their part (cf. Foucault 1979; Weeks 1985). 'What is homosexuality?' and 'Who is homosexual?' will be answered in very different ways according to the diverse cultural meanings and practices.

In researching homosexuality in Turkey, I have come to see it as a relationship, *a social contract*, where rules are initially based upon the agreement of various participants, rules which are ultimately defined by society. This means I look not just at homosexually identified people, but also at non-homosexually identified people, who may engage permanently or 'accidentally' in homosexual behaviour at some point in their life span.[2] Put this way, it becomes possible to ask about the cultural constructions of homosexuality versus 'the homosexual', and the boundaries drawn around differing forms of experience. It becomes possible to ask questions about the social contract which operates between the two social actors, *the one* and *the other*, and to see the ways this is regulated by society. It becomes possible to see how Turkish homosexualities are linked to both sexuality and the prevalent gender system. This is not new for those who understand the workings of homosexuality in the West; but it is an important first step in the grasping of what homosexuality means in the East.

MODELS OF MALE HOMOSEXUALITIES IN TURKISH SOCIETY

To understand how male homosexuality works in Turkish culture, I will suggest four alternative models of homosexual relations found in Turkey.[3] These models highlight the sexual meanings attached to homosexual behaviour by each participant, along with their assumed gender role.[4] Each model considers how the actor, *the one*, relates to *the other*, and how the gender role held shapes the sexual/gender identity of the individual in the final instance. Each of these models will be discussed in turn, but special emphasis will be placed on the second and third models, which seem to be the most decisive in Turkey.

Model A: the masculine 'heterosexual'

In sharp contrast to other models of homosexuality, in Model A sexual behaviour is confined to mutual masturbation and excludes oral and anal sex. Men who participate in this sexual behaviour regard it a part of heterosexual conduct, and, thus, no one ends up with homosexuality orientated sexual/gender identity. What this suggests is that the organization of sexuality in Turkish society dehomosexualizes the act of mutual masturbation, in contrast to much Western experience. For it does not jeopardize the value of the phallus at all and, more significantly, it naturally excludes penetrating sex, which appears as a decisive criterion in the conceptualization of homosexual and homosexuality in Turkey (as will be outlined soon in relation to the other models).

Model B: the masculine 'heterosexual' and feminine homosexual

In contrast, Model B takes masturbation, oral sex, and anal intercourse into the category of sexual behaviour, and this, in turn, requires the analysis of sexual meaning with the dimensions of 'activity', 'passivity', and 'mutuality'. The gender role and consequent sexual/gender identity of the individuals are then formulated on the basis of this meaning.

The key aspect of this model is the clear distinction between the masculine, 'active' inserter and the feminine, 'passive' insertee, who regard their sexual/gender identity as heterosexual and homosexual, respectively. The most common sexual practice among individual participants is expected to be anal intercourse and then fellatio in which the well-defined conventional sexual roles, being 'active' and 'passive', persist in both sexual acts.[5]

This socially recognized separation between 'active' inserter and 'passive' insertee roles in homosexual behaviour enables many heterosexual men to engage in homosexual relations which are considered to be a 'secondary sexual outlet', since, for them, although the sexual relation takes place in a 'homosexual context', it satisfies a 'heterosexual need'.[6]

> Men with a strong sense of their male gender identity and their masculine gender role could entirely enter same-sex sexual relations without challenging their heterosexual sense of self.
>
> (Marshall 1981: 136)

Hence, it is once more possible here to suggest that engaging in homosexual conduct is not strong enough to 'challenge one's heterosexual sense of self', for it is ultimately the gender role which demarcates one's sexual/gender identity rather than sexual orientation. And the mentality which preserves 'the heterosexual sense of self' in homosexual relations springs from the predominance of traditional gender roles which considers the 'real' man as a penetrator.

This suggestion in fact echoes the widespread preference for and occurrence of anal sex in which the masculine, 'active' inserter partner (not necessarily homosexual) represents the almighty power of the penetrating phallus, while the feminine, 'passive' insertee (and homosexual) stands for the anal powerlessness (Hocquenghem 1978) In fact, this relation of power is analogous to heterosexual sexuality in which the man with his phallus exercises power over women who lack it. A brief analysis of Turkish words which are used for sexual relations will make this clearer.

In the Turkish language two words are used most frequently to define the position of those involved in a sexual encounter, heterosexual or homosexual. One is 'to give', *vermek*, and the other is 'to put', *koymak*, and it is always the woman or 'real' homosexual who 'gives' and the 'real' man who 'puts'. This, indeed, in the end refers to receptive and active roles of penetration, respectively, either in anal or vaginal sex. Moreover in their study on the patterns of verbal duelling among Turkish boys, Dundes, Leach, and Özkök (1970) suggest that one of the most important goals in verbal

41

duelling is to force one's opponent into the role of either a woman or a passive homosexual, and the latter seems to be the major theme in the Turkish tradition of cursing.

> This may be done by defining the opponent or his mother or sister as a wanton sexual receptacle. If the male opponent is thus defined, it is usually by means of casting him as a submissive anus, an anus which must accept the brunt of the verbal duellist's attacking phallus. . . . Of course, the victim normally does not simply remain passive. Rather he tries to place his attacker in a passive, female role.
>
> (Dundes, Leach, and Özkök 1970: 326)

It is at this point that the set of societal definitions of homosexuality can be introduced. In Turkish culture the conception of homosexuality originates around the schema of penetration, and in this conceptualization the label of *the homosexual* is attributed to any individual who is being penetrated or thought to be penetrated, whereas the other one remains free of this label regardless of the fact that he is engaged in homosexual sex as well. In other words, *ibne*, the colloquial word often used for *the homosexual*, is the person who 'gives' his arse to another man. Furthermore, the word *ibne* is not used to refer only to effeminate homosexuals but also to other individuals who are thought to lack certain aspects of masculinity. In a word, *ibne* as an adjective becomes a floating signifier to despise, ridicule, and degrade a man in any social encounter in the male world. This assists in clarifying the affinity between the conceptualization of homosexuality and its relation to masculinity in Turkish society. Thus, as a consequence of this stigmatization, *ibne* appears to be the person who is expected to fulfil the effeminate and 'passive' role as *the homosexual*, condemned and despised in society. Interestingly enough, many homosexuals and gays themselves in Turkey adopt this mainstream/malestream distinction, and they have adapted two slang words, *laço* and *lubunya*, derived from gypsy slang, which refer to masculine, 'active', and not necessarily homosexual individuals and to feminine, 'passive' homosexual people, respectively.

Model C: the masculine homosexual and feminine homosexual

The specific nature of this model in many respects resembles Model B and refers to individuals who are masculine, 'active' homosexual and those who are feminine, 'passive' homosexuals. In sharp contrast to Model B, however, they define their sexual/gender identity on the basis of the sexual orientation they hold instead of merely on that of gender roles they assume. Nevertheless, gender roles still persist as important elements in the determination of individuals' homosexuality; that is to say, one partner is always expected to be the masculine, 'active' inserter, while the other one is to be the opposite. The reason for this manifest distinction could be detected in the polarized and inflexible gender system of Turkey, which largely originates from the functions in the family context. A brief exploration of the gender structure of the society would reveal that each sex possesses a highly segregated and autonomous space in both the private and public spheres.[7] In other words, the social network of Turkish society is organized not only by the division between private and public spheres but also through further segregation of these spheres by the category of sex as well.

The consequence of this social network seems to be the 'desexualization' and 'de-eroticization' of social relations between the sexes. Furthermore, it perpetuates the existing relations of power between the sexes/genders in which male/hegemonic masculinity exercises power over the female/femininities and subordinated forms of masculinities, especially homosexual and gay masculinity as a consequence of, to coin a term, 'degendered' relations. To elaborate, this configuration, on the one hand, embraces socially significant homosocial relations among same sex members of the society and, on the other, further polarizes the gender roles.

One of the most apparent characteristics of homosocial relations in Turkish society is the maintenance of deep emotional and tactile relations among men who spend most of their time in men's settings, for instance, coffee houses, pubs, and *meyhanes*. Kürşat Kahramanoğlu, a gay Turk who now lives in England, expresses his own observation on how male–male social relations take place in Turkey in *Walking After Midnight*.

> male friendship and the physicality between men is continuously encouraged. You hold the hand of a friend, your brother; you kiss your father and male members of your family, and you kiss your male friends. It is an insult if you don't kiss a friend after not seeing him for a week or two.
> (Hall Carpenter Archives Gay Men's Oral History Group 1989b: 148)

In relation to the affinity between the construction of homosexuality and male friendship, Segal (1990), in her book *Slow Motion: Changing Masculinities, Changing Men*, refers to Foucault who argued that the emergence of homosexuality as a distinct category is historically linked to the disappearance of male friendship. Giving credit to this affirmation, yet emphasizing the emergence of 'gay' as a distinct category rather than that of 'homosexuality' in the Turkish context, in this culture, too, this 'socially encouraged' male friendship, based upon a blurred division between the notions of 'private' and 'public' matters in social relations, embraces deep homo-emotionality; however, the border between intimate male relationship and sexuality seems to be an unambiguous one. The homosocial relations among men in fact keep them apart sexually and perpetuate the existing myth of masculinity, particularly its hegemonic form.

43

To elaborate upon the polarized gender roles, it is worthwhile to bring the institutions of both the Turkish family and the Islamic religion into focus, for the cultural construction of homosexuality is interwoven with them in the final instance.

Turkish families and Islamic religion

The institution of family in its conventional form is still prevalent culturally, economically, and politically in contemporary Turkish society. To refer to statistical data on marriage in Turkey, according to the findings of the *1988 Turkish Population and Health Survey*, carried out by the Hacettepe Institute of Population Studies (1989), only 3 per cent of the marriages in the country end with divorce. One of the reasons why marriages are more persistent in Turkey than in its Western counterparts can be detected in the power of marital status determining an individual's position and status in the society. This is more true for women than for men. While, for the latter, marital status is dichotomized socially as married or single, for women it is differentiated into further groups, and it is the unmarried women, especially after a certain age, who have the lowest status in society, compared to widows and divorced women (Özbay 1988). To elaborate further, among the family structures it is the nuclear family which is predominant in both the rural and urban settlements of Turkey. According to the findings of Timur (1972), 59.7 per cent of families are nuclear families, and the figure was put at 68.4 per cent in a survey held in 1986 (Tüsiad 1986). What is interesting about this dominant family structure and what is different from its Western counterpart is that it operates within an institutionalized system of wider kin relations which provide continued support and solidarity in various forms.

All these figures on the marital status of women and men and family structures in Turkey do not enable one to grasp the existing numbers of studies which uncover the second-class status of Turkish women (Kağıtçıbaşı 1982; Kandiyoti 1977, 1982; Kiray 1976: Melker 1976; Magneralla 1974) as well as those which reveal the strategies developed against this situation (Bolak 1990; Sirman 1990). Moreover, limited communication and role sharing between spouses and widespread male decision-making in the family epitomize intra-familial relations in the Turkish family. Hence, the kinship system and the Muslim communal social structure based upon the segregation of the private and public spheres by sex, serves to reproduce the dominant gender ideology as well as the gender-dominant ideology in Turkish society.[8]

Apart from the institution of family, there exists another social institution which helps reproduce the 'conventional' organization of homosexuality in Turkish society. It is religion, in this context Islam. In sharp contrast to the tradition of Christianity, which deems sex as sacramental and threatening, sex in Islam is regarded as a site of pleasure, and sexual function is one of those signs by which the power of *Allah* may be recognized (Bouhdiba 1985).[9] According to Islam, the pleasure of sex, which is creative and procreative in orientation, may take place only within the framework of *nikah*, the legal form of marriage. Any sexual encounter outside marriage is a crime; and it is homosexuality, *livata*, which is subject to the strongest condemnation and the 'most horrible punishment', the death penalty. For homosexuality is a challenge to the order of the world as laid down by God and based upon the harmony and radical separation of the sexes. On the authority of one hadith, there are three sorts of male homosexuals in Islam; those who look, those who touch, and those who commit the criminal act (Bouhdiba 1985). To expand:

> Do not sit next to the sons of the rich and noble: they have faces like those virgins and they are even more tempting than women.
> (Al-Hassan Ibn Khakwarn cited in Bouhdiba 1985)

With the support of this statement, it is possible to discern the importance of age as a criterion in the religious construction of homosexuality in which the young are identified with women. In the practice of Islam, including the Turkish case, 'those who have faces like virgins', that is to say, men with the beauty of women, *kız güzeli erkek*, are put in the same category with women. It is a consequence of this identification with women that homosexuals become an object of oppression by Islamic ideology. To elaborate, in Islam women are expelled from the public sphere and confined to the private one because of the omnipotent sexuality they have which is regarded as a threat to the social order. In conjunction with the identification with women, homosexuals, particularly feminine and 'passive' ones, are assumed to possess the omnipotent sexuality, and, in turn, they are regarded as agents of the sexual threat to the male world.

In such a polarized and fixed gender structure, which hinders the emergence of alternative models of identity for individuals, homosexuals are left with nothing but clearly defined gender roles. In fact, this is one of the reasons why the majority of homosexuals in Turkey, once they recognize their homosexuality, accept the effeminacy through identifying themselves with women and the images of womanhood. An analysis of the interactive processes taking place within the male world would show that the second social actors of Model B and Model C, *the homosexual*, are exiled from the male public sphere by other men in the name of 'honour of manhood'. For straight men, homosexuals are the 'disgrace of manhood'. Hence, it is not surprising at all that once you give up your culturally defined 'manhood' the only place to find space is in the sphere of women. In addition to this, the cultural idolization of particular aspects of masculinity results in the adoption of feminine traits by some homosexual individuals, which contributes to strengthening of the myth of masculinity as well as to the

45

ridiculing of it. Above all, it enables many homosexual people to 'practise' their sexuality.

There is, then, an underlying mechanism of identification with woman closely linked to penetration, which is found in Model B as well. Thus, it is once again feminine, 'passive' homosexuals, to be culture-specific, *ibne*, who are labelled as homosexuals, and, in turn, are expelled from the male public sphere and condemned, sanctioned, and ridiculed by society at large. However, the masculine, 'active' homosexual can still keep his place in the men's world so long as he 'announces' his 'activity' in social encounters. Yet, this does not suggest that being an 'out' 'active' homosexual is valued in Turkish society. On the contrary, he is subject to the devaluation of society in the final instance as well, but this devaluation differs in both degree and kind from the one *the homosexual* is subject to.

Model D: the masculine gay

The final alternative type of homosexuality, however, emerges as a recent phenomenon in Turkish society. Briefly speaking, this model, in which the traditional distinction between 'active' and receptive sexuality disappears, is found widely among urban, young, educated, and middle-class homosexuals. Most gays in Turkey regard themselves as 'real men', differentiating themselves from the so-called feminine homosexuals by adopting a male identity in the urban arena. They represent a new sexually conscious stratum of the homosexual population in society, and have introduced the word 'gay' with which to identify themselves. This, of course, suggests a modernizing 'Western connection' in the emergence of gay identity, gay culture, and gay politics in Turkish society.

TOWARDS A POLITICS OF GAY SEXUALITY?

Starting from the mid-1980s, Turkish society started to hear about the existence of homosexuals/gays in society from their own voices for the first time. This voice was raised, generally, from within the Radical Party, now called the Radical Democratic Green Party, officially the non-established party. This 'party' contains not only gays but also anti-militarists, atheists, greens, and feminists. Indeed, it is through its political and social activities as well as its magazine *Yeşil Barış* that Turkish society started to familiarize itself with the notion of homosexuality from a different perspective.

The history of establishing an organization by homosexuals in Turkey can be traced back to the late 1970s. In Izmir, the third largest city, a closed organization was instituted in alliance with ecologists/greens and radicals, and the goal was set to erect a political party in which homosexuals would be represented. The political climate of the pre-1980 period did not allow this organization to become a political party, and the coming military regime exercised repressive policies against homosexuals following which many of them moved to Istanbul. The idea of establishing an organization flourished once again in the mid-1980s, and in contrast to Western experiences, gay politics in Turkey emerged from within a 'political party'.

The birth of sexual/gender identity politics and discourses is interwoven with the larger social and political system. The emergence of the 'homosexual movement' in Turkey within the body of a 'political party' provides clues to the political culture of Turkish society which is dominated by 'vertical political relations', policial parties in antagonistic relationship with the state. Even though, at first sight, the birth of the homosexual movement seems to be embedded in this culture, its politics of sexuality and gender identity also signifies the advent of 'horizontal political relations' in Turkey, a politics among social actors within civil society on the strength of personal identities.

The advent of gay politics from among the Radicals in the early 1980s, concurrently with the emergence of an autonomous feminist movement, enabled the organization of various political demonstrations, sit-ins, and hunger strikes (particularly by transvestites) against the brutal oppressions of the police force in Istanbul and the proclamation of the 'gay situation' in society in public discussions and publications. However, today's political gay scene in Turkey seems to be dominated by an unfortunaté and early pernicious 'silence'.

CONCLUSION

My central argument suggests there exist homosexualities rather than one single category of homosexuality in Turkish society, and these are stratified within themselves. Alternative models of homosexuality are constituted on the basis of the meanings attached to same-gender erotic behaviour; and both the schema of penetration and the gender role each individual participant assumes are the decisive criteria in the conception of homo-sexuality. The former serves as the initial step in the cultural definition of homosexuality in the sense that the very occurrence of non-occurrence of penetrative sex sets a boundary between homosexualization and dehomosexualization of sexual conduct. Furthermore, the effects of penetrative sex manifest themselves in relation to the gender role each social actor holds, which, in turn, generates three possible types of homosexualities on the strength of existing separation between the masculine, 'active' and the feminine, 'passive' men who regard their sexual/gender identity as either heterosexual or homosexual. To put it differently, the strict division of sexual roles among participant individuals, in fact, perpetuates the myth of heterosexuality as well as that of masculinity. This point becomes clear if one glances over societal attitudes toward homosexual people. As suggested, Social Actor 1 of Model B is in no way regarded as homosexual by the society. On the contrary, he appears to be a *hyperheterosexual*, and *hyper-masculine*: 'he can screw a man as well as a woman'. It is the feminine, 'passive' individual, Social Actor 2 of Model B and Model C, who emerges as *the real homosexual, ibne*, in society. The masculine, 'active' homosexual individual frees himself from this stigmatization providing that his sexuality remains covert. The Social Actors of 1 and 2 of Model D, however, come into view as individuals who *dehyperheterosexualize* homosexual behaviour and *dehyperfeminize* the homosexual in the society. They are the agents of the masculinization of homosexuality in Turkey.

The introduction of the politics of body, along with radical interpreta-tions of the social definitions of gender and sexuality in Turkish society by gays in the mid-1980s, will certainly shift the basis of local cultures and identities. However, the very operation of this body politics will also contribute to politics on a global scale, revealing the existing relations of power both in the world of men and male homosexuals in particular and among genders in general.

NOTES

This essay is to Tim: for being 'there'.

1 This article focuses upon male homosexualities in Turkish society, excluding female homosexualities which remain as the 'dark continent' of the female world. Turkey is like many other countries in rendering lesbianism invisible. What is especially interesting in the Turkish case is that this invisibility persists in both feminist organizations and the only gay bar in Istanbul, Pub 14. This invisibility has been broken recently both by the publication of two books (*Sevginin Rengi (The Colour of Love)* by D. Kuban and *Lezbiyen (The Lesbian)* by R. Eser) and by the increasing visibility of lesbians in the first gay disco of Istanbul, Dancing 20, which opened in 1990.

2 By 'accidentally' I refer to relatively rare homosexual acts accompanied by 'excuses' such as 'I was drunk' or 'I was seduced' (Hencken 1984).

3 These alternative models of homosexuality have been derived from the typology of John Marshall (1981), who aimed to clarify various assumptions about gender and sexuality in early twentieth-century Britain.

4 From now on in this article the notion of 'homosexual behaviour' will refer to three sexual conducts: masturbation, fellatio, and anal intercourse. Problematic as this is, it will exclude other conducts.

5 With fellatio, the distinction between 'active' and 'passive' persists in Turkish homosexuality, contrary to the Western case.

6 A similar case is witnessed among Latin American cultures, as discussed by Murray in the previous essay. See also Carrier (1976, 1989a, 1989b); Parker (1985); Paz (1961).

7 Olson (1982) describes the duofocal family structure in Turkey where each spouse holds segregated and autonomous spheres of social life within the family. This model could be extended to understand the nature and internal dynamics of social relations between the sexes in Turkish society.

8 Both the family and the status of women became political issues in the 1990s

in Turkey when the neo-liberal/conservative government of the Motherland Party decided to establish 'The Institute of Family Research' and the 'Administrative Office of Women's Status and Problems' as part of the Ministry of State. The constitution of these ministerial bodies portends the intervention of the state moulding the family with Turkish Islamic ideology, while controlling the feminist movement. The creation of these state bodies underlines the fundamental place which the family occupies in Turkish society.

9 For an excellent counter-argument to Bouhdiba's position on the relation-ship between Islam and sexuality, see Sabbah (1981) which shows how Islam separates sexual desire from sexual acts so as to regulate the heterosexual life not only of Muslim women but of Muslim men as well, reinforcing a negative religious attitude to sexual orientation.

Part III

CONSTRUCTING COMMUNITIES AND IDENTITIES

Two ideas have dominated research into modern gay and lesbian lives over the past twenty years: community and identity. Indeed, what sets off the modern world of same-sex experience from other forms is the move towards it being based in ideas of a personhood belonging to a distinctive culture.

These articles add to this abundant literature. Judith Schuyf shows the importance of a growing sense of the social nature of lesbianism and documents some of the earlier patterns of the lesbian community in the Netherlands. These patterns have parallels with much of Western culture, and still exist today; but they are being supplemented with an ever growing range of possibilities. Valerie Jenness and Peter Davies turn to the thorny problem of identity, looking at lesbianism in the USA and gay men in the UK – but, in fact I suspect, curiously talking about common experiences. 'Coming out' is the momentous point of the modern gay and lesbian life: the moment of entering that personhood, and these articles, drawn from research, analyse critical features of this process. There are hints of the future here in these modern concerns: of communities diversifying and identities proliferating.

4

THE COMPANY OF FRIENDS AND LOVERS

Lesbian communities in the Netherlands

Judith Schuyf

I felt I alone was so inclined. Often I thought 'could it be that there were others like me?' Reading 'The Well of Loneliness' by Radclyffe Hall was a revelation for me; in Stephen, the central figure, I found much that was familiar to me. Now I knew I was not alone. There were many like me and from then on I spent my life looking for them.

(Stokvis 1939)

The feeling of loneliness conveyed by this Dutch woman's autobiographical note from the 1930s is a familiar theme in lesbian writing of that time. No wonder: in an age when lesbianism was primarily defined as an individual defect there were few possibilities for women to imagine what we call nowadays a 'lesbian existence'. Yet here we find already a sense of the social: the company of like others – not just one 'special friend' – was essential to a lesbian's life.

The fact that homosexuality could also be studied as a social phenomenon was recognized by sociologists only in the late 1950s (Leznoff and Westley 1955; Hooker 1961) and the 1960s (Simon and Gagnon 1967b).[1] The latter coined the phrase 'the lesbian community' by which they meant not actual spatial communities but loosely organized groups of lesbians whose prime function was mutual support.

The fact that these groups could also play an important role in identity formation was recognized and elaborated by Barbara Ponse. In her work about the relationship between the lesbian subculture and lesbian identities (Ponse 1978), Ponse described this relationship from an symbolic inter-actionist perspective. Subcultural resocialization entailed a process of secon-dary socialization using sets of standards specifically tailored to the lesbian situation in life with the aim of making lesbianism an accepted part of the women's identity. Lesbian groups or subcultures played an important role in this resocialization process. Central to this process were the 'homosexual assumption' (putting a lesbian or homosexual perspective in place of the heterosexual norms of society) and a standard of identity development, the so-called 'gay trajectory' to which every lesbian was supposed to adhere. She recognized closeted groups, in which the norm of secrecy was important, and activist groups, where the norm of secrecy had been replaced by the norm of coming out.

IDENTITY AND COMMUNITY IN LESBIAN WORLDS

Regarding lesbianism as a social phenomenon gave an extra dimension to the theories on lesbian identity, which prior to that had been seen as a purely individual experience. This led Betsy Ettore to describe *social lesbianism* as a specific form of lesbianism. Social lesbians were those lesbians involved in some form of group awareness. This group awareness included for the first time the possibility of political action. Ettore described two different identities, which she called 'sick, but not sorry' (defined as pre-political and comparable to Ponse's closeted groups) and 'sorry, but we're not sick' (defined as potentially political and comparable to Ponse's activist groups) (Ettore 1980).

Changing views of community

During the 1970s the recognition therefore grew that lesbian communities played an important part in shaping individual lesbians' lives. The idea of 'community' however changed during this period. At first communities were seen as *actual* communities, defined as groups whose members acted as support for each other (Ponse 1978; Lewis 1979). From the early 1970s the rise of the lesbian-feminist movement brought to the fore a powerful ideology. Lesbian-feminism represented a politicized view of lesbian identity, consisting of a radical rejection of patriarchal heterosexist society. The lesbian-feminist community therefore was defined as an *ideological* entity: groups of lesbian-feminists who shared the same political views (Wolf 1979) and from that base could (and in the US and UK actually did) form integrated *spatial* structures from which men were bodily excluded (Ettore 1980; Lockard 1985).

The potential for these spatial structures led Jill Johnston to assign a name to this form of lesbian community: 'Lesbian Nation' (Johnston 1973). The shared ideological base could not conceal the fact that if – perhaps – all women were equal, some turned out to be more equal than others. This led to the question of whether there were unique mechanisms at work when women got together to form communities against oppression. Susan Krieger reviewed several studies on the relationship between community and identity and found them to highlight a number of negative mechanisms, especially the way in which these groups intervened in the personal lives of their participants (Krieger 1982). These aspects were partly brought forward by the socio-psychological line of approach taken by their authors. But there appeared another problem: most groups studied were white and middle-class. The mechanisms that were active in non-white, non-middle-class communities were not identical to those active in white and middle-class ones (Sandoval 1984). This same point had indeed been made before by Joan Nestle as she reinstated the erotic power of the working-class 'butch-and-femme' cultures of the 1950s (Nestle and Edel 1981) and by Davis and Kennedy when they emphasized the role 'bar communities' played in the formation of this lesbian life-style and in the standardizing of sexual mores (Davis and Kennedy 1986, 1987).

Although the shift to differentiation meant the end of feminist-inspired all-encompassing unity, it was not the end of a specifically lesbian theory of community. Zimmerman has recently revisited Lesbian Nation. Lesbian novels written in the 1970s and 1980s describe lesbian communities that can be seen as *Utopian* – but not uniform – visions of lesbian futures. The land of Lesbian Nation can be visited and reified by every reader according to her wishes.

Life-style and community in Europe

In Europe writers were interested in the practice of lesbian communities. The focus of this research was on the diversity of local subcultures and the way in which they supported different lesbian identities. Kokula wrote about closeted and activist groups in the Berlin subculture and the function these groups had in structuring the lives of their participants (Kokula 1983). Schreurs tested the viability of Ponse's 'gay trajectory' in a Dutch non-political lesbian group (Schreurs 1985). If anything, this research showed that there was an almost infinite number of lesbian identities.

This same point was emphasized in Britain where Kitzinger mapped out different identities by letting women sort out different statements which they could or could not apply to themselves (Kitzinger 1987). She found five different identities: 'radical feminist', 'special person', 'traditional', 'personal fulfilment', and 'individualistic' that differed according to the position lesbianism took in the women's lives. A Dutch replica of her research by Smit also found five identities, albeit slightly different ones (Smit 1987). Membership of a lesbian-feminist group did not cause any differences in adherence to type.

In Kitzinger's research the single types are connected to individual choices made by lesbians according to their own interpretation of lesbianism. They do not connect to wider social issues. Persons are however rarely free to 'construct' their own identity without a number of influences from different levels of the outside world. Identity is always shaped by interaction: lesbianism may be a part of it, but other parts of identity are shaped by the dominant culture, by class cultures, religion, geography.

55

The Dutch experience

In the second part of this article I will look into these other aspects of identity more closely and describe the connection that exists between society, different lesbian communities, and lesbian life-styles.

In order to do so I use part of the material gathered for a book on lesbian life-styles in the Netherlands in the fifty years prior to 1970 (Schuyf, in prep.). I interviewed a number of women who had their formative years in the 1960s or earlier. I was not interested only in the relationship between lesbian individuals and lesbian or gay community organization, but also in the relationship any norms and values in the community might have to standards set in the dominant or parent culture.

The clique

Lesbian communities in the Netherlands were organized as cliques. The form and purpose of these cliques changes according to life-style. At the same time cliques are the formative element in the relationship between culture and individual. A clique is an informal group, usually consisting of five to ten persons, who meet regularly. The members are more or less of the same age and class. Cliques as the constituent form of lesbian communities have been recognized both in the United States (Cory 1965; Ponse 1978) and in Germany (Kokula 1983). In the Netherlands too they were important. Their importance varies, however, according to the position they take in the life-course of their members.

For some, the cliques were primarily a vehicle to 'try out' what it meant to be lesbian. They were places of experiment where lesbian life-styles could be practised. These had the same function as adolescent peer groups have for heterosexuals. This type of clique functions only for a limited time, as its importance is over once a lesbian life-style is established. In the period before 1970 this usually meant when the women had reached their early 20s. This type of clique is mainly found among middle-class lesbians. Young middle-class women are allowed their own 'space' (to experiment) after they are able to leave home (usually at 18, 19). Realization of the sexual aspects of lesbian preference usually started at that time in the early 20s.

Other cliques served as non-sexual friendship groups consisting of several 'married' couples. These groups had a social function and lasted usually for quite a number of years. This type of clique is found among butch-femme lesbians.

A third type served as a sexual circle for lower-middle-class women who could find 'safe' relationships within their own circle of friends. This type is found among bar dancers.

FIVE LIFE-STYLES

During the 1950s and 1960s at least five different life-styles were found among Dutch lesbians. In the following description special care is taken to show the way in which these life-styles are part of specific communities.

Butch-femme

During the 1950s and 1960s butch-femme relationships were very common. Although butches were often perceived by others as male, they themselves stated that they never felt 'real males', although they almost all ascribe their feeling 'different' from early on to a congenital condition. Their 'difference' in earlier life consisted of hating female beings, games, and things, loving to play with boys and boys' games (the manufacturer of Meccano has probably made more lesbians happy than any man in the world). This 'feeling different' in earlier life is what now seems to distinguish butches from other lesbians. In fact, they rejected the conventional socialization destined to turn young girls into prescribed women's roles. At the same time, they reflected strongly conventional social norms. Part of these norms reflected the importance given in society to males. On the other hand, they kept a large part of the traditional female socialization such as the extreme importance they laid on faithfulness and caring for their partners. Politically they were rather conservative.

Butches were the most 'visible' of lesbians; femmes were much more vaguely defined. In fact, the butch's partner could be anybody (except for another butch as 'wood cannot cut wood', as the 'mates' used to tell each other). This is one of the reasons there is so little known about femmes, even to the extent of not knowing whether 'femmes' existed in the same way as 'butches' perceived themselves to exist. Perhaps the partner of a butch was automatically labelled a femme. Some butches liked only partners who had up till then led an heterosexual life. The taint of heterosexuality led to them being viewed with some ambiguity. They were desired but at the same time hated, as there was always the risk of them returning to heterosexual life.

The community played a large part in shaping role play in butch-femme relationships. Great store was set by public role play, as it embodied the existence of this specific lesbian way of life by creating specifically lesbian orientated norms and values. This public lesbian life of the butch-femme couples centred around the bar, of which there were only a few in the larger towns of the Netherlands at that time. Life in the bar was a very hierarchical affair in which the butches were highest in status. They could however maintain this status only by acting 'butch', a very prescribed role. Most people 'knew' this was a role and commented on people who fell out of it, such as women from the provinces, who did not have much 'training' behind them when they went out on the town once in a while. This maintaining of status went by strictly adhering to the prescribed roles of butches and femmes – a butch had to help her partner out of her coat, light her cigarettes; a butch who wanted to dance with somebody else's femme had to ask her butch permission. Adhering to the sexual codes meant absolute faithfulness for 'married' couples, but a hunting life for single butches. Even here there was a hierarchy, seducing (married) heterosexual women carried the highest status. Adhering to the dress codes meant tailor-made suits and short hair for the butches, a dress for the femmes. Another part of the butch's role meant displaying the kind of conduct that is known in anthropology as 'conspicuous consumption' – drinking and standing expensive drinks, showing off expensive clothes and cars.

Several 'married' couples together formed a clique. Usually two or three pairs went out together.

> I was always very faithful to my partner, but at the same time I acted tough, standing drinks to women, nattering, meddling when there was a fight, but at the same time clearly stating *that* was my friend. And if somebody would so much as look at her, I would punch her or him. . . . There were six of us. I was – in a manner of speaking – the man; which was how I acted already anyhow. So we were with three women and three men. And the women always sat on a bar stool and we sort of stood behind them with our hands in our pockets. When somebody offered my friend a drink, I had it sent back – not very nice of me of course. First she would have to ask me – the one who was offering a drink to my friend had to know that she was my friend and I had to agree. . . . In this little club you would not steal each others' women. There were six of us, but there were also three of us. You cared for each others' women.
>
> (taped interview, Lies, born 1942)

If somebody or other in the bar broke the code of faithfulness, she was publicly corrected. Loud remarks made sure that such conduct was publicly condemned.

In private life this role play was much less pronounced. There either could or could not be a role difference in domestic work, although most had some sort of division of labour. Although a butch who seduced another woman was supposed to initiate sexual play, there is not much evidence of prescribed sexual roles.

It is interesting to compare Dutch butch-femme relationships with American ones to see the way in which cultural differences play a role in shaping butch-femme identities. Dutch butches differ both in their outlook on life and in the way they regard their relationships from American butches. Sexuality played a minor role in the Dutch relationships; in fact a number of women told me that they had lived for quite long periods of their life with partners with whom they no longer had sex or had never had any sex at all. This partly had to do with the important norm of faithfulness. Another notable difference is the importance butches gave to the position of paid work in their lives. It was seen as a way of self-realization much more than just a way to make money. Both norms are very much a part of the general norms of middle-class society during the post-war reconstruction of the Netherlands and serve to illustrate the fact that butch-femme life-styles mainly reflected dominant norms in each particular society.

The bar-dancers

The bar-dancers did not get on very well with the butch-femmes, which was not surprising as they did not accept the same values that were important for butch-femmes. They were not visibly different from heterosexuals. This meant that they were not 'out' except to the members of their own clique. They led classic 'double lives'. These women were in their 20s or early 30s. Fashionable clothes, the beauty parlour, and the hairdresser played a large part in their lives. As meeting-places they had the beach and the bar: drinking, dancing, and in general having fun was deemed important. They usually went around in cliques of fifteen to twenty persons among whose members they found their sexual partners, switching frequently (i.e. every few months to every year) but at the same time presenting themselves with each new friend as a 'married' couple.

Members of the bar-dancer circuit were usually employed as lower office personnel: secretaries, tea ladies, shop assistants, cleaners. They came from (lower)-middle-class backgrounds. As they did not 'look' lesbian ('they were stunners, some of these secretaries' somebody remembers), they were more or less 'safe' against discrimination. This safety was heightened by the fact that they found their sexual partners only within their own clique.

They saw their work as a means to earn money for their parties.

> Some shop assistants were in the bar every Saturday evening; one of those used to say 'we are sick, society is against us, you know, we don't have any responsibilities. We'll just stay in bed, won't go to work in the morning, let's have another genever!'
>
> (taped interview, Joke, born 1942)

The possession of a safe place to have a party was a cause of concern. They had to go either to bars or to other meeting-places (e.g. the club-rooms of the Dutch gay and lesbian organization, COC; this led to protracted hassles with the more serious members of this club). Or they would have to find a private apartment. This was not easy in the years after the Second World War when the housing shortage was so enormous that it was almost impossible for non-married people to live on their own, unless they were willing (and able) to pay through the nose for it.

This problem was sometimes solved in an original way. One of the women told me she knew (during the 1950s) a couple of women who had regular parties on Sunday afternoons, when they used to undress in the hall, before going in to the living-room, to drink and make love.

> There was the secretary of a car dealer who had a relationship with the daughter of this car dealer as well as with the car dealer himself. Tuesdays they would buy second-hand cars and afterwards he'd go with the secretary to a hotel to make love. At a certain moment this secretary said: 'Well, this is all very nice, but I want you to buy me a flat, because I don't want to go to a hotel every week.' So there came this flat. And that's how it started: she had her own flat so all her friends could visit her. There were six, seven women in this group, and in the end they had all had one another, days, weeks, months. Then the group fell apart.
>
> (taped interview, Klun, born 1932)

Changing partners happened quite frequently. After changing partners the couple would not be thrown out of the clique (as would be the case in the butch-femme friendship circles) but the deserted partner would be taken 'care' of. Although everybody paid lip service to monogamy, these cliques were quite promiscuous.

Among themselves the bar-dancing types gossiped endlessly. Gossip was clearly used as a means to reify the norms in this life-style – who was with whom, and who no longer; what books to read (in the sense of American lesbian trash), what films to see.

We now know about this life-style mostly because other people talked about it: women who participated in it are rather reticent about it. Their promiscuity, their wild parties, and especially their flippancy in general attracted a lot of (negative) comment. These comments reflected among other things a difference in class.

This general attitude to life, sometimes called the hedonistic attitude, is in this form typical of the 1950s and 1960s. For the first time lower-class people, especially younger lower-class people could start to earn money slightly above subsistence level. The rise in England of youth cultures such as the Teds and the Mods has been explained as part of the same phenomenon.

Ordinary people

'It was not important. It was not something special, like "Now we are like *that*". On the one hand it was very natural, but on the other hand it was of minor importance', a woman who was active in the national Dutch gay and lesbian organization COC told me. This ideology of being 'ordinary people' was the one propagated by the COC and is typical of the reform movements of the 1950s. From the start in 1946 the COC aimed at integration of homosexuality on an equal base with heterosexuality in Dutch society. Especially in the 1950s and 1960s this meant that what were regarded as the more unsavoury sides of homosexuality (such as campy, gender-crossing behaviour, cruising, and excessive drinking) had to be suppressed in order to show that homosexuals were worth being treated equally. Discussions in the 'Little Circle', the think-tank of the COC in the 1950s, were about whether homosexuality was a special condition which made homosexuals a special kind of human being or whether the problems of homosexuals were caused by the negative societal response to homosexuality. This last opinion prevailed,[2] leading to a change of course in the COC in the mid-1960s. The COC would become more open to society (Warmerdam and Koenders 1987). A number of people in the COC internalized the ideology of 'ordinary people'. Among the different life-styles they were the ones with a definite ideology. They were the vanguard of the movement, usually quite highly educated. In other aspects they show the same moderation. Choice of partner, faithfulness, and sexuality were deemed important but not to the extent of ruling life. They were open about their homosexuality when it was necessary, but only then; they dressed themselves 'casually' (showing their homosexuality only to the insiders).

Romantic friendship

Romantic friendships have been seen as the most characteristic forms of pre-twentieth-century same-sex love (Vicinus 1988). Two women, usually intellectuals, shared their lives and work. One of them was usually active within the women's movement (Faderman 1981). Athough we are not able to say anything about the presence or absence of sexuality in such relationships (Jeffreys 1989), it is clear that romantic friendships were at one time a common lesbian life-style. According to Lillian Faderman, this was the life-style that was stigmatized into non-existence with the advent of medical-based theories on homosexuality, which reached the United States somewhere during the late 1920s (Faderman, 1986). Leila Rupp has recently noted that the fact that there was a very circumscribed notion of what a lesbian was supposed to be did not deter American women in the 1940s and 1950s from having intimate friendships with other women while refusing to call themselves lesbian (Rupp 1989).

The life-course of one of my respondents shows how romantic friends describe themselves. Here also there is a connection with the women's movement and the devotion to an older woman that are familiar from earlier descriptions of this life-style.

As a child she was very close to her parents, especially her mother. Caring for her mother after the untimely death of her father was one of the reasons she never married. She was not 'against' men, but was loath to give up her independence. 'Men always want you to do what they want and take all the nice things for themselves'. She wanted a career in science. As a student she adored her female professor, for whom she was a favourite student. They played music together. It is not very clear whether this relationship was physical or not ('well, perhaps, once or twice') but it was *seen* by others as a lesbian relationship. A scandal ensued, which she now sees as detrimental to her career (she never made a full professorship).

She remembers always having had special friends. 'Not very intimate, no. Sometimes *they* wanted intimacy, but it always frightened me a little .... I never started it, but I sometimes put up with it.' These repeated contacts with women did not lead her to a lesbian identity. 'I was too busy with a lot of other things'. Sexuality never played an important role in her life, although she has been in what she calls a real relationship with another woman for the past ten years. She put this down partly to some gynaecological disorder, partly to the fact that they find many other things of much greater importance. To her, her relationships with her friend and with other women from the women's movement are the important facts of her life. Her whole life has been defined by men and she does not want it to be like that.

Intermittent lovers of women

Vicinus supposed the intermittent lover of women may have been a quite common type of lesbian. She lacked a visible lesbian identity; what little documentation we have is gossip or pornography. In my research, references to prostitution kept on cropping up. Apparently there was a group of women for whom heterosexuality, homosexuality, and prostitution went together in the sense that there were payments (in money or in kind) for sexuality. These could be occasional contacts, in which sexuality was the main purpose. Faithfulness was not important. Most people involved in these kinds of contacts lead a double life. They lived as heterosexuals. They were apparently mostly attracted to butches.

Some lesbians had relationships with prostitutes who need not themselves be lesbian ('for her I was just an easy trick'). Others were propositioned by women, e.g. businesswomen. One of the respondents was a woman who worked as a singer in the 1950s. She often got proposals while on stage from both men and women. One day the female owner of three shoe shops offered to keep her. Another time somebody who worked as a whore offered to pay her a thousand guilders a day. She never accepted any of those offers, but they show that anything was possible. Other people also mention that some lesbian prostitutes either went with women or even paid women for sex.

Women who lived more conventional heterosexual lives also sometimes paid for lesbian sex. Usually they were businesswomen (or women married to businessmen) – these women had the money for that type of contact. They could keep their lesbian preferences a secret and out of their daily lives in that way.

At the same time we must reckon with the fact that probably most Dutch lesbians lived in some form of heterosexuality and probably did not have the support of a community at all. A survey into the sexual habits of the Dutch show that in 1968 4 per cent of the then married women (a total of 112,000) said that they were predominantly or somewhat attracted to members of their own sex (Witte 1969).

LET A THOUSAND FLOWERS FLOURISH

In what way do these Dutch communities compare with lesbian communities in other parts of the Western world at the same time? The answer to that question can be found in realizing that lesbian communities are closely connected to what has been recently called different 'modes of patriarchal sex/affective production' (Ferguson 1990).

As societies change, so does the perception of lesbianism, the possibilities for creating lesbian subcultures, the independence of women. In fact, we recognize in each of the five different life-styles a lesbian way of life that is firmly placed in history. To the nineteenth century belong the hetero-sexuality/prostitution model (so celebrated by French authors!) as well as the romantic friendships. The last type was enhanced by the early waves of the women's movement. The two bar life-styles, butch-femme and bar dancing, were brought into existence by the urbanization process of the latter part of the nineteenth and the early twentieth century. 'Ordinary people' belong to the homosexual reform movements of the 1950s.

Most lesbian life-styles have shown themselves to be remarkably resilient since their period of origin. Their basic pattern remains the same, although their internal meaning can change in each phase of history.

The 1970s and 1980s have shown us that the multiplication of life-styles goes on. To the five life-styles recognized in the 1950s at least three have been added: the lesbian-feminist, the lesbian mother, the lesbian anarcho-squatter. This multiplication of identities adds an extra dimension to the elusiveness and diffusion that is lesbianism. Others will no doubt appear in the future. Whether such diffusion will add to the force of the lesbian movement, or render it more invisible, remains to be seen.[3]

NOTES

1   In the mid 1950s the term 'homosexual community' was first used. Although the equivalent 'lesbian community' was only described in the late 1960s, this des-cription owed much to articles on lesbians published in the 1950s in early lesbian magazines such as *The Ladder* in the USA and *Vriendschap* in the Netherlands.

2   The ideology of ordinary people was finally codified when one of the most influential psychiatrists in the Netherlands coined the phrase for one of his books on homosexuality (Sengers 1968).
3   After the completion of this article, an important new social history of lesbian life in the USA was published (Faderman 1991). Many of my themes are echoed in her book.

5

COMING OUT

Lesbian identities and the categorization problem

Valerie Jenness

For the last twenty years, gay and lesbian studies have focused on under-standing lesbianism as a particular form of homoerotic and political experience. Central to this pursuit has been a preoccupation with render-ing visible heretofore 'invisible lesbians' of the past, documenting the bases upon which women have come to engage in behaviour that may be identified as homosexual by themsleves or by others, and describing the multitude of ways in which women come to identify themselves as lesbians. At this point in the early history of gay and lesbian studies, there is an abundance of literature which conceptualizes and comments upon these types of concerns. In general, this literature has been sensitive to the historical and cultural context in which these processes occur and produce different types of women, lesbians, and lesbian communities.

A clear message emanates from the *mélange* produced by this literature: there is a theoretical and an empirical difference between 'doing' behaviours associated with lesbianism and 'being' a lesbian. For example, in her now classic article 'The female world of love and ritual: relations between women in ninteenth-century America', Carol Smith-Rosenberg (1975) documents the way in which romantic female friendships were comparatively common in the ninteteenth century. Yet, imputations of lesbianism were absent from these relationships as they were understood to be socially acceptable and fully compatible with heterosexual marriage. Similarly, Lillian Faderman (1981) examined various psychological and social reasons why romantic friendships between women were accepted and flourished during the eighteenth century, although they did not become understood as lesbian relationships by the participants. More recently, Martha Vicinus (1984) has examined the social origins and various phases of adolescent crushes between women in the late nineteenth and early twentieth centuries, including the ways in which participants in these relationships spoke of them as replications of heterosexual love rather than emergent lesbian relation-ships. In short, a 'doing' is not a 'being'.

Taking this well-documented gap between women's behaviours, the cultural imputations of lesbianism, and the adoption of lesbian identities as a starting point, this chapter discusses the ways in which women who ultimately come to define themsleves as lesbians understand the very concept of 'lesbian' and relate themselves to this cultural construct at different points in their lives. The specific question pursued here is: *what is the nature of the process by which some women come to see themselves as* being *lesbian?* I grapple with the question of self-categorization by focusing on the interaction between culturally available categories, the interpretation of experiences, and the adoption of identities. To this end, this chapter relies upon existing autobiographical accounts of self-defined lesbians.[1]

Although others (Cass 1979; Dank 1971; Plummer 1975; Ponse 1978) have enumerated sets of sequences as a way of offering insight into the possible stages one might go through before and after arriving at a lesbian identity, I argue that the adoption of a lesbian identity – the difference between 'doing' and 'being' – fundamentally hinges upon a process that I refer to as detypification. *Detypification is the process of redefining and subsequently reassessing the social category 'lesbian' such that it acquires increasingly concrete and precise meanings, positive connotations, and personal applicability*. Transformations along these lines point to a patterned process of interpreting, evaluating, and adjusting to the social world that women proceed through in order to arrive at a lesbian identity, and thus claim membership in the social category of lesbian. Of course, the corresponding substantive changes in meaning associated with these shifts vary along a variety of dimensions, such as race and class, religion and ethnicity, region and nation, and education and political beliefs.

In what follows, I discuss the nature of this process. First, I note the relationship between social categories and personal identities, and argue that an awareness of the concept lesbian is a necessary prerequisite for the adoption of a lesbian identity. Then, I detail the way in which 'lesbian' is detypified in the process of women coming to understand themselves as an instance of that particular construct. Finally, I conclude this article with some thoughts on gay and lesbian studies' participation in the detypification process, as well as the construction of lesbianism, as we enter the twenty-first century.

SOCIAL CATEGORIES AND PERSONAL IDENTITIES

In the first instance, we interpret our world in terms of social categories. Social categories serve as a basis for self-evaluation in so far as we utilize our understanding of them as interpretative schemata to assess our experience of ourselves as an object existing in a larger social world. Put simply, identities emerge from the 'kinds' of people it is possible to be in society. Accordingly, our identities emerge and are transformed as we place ourselves in various categories recognized in the community.

66

Important

The construction of a lesbian identity is firmly located in a developmental process that begins with an awareness of the social category 'lesbian'. Regardless of how the category is understood, an awareness of the social category lesbian must be present for a woman eventually to categorize herself as a lesbian and adopt a lesbian identity. If the woman is not aware of the social category, she cannot assess her experiences in terms of that social construct and its affiliated identity. In essence, the commitment to a lesbian identity cannot occur in an environment where the social construct 'lesbian' does not exist (D'Emilio 1983; Ettore 1980; Weeks 1977). Although various behaviours, emotions, and thoughts may be experienced prior to an awareness of the social category lesbian, they cannot be (retrospectively) interpreted as such until the woman acquires an awareness of the social category lesbian.[2] Indeed, the term lesbian provides a necessary interpretative framework for women to utilize in assessing themselves.

Typifications of the social category lesbian

There are many ways of becoming aware of and understanding any social category in a given socio-historical milieu. How one becomes aware of the social category lesbian is historically specific, yet diverse. For the purposes of this chapter, how a woman becomes aware of the category lesbian is not at issue. Instead, the nature of the meanings associated with the category lesbian is of importance.

Not surprisingly, prior to the adoption of a lesbian identity, the meanings associated with the term lesbian derive from cultural typifications. Typifications are cognitive representations of a supposed banal group; in this case, the woman's image of lesbians 'in general'. As a function of our stock of common knowledge, typifications are unexamined understandings that represent oversimplified opinions and images. Thus, by definition, typified understandings abstract from the concrete uniqueness of objects.[3]

For women who ultimately come to adopt a lesbian identity, the social category lesbian has three critical characteristics prior to self-categorization. First, understandings of the social category lesbian are relatively vague and derive from sources fairly removed from direct experience. Second, with rare exception, the connotations associated with the term lesbian are at best neutral and usually negative. Third and finally, the imagery associated with what it means to be a lesbian is perceived as incongruent with individual lived experience, and thus prohibits self-categorization.

During periods of their lives in which women reported understanding the social category lesbian along these lines, they did not identify themselves as lesbians. Regardless of content, typifications with these characteristics effectively allow women to disassociate themselves from the category lesbian. As Nancy clearly expressed:

I compared this information with my own 'case history'. My childhood had been relatively happy. I possessed no glaring deformities that I had noticed and my biggest sexual thrill had been holding Joanie's hand. Half of me felt relieved. If that was lesbianism, clearly I had nothing to worry about.

(Quoted in Cruikshank 1980: 141)

Similarly, Cynthia explained:

It's funny, I had no idea at that point. First of all, I didn't even know what a lesbian was – well, no that's not true. There were always queer days in high school and things like that, but I never thought about it in terms of myself. I can't remember thinking about it ever – except to wear the right color on the right day so that you wouldn't be considered a queer. On the other hand, I was really programmed to be a heterosexual. But – I don't know – I don't think any more so than most kids. On the other hand, when I thought about it, my whole vision of it was just of the sleazy, gutter kind of depressing life, you know? I don't know where I got that! 'Cause I don't remember reading any books, or really hearing anything concrete. I don't remember anyone ever talking to me about it. So it had just seeped into my head is all I could figure . . . it sounded so creepy to me; I couldn't imagine doing it with someone of the same sex . . . I wasn't defining myself as a lesbian.

(Quoted in Adair 1978: 141)

Finally, consider the words of Ruth who, after living with a woman for over five years, did not define herself as a lesbian:

We considered ourselves married, although of course it was unofficial: we were both women. Never did I attach the label 'lesbian' to either of us. I rarely thought of the term, and when I did I simply assumed that lesbians were women 'out there' who were probably sick or deranged and at any rate were trying to be men.

(Quoted in Baetz 1980: 17)

These comments suggest ways women implicitly and explicitly assess themselves through their general understandings of what it means to be a lesbian and then exclude themselves from membership of the category lesbian based on their typifications.

The practice of excluding oneself from the social category lesbian when it is typified in the above described manner contradicts the findings of others. For example, Grammick (1984: 35) found that 'physical/genital behaviour and the establishment of a physical relationship directly and substantially influenced the woman to define herself as a lesbian'. However, I argue that critical changes in the categorical meaning of lesbian are the decisive factor for self-categorization. The presence or absence of same-sex genital behaviour or whether or not other women are found to be erotic or worthy of primary affiliation is crucial in the process of self-categorization only in so far as it facilitates a change in the typification of the social category lesbian.

CRITICAL REVISIONS AND DETYPIFICATION

While the social categories we apply to ourselves are in a constant state of flux, they are not arbitrary. We are active in the establishment of our identities as we undergo changes in our knowledge base, including our understandings and interpretations of social categories and ourselves as an instance of them. As our understandings of the meanings associated with the kinds of people it is possible to be in society undergo substantive changes, we continually reassess the personal applicability of any given category.

Typified understandings are assumed to be an accurate assessment of reality until demonstrated otherwise. Our understandings of the world, including ourselves as an object, are generally held intact until a problematic situation allows – or forces – us to suspend belief in previously unquestioned assumptions. As pragmatists have stressed, habitual behaviours, thoughts, and beliefs are often interrupted and suspended when the individual encounters a problematic situation, or what I refer to as a crisis.[4] Dewey succinctly explained:

> The individual has a stock of old opinions already, but she meets a new experience that puts them to a strain. Somebody contradicts them; or in a reflective moment she discovers that they contradict each other; or she hears of facts with which they are incompatible; or desires arise in her which they cease to satisfy. The result is inward trouble which she seeks to escape by modifying her previous mass of opinion.
>
> (Quoted in Thayer 1982: 216)

These modifications often result in 'critical revisions' wherein typifications become detypified (Bittner 1963).

Since typifications are inherently general and undetailed understandings of social objects, they inevitably fall short of complete understanding and are thus susceptible to change at any moment. By definition, typifications are indeterminate, open-ended, and capable of revision. The question then becomes: in what ways is the social category lesbian shaded by individuals who ultimately define themselves as a member of that category? Specifically, are the meanings and connotations associated with the term lesbian modified in specific ways which facilitate women being able to categorize themselves as lesbians?

Detypification of the social category lesbian

I argue that the detypification of the social category lesbian is a prerequisite for self-categorization. Detypification refers to a process through which the acquisition of a new (alternative) interpretative schema allows women to redefine the social construct lesbian such that it is altered in three characteristic ways. First, understandings of the social category lesbian are enriched with detail as they are subjected to lived experiences and located in biographical contingencies. In the process, more concrete and precise understandings of what it means to be a lesbian are embraced. Second, the connotations associated with the term lesbian become increasingly positive. And third, the imagery associated with what it means to be a lesbian is perceived as congruent with individual lived experience, and thus the possibility for self-categorization is enhanced.

The process of detypification is prompted by a crisis, either large or small, which results in the restructuring of the category lesbian. Quite often, rethinking what it means to be a lesbian is sparked by new knowledge:

> Then, in a magazine shop in Greenwich Village, I found *The Ladder*. This small, rough periodical was not full of unhappy endings. I sensed that its very existence proclaimed a kind of healthy survival I hadn't imagined possible. There were stories and poems and articles, advertisements and letters and editorials, just like in a real magazine. To a sadsack little kid who'd been badly beaten by the blows of persuasion to hide and mourn her very being, *The Ladder* allowed entry into a legitimate universe.
>
> (Lynch 1990: 45)

As another example, consider the words of Cynthia, who was introduced in the previous section:

> A girl I had known in high school who had gone out to California came through town . . . she started telling me about all these people in California who were bisexual! I'd never heard that term before. I don't know where I'd been all my life . . . I just started thinking 'Weird'. That sort of started me thinking about myself and about how I didn't seem to get along that well with men – in terms of romantic, I mean, it just didn't seem to happen. I started thinking. Like I had this one girlfriend who was a very physical person. Whenever she talked to people she touched them, so from then on, whenever she'd touch me I would think 'Am I enjoying it?'
>
> (Quoted in Adair 1978: 141–3)

Cynthia failed to consider herself a member of the social category lesbian prior to this moment. At this point, however, she 'rethinks' the nature of the construct lesbian as well as her relationship to it. Specifically, as she (re)defines what it means to be lesbian, she re-evaluates herself with reference to those images.

Typifications get revised to become less general and more specific as they are employed to clarify ambiguous situations. That is, typifications undergo elaboration and/or qualification as they are shaped by experiences that arise in the course of women's lives. For example, Carol reported that she:

Finally did make love [with another woman], but it happened just because we loved each other a lot, and I didn't connect it to lesbianism. It was a separate unit in my life. Then, I joined a consciousness-raising group in Mobile. A few months after I joined, the first two lesbian feminists ever to hit Mobile joined it. They said, 'We are lesbians. We've been lovers for five years'. Things started connecting in my mind. The more they would say, the more I would think, 'Oh wow! This is what is going on with me.' They just made everything fit together.

(Quoted in Baetz 1980: 62)

As another example, Donna reflected:

I might not have made this connection if I had only my vague attachments to women to go on. But there was a second development in my psyche when I was in my early twenties: the knowledge I got from reading a few lesbian novels and one or two studies on homosexuality. The sketchy reading did tell me a great deal about myself. In fact, by giving me a tentative sexual identity, it gave me a great deal. I was quietly satisfied to have figured it all out ... thus was confirmed my suspicion of my emotional preferences for women which had come from reading. No longer could I interpret my unsatisfactory dating experience as a matter of mismatched minds.... All of the pieces of the puzzle had finally sorted themselves out and their configuration stood the test of everyday life.

(Quoted in Cruikshank 1980: 55)

Passages such as these reveal that women simultaneously reconstruct what it means to be a lesbian and reassess themselves as an instance of that particular category.

However, just because a woman retypifies what it means to be a lesbian does not ensure that she will come to understand herself as a lesbian. Retypification of what it means to be a lesbian is necessary, but not sufficient, for self-categorization. Women who categorize themselves as lesbians ultimately perceive similarities between themselves as objects and the cultural category lesbian. Congruence along these lines is *achieved* to the degree that personal experience converges with the retypified understandings. However, this in no way implies that the source or the content of the retypified construct is similar for all women. Obviously, the source and content of the retypification varies to the degree that individual lived experience varies.

71

FUTURE LESBIANISMS

Clearly, the process of detypification does not account for all that is included in the adoption of a lesbian identity. However, it does lie at the core of the difference between 'doing' and 'being', or what I call 'the categorization problem'. The process of detypification points to the way in which women are actively involved in ordering and interpreting their world, including themselves as an object in a larger social milieu. This is evidenced by the delicate interplay between the awareness of 'lesbian' as a kind of person that it is possible to be in the world, the typification and detypification of what it means to be a lesbian, and the achievement of convergence between imagery and experience. Self-categorization as a lesbian arises out of a partial reconstruction of the social world, including ourselves, as type constructs. In essence, lesbian identities are simultaneously products of and resources for social categories.

The development of a lesbian identity is, in the first instance, dependent upon the meanings that women attach to the social category lesbian. Such meanings are directly related to the meanings that are available in their immediate environment, as well as the meanings that are allowed to circulate in the wider society. Indeed, the historical invisibility of women's relationships with each other in general and lesbianism in particular, coupled with the insistence that sexual expression within women's relationships is deviant and unnatural, has constituted the greatest barrier to women's untroubled assumption of a lesbian identity.

Regardless of the now well-documented historical shifts and corresponding individual variation in the meaning of the term lesbian, since the concept 'lesbian' emerged in common usage in the 1890s it has mostly been ideologically linked with invisibility and with deviance (Jay and Glasgow 1990; Katz 1976; Schur 1984). However, over twenty years of gay and lesbian studies have done much to challenge these links by making visible the range of women's experiences with each other, as well as the contexts within which they occur. In the process, lesbian research has implicitly or explicitly constructed new images of lesbians through the production and dissemination of 'gay affirmative models' (Kitzinger 1987).

With the help of the gay and lesbian movement, as well as the women's movement, there has been and continues to be a proliferation of understandings of what it means to be lesbian (adjective) or *a* lesbian (noun). O'Brien (1984) has pointed out that same-sex genital sexual behaviour experience has often been used as a least common denominator criterion. However, many have taken issue with this understanding by offering alternative conceptions which make genital experience and an erotic component only secondarily important. For example, Cook (1979) and Rich (1980) extend the term lesbian to refer to a range of woman-identified experiences, while radical feminists and lesbian separatists understand lesbianism as

72

fundamentally a political statement representing the bonding of women against male supremacy. Others, such as Martin, argue that the word lesbian is 'not an identity with predictable content constituting a total political and self-identification. It is a position from which to speak' (quoted in Jay and Glasgow 1990: 6). From this perspective, lesbian is not a type of person at all, it is a metaphor.

In short, throughout the 1970s and 1980s the term lesbian has become increasingly expansive – some would say problematic. For over two decades, gay and lesbian studies have contributed to this expansion by providing a now institutionalized forum for lesbians' voices to be heard in the articulation of what it means to be a lesbian. At this point in the history of lesbian studies, it may be useful to step back from our 'cumulative discoveries' and examine them as our 'collective constructions'.

It is well past time to take inventory of the typifications of what it means to be a lesbian that emanate from lesbian studies and assess the degree to which they adequately capture and reflect distinctive new forms of women's same sex/gender relations in the so-called 'post-modern era'. As Stimpson surmised:

A 'lesbian identity' once entailed invisibility because no one wanted to see her. Now a 'lesbian' identity might entail invisibility because the lesbian, like some supernatural creature of myth and tale, shows that no identity is stable enough to claim the reassurances of permanent visibility.

(Stimpson 1990: 381)

Accordingly, are the conceptualizations of lesbianism emanating from gay and lesbian studies and remaining in common currency currently rendering invisible certain types of women, women's experiences, and women's relationships? Put another way, have the typifications emanating from lesbian studies been constructed in such a way that enable a diversity of women to locate themselves in that construct in light of their racial, class, ethnic, and religious identities, as well as the practical experiences and relevances of their lives in the course of engagement with their socio-symbolic world? At this point in our collective efforts, it is time to think seriously about the ways in which gay and lesbian studies have generated typifications which simultaneously facilitate and hinder the adoption of lesbian identities for particular women.

NOTES

1   Due to space limitations, a discussion of the materials used for this work has been reduced to a footnote. For a more lengthy discussion, see the larger work from which this article derives (Jenness 1987). What follows is a brief overview of the types of 'voices' that were considered in this work. I relied upon a corpus of published material by surveying literally hundreds of autobiographical

accounts of self-defined lesbians. While availability and usefulness ultimately directed the selection process, in each case the narrative was written in the first-person singular by a woman who defined heself as a lesbian. Ultimately, a diverse selection of lesbians was considered. That is, self-defined lesbians who account for a number of historical periods, a range of ages and socio-economic statuses, a variety of political camps and religious backgrounds, and a multitude of races and ethnicities were incorporated.

2 Zimmerman (1984: 558) has pointed out that 'many of us would like to believe that we were born lesbian, free from the original sin of heterosexuality. Thus, as the Furies collective demonstrated, lesbians tend to reconstruct personal histories in accordance with norms established by either the dominant culture or the lesbian subculture.' In her more recent work, Zimmerman (1990) has made evident the array of meanings attached to lesbianism through the proliferation of novels with lesbian themes, characters, etc.

3 The term typification should not be confused with the term stereotype. A stereotype is an image that conforms to a fixed pattern that constitutes a stan-dardized mental picture that is held in common by others. While both stereotypes and typifications both represent oversimplified opinions and understandings, the critical distinction is that a stereotype is assumed to be held in common by others, thus lacking variation in imagery. A typification, on the other hand, is not necessarily held in common by others, nor does it lack variation in imagery.

4 Crisis situations arise whenever new events are incomprehensible in terms of established assumptions. When existing expectations are violated, new sensi-tivities arise and new ideas emerge to be tested (Shibutani 1961, 1966).

6

THE ROLE OF DISCLOSURE IN COMING OUT AMONG GAY MEN

Peter Davies

> Becoming is younger than Being just as being is older than value. This concept of Being and its affirmation amount to a question of courage.
>
> (Tillich 1964: 164)

Coming out is a central feature of the experience of lesbians and gay men in the Western world. It forms the subject of a wealth of (auto)biography and fiction and is perhaps the central area of academic research. But for all this interest, there remains much disagreement about what coming out means, how it happens, and what drives the process forward. There is general agreement that coming out begins with an individual who is either unaware of her/his sexual orientation or shares the general view that to be homosexual is to be 'degraded, denounced, devalued, or treated as different' (Plummer 1975: 175) and ends with a person relatively happy with her/his sexuality, acknowledging this to self and to others. But this unanimity is largely illusory. On the one hand, there are those who regard coming out as a 'road to Damascus' experience, a single moment of recognition of one's 'true' self, a gestalt shift in which the label of the derided other is applied to one's self (Simon and Gagnon 1967a: 181; Sartre 1963: 78, Dank 1971). On the other hand, there is the more popular and realistic view that coming out is a 'long and winding road': a series of realignments in perception, evaluation, and commitment, driven by the affirmation 'I am gay' (e.g. Cass 1984; Troiden 1988b; Weinberg 1978).

Second, the great diversity of individual experience is a problem for those who seek to describe *the* coming out process. Is there in fact, one essential process, of which each individual biography is an idiosyncratic variation, or is there a multiplicity of paths and experiences which bear only superficial resemblance each to the others? Perhaps, as Coyle (1991) has recently suggested, individual biographies become assimilated to, or at least are presented as following, a script which is subculturally prescribed. The matter remains unresolved.

Third, psychologist and sociologist (perhaps predictably) disagree over the underlying dynamics of coming out. The former propose an internally generated process, driven by cognitive dissonance, while sociologists prefer an account which emphasizes identity as a social production: a process of social exclusion, labelling, and individual accommodation. Perhaps the most influential, certainly the most prolific writers on coming out are those who describe 'stages' of the coming out process (see Troiden 1988b). These 'stages' are periods of relative equilibrium which involve some unresolved conflict. Resolution of those conflicts facilitates movement between stages. It is, therefore, a description of a dialectic process. It is unfortunate that the focus of interest has been on what is stable at different stages, rather than on the nature of the conflicts that encourage movement from one to the other.

INDIVIDUATION AND DISCLOSURE

It is convenient to distinguish two processes which have sometimes been treated separately, sometimes confused: individuation, an internal, psychological process whereby I come to recognize my gayness, and disclosure, the process whereby others are appraised or learn of the fact that I am gay. One focus of this chapter will be the process of disclosure, specifically regularities in the patterns of disclosure by gay men.[1] The main argument will be, however, that disclosure and individuation are not parallel processes, each proceeding by its own, separate, internal, dynamic logic. Nor is disclosure merely the dual of individuation, lamely following as individuation proceeds, but they exist in a dialectic relationship: coming out to others constantly redefines one's notion of self and the development of a self-identity drives the process of disclosure.

In our culture, no one (well, hardly anyone) grows up assumed to be gay. The man[2] on the brink of coming out therefore inhabits a social matrix, a social structure which assumes, expects, and enforces heterosexuality. Typically (though not universally) the individual becomes aware of sexual desires that run counter to these expectations. It is tautological (though, in the manner of tautologies, nevertheless true) that these desires have themselves been engendered in that individual by the interaction of his body with the social structure. So, the individual is faced with a psychic dilemma: a contradiction between the expectations of society and its creation: himself.

Very broadly speaking, there are, at this stage, three options facing the individual. He can (i) deny his desires, (ii) deny the expectations, or (iii) live with the contradiction. The first option involves suppressing his feelings, living as a heterosexual. In the second option he asserts his homosexuality and begins the process of coming out. In other words, he accommodates either his self to the structure or the structure to his self. In the third case, he seeks to construct an accommodation between the two. The ways in which this may be achieved and sustained over time form the subject of this chapter. This third option has often been ignored. Because it can create potentially devastating strain on the individual, it is regarded as (at best) a short-term strategy doomed to failure as the individual seeks to consolidate his identity and his social life.

The crucial point for the individual starting to come out is that he lives in a social structure that is not of his own choosing. He can and will change that structure: acquire gay friends, frequent gay venues, perhaps become involved with a lover. He may also lose other friends, move house, cease to frequent other venues, etc. In this process of social relocation, he changes not only his friends and life-style, but also himself. A different social network, different social and sexual contacts will impose on him different expectations. *He becomes, in a real sense, a different person.* Becoming a gay man is a process of reaction to the expectations of the gay world and, in that sense, the processes of individuation and disclosure are inextricably linked.

But while there are parts of the social structure that are relatively permeable, others are relatively intransigent and these impose limits on this process of self-(re)creation. Whereas we can choose our friends, we are, by and large stuck with our family. Jobs which are conducive to gay men are relatively few. These and other features of the individual's social matrix can militate against total disclosure and leave the individual with areas of his life where he is known as gay and others where he is presumed to be, and must act as, straight. This disjuncted social life creates conflicts which require management (which are dicussed below) but also impinge upon his sense of self and put constraints on the process of individuation.

The assumption behind most accounts of coming out is that the process tends to produce an open gay man, open about his sexuality in all areas of his life. Moreover, it is implicit that this sexual identity will come to predominate over other aspects of identity and prove the prime mover of the ways in which he creates his life. Since many of us who write on this subject are just such men, there is a need to beware of solipsism: seeing our personal experience as universal. For it remains the case that, for many men, sexual identity is not the central feature of their lives; and there are yet others for whom it is simply not feasible to construct a fully gay life-style. We should not be tempted to see these individuals somehow as 'failed gays', men who have not managed to attain the final stage of a process that we have followed. Rather, we need a postmodern account of identity, which recognizes multiple identities and life as a process of achieving a more or less satisfactory *modus vivendi* with them. Rather than the idea of a gay identity as a superordinate organizing principle, we might pursue the idea of the sexual identity as one element of a man's life vying for space and energy with other aspects.

PATTERNS OF DISCLOSURE

The question therefore arises: are there patterns of disclosure which recur in the process of coming out? Writers have tended to concentrate on what features facilitate disclosure, particularly the 'stranger on a train' phenomenon: the tendency for an individual to be honest with a complete stranger. Telephone helplines, with the added guarantee of professional confidentiality, rely on this (see Macourt 1989). Few, if any, have considered the structural features of the disclosure process. It is usually assumed that the process of disclosure is ever onward and outward: the tendency will be to tell more and more people – and to an extent this is inevitable: you cannot un-tell someone that you are gay. They almost certainly would not believe you. This diffusion process is further assumed to be correlated with the process of individuation: the progressive retreat from living a lie. But it remains an undeniable feature of the society and culture in which we live that disclosure can, in many circumstances, have damaging, indeed disastrous effects: the loss of job, friends, house, family, etc. Thus, for some, indeed many individuals the costs of full disclosure quite heavily outweigh the benefits. Some individuals will, therefore, seek to maintain a partial disclosure over a period of time.

A useful analytical tool for understanding the process of disclosure and in particular its structural features is the idea of a social network (or what Sartre calls nexus). The individual invests significant amounts of emotional and psychic energy in only a relatively small proportion of those with whom he daily comes into contact. Each of the individuals in this social network will, in turn, have her/his own network of friends, etc. Individual networks overlap and networks of friends commonly overlap to a greater or lesser extent. Where there is much overlap, the networks form a clique, a tightly defined group of friends. In other cases, individuals draw their friends from disparate sources and the friends will not know each other, so their networks do not greatly overlap.

Two important corollaries follow from the observation that my friends will have some friends that are also my friends, First, it allows the possibility – indeed the likelihood – of gossip. Information can and will circulate among this group – especially information about me. The observation[3] that 'it's not me who can't keep secrets, but my friends' succinctly acknowledges this. Thus, two sets of considerations accompany the decision to make a disclosure to one of a group of friends. I must not only assess her/his individual reaction and decide whether the benefits (greater honesty, closer friendship, etc.) are likely to outweigh the dangers (distrust, dislike, shunning, etc.). I must also assess the structural consequences. Is it the case that this individual will disseminate this information among the rest of our mutual acquaintances? Now, this may be, from my point of view, either a good thing or a bad thing. I may tell so-and-so because s/he is a known gossip and will save me the trouble of coming out individually or collectively to a large group of people. Conversely, I may wish the disclosee to keep the piece of information secret and will extract a promise of confidentiality – and clearly, in the latter case, I will assess the likelihood of that promise being kept. There are, as we all know to our cost, those who seem congenitally incapable of keeping a secret. Telling some individuals a secret is equivalent to taking out an ad on the local radio station.

Second, partial disclosure creates potential situations of social strain. If some of my friends know that I am gay and others do not, and these friends know each other then situations in which I am in the company of at least one of either group will be difficult and, if the one(s) who know me to be gay are not aware of my desire not to tell others, at least potentially disastrous.

These two features underline the proposition that partial disclosure is inherently unstable. Over time, these two features will promote the diffusion of disclosure within the network. The individual who wishes to keep his gayness secret from one part of his network will be successful in the long term only if he is judicious in his disclosure. It turns out that, in the disclosure patterns of gay men, there are two broad strategies for the containment of partial disclosure: compartmentalization and collusion.

Compartmentalization

Simply put, this strategy involves ensuring that none of the people who know I'm gay knows any of those who do not know. In other words life is compartmentalized into areas where I am known as gay and those where I am not and those areas are kept apart, thus severely reducing the incidence of stressful encounters and the possibility of information flow between mutual friends (see Goffman 1970: 104; Warren 1974: 93–9). The crucial feature which determines the form of compartmentalization which is preferred in a particular case is that group from which gay identity is to be kept a secret. As has been suggested above, this is usually either family or people at work.

Where it is people at work from whom the secret is to be kept, a common strategy is to maintain a network of gay friends which does not intersect with the work networks. As 'Paul' said:

R: I'm only really gay, y'know, at weekends. The rest of the time I'm just John Jones, bank clerk.
Q: Isn't that ... doesn't that create problems?
R: Not really, that's how it is. It's easier like that.

The socially sanctioned segregation of life into public and private helps in this case, although there are established circumstances in which the private becomes a relevent topic of public conversation (see Plummer 1975: 175ff). The strategy is more likely to be a success if the individual works in a large town or city, where anonymity is a more realistic option than in a small town or village where all social networks are interconnected and private matters soon become public concerns.

Where it is members of the family who are to be insulated, a move away from home is commonly used to reinforce the compartmentalization. Obviously, this strategy is not always available and is likely to be more accessible to the middle class. The strategy of geographical compartmentalization is, in general, likely to be successful because it tends to minimize (if not entirely to exclude) a major problem with compartmentalization, that of friends of friends. While I can exercise a degree of control over whom I choose to associate with and thus, to a degree, create my own network, I am progressively less aware of and unable to control the friends of my friends and their friends and gossip can just as easily circulate between these as between my immediate circle of friends. Indeed, it may be only when it is too late and someone is found to have acquired the information that I sought to keep away from her/him that a path of acquaintances and breaches of confidence becomes apparent.

A good example of a segregated network is that of 'Richard', who has so arranged his life that it is segregated into three discrete milieux, reinforced by geography: his home village, where his family live; his work in a town some fifty miles away; his gay friends in a city twenty miles from the village and forty miles from the town. He is out only in the city and wishes to keep this information from his family and his work colleagues. The only structural weakness to this plan is a schoolfriend who now lives in the city where Richard is gay and they see a little of each other. Richard recognizes that he may have to collude with this friend in the medium term. Otherwise, as he says, the only way that news will get back to the village is if 'One of the neighbours has come down to Marks and Spencer and sees me draped around Justin.' (Justin is a young man whose flamboyant demeanour suggests that, even should he wish to do so, he would have difficulty in keeping his sexuality secret from anyone.)

Collusion

The second broad strategy is that of collusion. In this strategy, the structural features of disclosure are played down but the discloser enters into an agreement with a person or persons to keep the information away from certain others. Within this strategy two forms may be distinguished. In the first, the information is kept away from a few people by many: in the latter, a few people keep it away from many. A common instance of the former strategy is an agreement among the other members of the family to keep grandparents unaware of a grandson's sexuality. Grandparents (typically in their 70s and 80s) are generally thought not only likely to be distressed by the information but to be unlikely to have an understanding of what to be gay entails. As 'Peter' says of his grandmother, who is 73: 'She just wouldn't know what I was talking about. She was brought up ... it just wasn't talked about. She'd think I wanted to wear dresses or something.'

The second form of collusion involves the disclosing individual along with usually one but sometimes two or three others 'in the know', with a wider group excluded. Within the family a sister, usually an elder sister, often plays this role; in work a close companion or confidante, also often female, can present a diversionary front, even to the extent of feigning romantic involvement to divert attention and suspicion. The confidante in either or these arenas functions not only as a 'front' but also as a 'listening post'. S/He can alert the individual if questions are asked, suspicions have been voiced, doubts are emerging, so that a strategy to allay or confront them can be prepared.

Because the strategy of collusion does not utilize the natural structure of the social network in the way that compartmentalization does, the long-term success of the strategy depends on the motivation and commitment of the colluding parties. In the case of grandparents, it is likely that the whole family will agree that the benefits of telling them are greatly out-weighed by the anguish it would cause. But in work, it is rather more likely that at least one individual will feel that her/his duty to or standing with the boss demands that confidence is broken.

The purpose of collusion is therefore primarily and specifically to render safer those triadic situations of psychic strain mentioned above by ensuring that the party 'in the know' will play along with the discloser's deception. However, in general, the larger the number of the confidantes, the less likely it is that this strategy alone will prevent gossip circulating. Individuals become less friendly over a period of time. Indeed, a quarrel and estrangement will leave a putative enemy with potentially dangerous information, which can, in the extreme, lead to blackmails of the moral or the pecuniary sort. It is hardly surprising, therefore, that the more successful partial disclosure uses a mixed strategy – whether this is from necessity or choice.

Having described these two broad strategies, it should be said that most men use some mix of the two. Even 'Richard', with his strongly segregated life, needs to collude in one case.

DRAWING SOME THREADS TOGETHER

We may then conclude the following.[4] Structurally, the safest cases are those where (i) no one knows or (ii) everyone –or, at least, everyone who is anyone – knows. These automatically reduce the number of stress-producing situations and the potential for the circulation of knowledge (as opposed to rumour). In the case of partial disclosure, some strategies are more likely to be safe (in the sense that they represent some sort of equilibrium, with relatively little inherent tendency to change) in the long term than others. Compartmentalization is safer if it is complete and if the various clusters are separated by existing social or geographical boundaries. Collusion is more likely to be successful in the long term the fewer the people involved and the closer (more committed) they are to the discloser.

The central point is that partial disclosure creates some strain. The better strategies reduce that strain, but in the last analysis the success of any such strategy will depend on the amount of energy which the individual is willing and able to expend on maintaining that unstable state of affairs.

The unkind critic might make a number of points. First, coming out is a process in more ways than the exposition so far has allowed. Coming out also involves a series of disclosures and accommodations to a new life-style, not merely the acquisition of a new and isolated piece of information, however explosive it might be. Coming out is a constant struggle against those who, on the one hand, accept the disclosure and then, on the other, refuse to accept its implications: refusal to accept a lover, etc. The answer is that this does not involve the gay individual in a process of passing. Rather, it involves a battle of wills on a different level, although collusive strategies might well figure.

Second, the account given in this chapter does assume that individuals have effective control over disclosure and this is clearly not always the case. A man prosecuted for cottaging, for example, will, if his name appears in the local press – and this is the real threat of such prosecutions – find his carefully nurtured disclosure network summarily destroyed. Likewise, the practice of 'outing', whether done for salacious motives by the gutter press or for political considerations by gay groups, deprives the individual of control over disclosure and social identity. The very fact that outing is so controversial underlines the importance that is accorded to this control. In the light of the argument set out in this chapter, it should be noted that arguments about outing are not essentially about privacy, although these are the terms with which this debate usually operates, but about the control of information, and while there is a coherent – though, not to my mind conclusive – case to be made for privacy, it is far more difficult to argue convincingly for absolute control over information.

Third, the scheme I have put forward seems to suggest that the individual, especially he who engages in the strategy of compartmentalization, has perfect knowledge of the structure of his network. This is clearly unlikely, especially, as has been noted earlier, in the more distant parts of the friendship network. The better his knowledge of the network, the more likely it is that the strategy will succeed. Indeed, the consequences of getting it wrong may be disastrous. It is for this reason that the individual will, if the model is correct, spend some energy in ensuring that he has got it right. But, even so, the successful compartmentalizer is the one who invokes, in the defence of his secret, entrenched social divisions rather than the fluid patterns of mere friendship or gay camaraderie.

In conclusion, I have suggested that the process of coming out is not an ineluctable one of psychological necessity, but one that is situated in and influenced by a real and immediate social context. A better understanding of the process and its ramifications than can be gained merely from endless refining of the stages of disclosure is possible if the social strategy is integrated into the process of individual becoming.

A central assumption of traditional accounts of coming out is that sexual identity will become the primary identity: the one around which the individual's life will be arranged and articulated. In this paper, I have suggested that there will be cases in which this is an impossible or highly unsatisfactory possibility and have suggested ways in which the resulting strains are accommodated and managed. Furthermore, I have suggested that identity is a process of accommodation to a social world, rather than a dominating and pre-disposing psychic force. This perspective allows, far more easily than traditional accounts of self-concept or identity, the possibility of multiple identities, which compete, collude, and compromise in the process of everyday life.

NOTES

1　This part of the paper reports, in brief, the results of a study undertaken some years ago. Full details, including a mathematical derivation, may be found in Davies 1984. My thanks are due to my supervisors, Tony Coxon and Anne Murcott, for all their considerable help in that work.
2　From now on, I refer to the process of male disclosure and identity formation. While there may be similarities between this and the female case, there are also salient differences which would overly complicate the exposition and are, therefore, outwith the scope of this paper.
3　For which I am indebted to my friend Tony Coxon.
4　These conclusions may also be derived from balance theorems of basic graph theory (Davies 1984).

Part IV

CREATING NEW RELATIONSHIPS

Pretending to be families?

One of the most common of modern attacks on homosexuality declares it is a threat to the family. Yet at the turn of the twentieth century it is clear that family experiences mean something very different from those at the turn of the nineteenth century. 'Families' are everywhere; but they are different. Their dark side is now clearly seen, but so too is their diversity and range across the life-cycle. Same-sex experience is increasingly a part of this rich diversity. All gay and lesbian lives touch upon families – as sons and daughters, aunts and uncles, mums and dads, brothers and sisters, grandparents, step-parents and stepchildren. They most surely are a threat to the family as traditionally conceived, but not in its newer, richer, and more complex forms. Here they are very much part of the new families.

The five articles in this section make us aware of these newly emerging forms, giving us a glimpse of the future. Families exist where one of the partners is gay or lesbian (French); families exist where children are being raised by gays and lesbians (Romans); legal recognition of gay or lesbian marriage is happening in quite a few countries (Hart and Bech). In addition, new families are being composed not out of 'blood' but out of deep friendships – a point so forcefully demonstrated in Peter Nardi's article.

Although all the articles highlight oppression as a backdrop to the modern lesbian and gay experience, they also signpost how new worlds are being made: vibrant, positive, and curiously familial. Is this the shape of things to come?

7

LOVES, SEXUALITIES, AND MARRIAGES

Strategies and adjustments

Maggie French

> I can at least understand that it is perfectly possible to love someone
> of the same sex and opposite sex . . . one can do both.
>
> (Wife of gay man)

In 1988 the United Kingdom's Parliament introduced Section 28 which stated that a local authority shall not 'promote the teaching . . . of the acceptability of homosexuality as a pretended family relationship'. This civil legislation consolidated the moral panic surrounding the hitherto unfounded political belief that homosexual relationships were being 'promoted' in schools; further entrenched legal and political heterosexist attitudes; and presented the Government's view that the only acceptable 'real' type of relationship is a union of a heterosexual man and woman. Indeed, this legislation reflects the persistent discrimination against gays and lesbians and their relationships. Clearly, these types of relationships are seen as a challenge to the Government's commitment to promoting traditional 'moral' family values – heterosexual, of course. At the same time there is an underlying assumption that all husbands and wives who live in 'real' families are naturally heterosexual. However, as I will illustrate in this chapter, not all who live in 'real' families are heterosexual, and being heterosexually married is not by definition a validation of heterosexuality.

For this is a UK study of married couples who discovered that one partner's sexuality was gay or lesbian. Some were aware of this sexuality before their marriage; others not. Regardless, they expected that marriage was a validation of heterosexual identity. On becoming aware of the lesbian/gay identity all the relationships and the partners' identities were hurled into crisis, chaos, and turmoil. They were confronted with a situation they had never expected. They had assumed that they would enjoy a 'normal' heterosexual married life 'until death do us part', and suddenly all this was under threat.

Between 1980 and 1984 I interviewed sixteen heterosexual wives, twenty gay husbands, seven lesbian wives and four heterosexual husbands – most of whom were members of a self-help group for individuals in such marriages. They were white, middle class, and their ages spanned from the early 20s to early 60s. They were employed in various jobs including teaching, clerical work, secretarial, engineering, executive, nursing, etc. Some had financial problems; others not. Most had children and faced the same sort of problems as other parents (French 1990).

Each person related their own experiences in open discussions and interviews, describing the various strategies they employed when coping with the changes in themselves and their relationships. What became obvious from their stories was the complexity and diversity of their loves, sexualities, and marriages. However, as I sat and listened to their descriptions of why they got married, why they stay married, and how they adjusted their relationships and identities, a pattern did emerge. From this I located four distinguishable turning points in their relationships: *Starting Together*, in which couples described the early days of their relationships; *Something's Happening*, where various warning signs of future problems are detected; *Coming Out*, where both partners acknowledged the gay/lesbian identity in the marriage; and *Negotiating a New Life*, when the partners attempt to find some solutions to their difficulties and, in interaction, negotiate satisfactory life-styles.

STARTING TOGETHER

In the earliest stages, the couples showed very little difference from many heterosexual relationships (Mansfield and Collard 1988). They met, became friends, got closer, got married, and 'honeymooned'. The main difference could be found in their motives for marriage and in their awareness of gay or lesbian sexuality. Of course, such awareness changes over time, as will become evident and will be illustrated in the following stages.

All the gay men said they had questioned their sexuality before they met their future wives; but this was not so for the lesbians. The men seemed to know about their gayness long before the women and hence faced different problems. The lesbians, by contrast, had their lesbianism revealed to them only during the marriage. Indeed some of the gay men had been actively involved in the gay world before marriage; others not. Some told their future wives; others did not. But they all said that they had questioned their sexuality before they met their wives.

Because of the stigma attached to homosexuality many of the men did not develop a gay identity even when they were aware of same-sex attraction. Most thought that the attraction would disappear if they formed opposite-sex relationships. Some husbands were aware of their attraction to men, but when they met and married their wives they were expecting this attraction to disappear. They assumed that such a relationship would be confirmation of their heterosexuality and said that they expected to live a 'normal' married family life. As Tim described it:

88

We were very much in love. . . . I imagined marriage consisted of love, companionship, children and family. . . . We had children about the time we wanted them. . . . We've had financial worries throughout our life which is what most have.

Most wives who were aware of their husbands' sexuality did not expect it to be a problem once they were married. Caroline, who met Ted at university, said:

We met in 1958 at university where we were friends with the usual chaste stuff of good night kisses of the 1950s. . . . I did know when we got married that he had had a homosexual experience but it did not worry me. We slept together before we were married and we were very much in love. I just put it down to youthful experience or whatever.

By contrast, for the lesbians it was only after marriage that they became aware of their lesbian identity. Most of these relationships began as friendships that developed emotionally and culminated in marriage. Kathy described this stage in her marriage:

The relationship worked well. . . . I did what society expected me to do. . . . I married a guy who was nice and supportive. I had a child and was led to believe that that would lead to ultimate fulfilment.

The lesbians were not aware of their sexuality until after they had been married for some time and their husbands had assumed that they were marrying heterosexuals. They, like others, defined this first stage of the relationship as 'normal'. As Robert said:

We had led what I felt was a perfectly normal life and had been married for twenty-six years. I had worked my way up the career ladder with my company and led a fairly conventional life-style with a home and a family.

What was strikingly clear from these couples' accounts was that regardless of their awareness they overwhelmingly defined their marriages as normal and conventional at the outset of their married life when 'starting together'. Gradually, however, they became aware of changes and that 'something was happening' in their relationship.[1]

SOMETHING'S HAPPENING

Gradually, some of the spouses became aware of changes in their marital relationship and that something was happening, yet there was some uncertainty about whether to define it as 'something unusual' or 'nothing unusual' (Emerson 1970). Indeed, they constantly shifted from one definition to the other and there was some confusion as to how to react or respond to the changes. Interestingly, there was a reluctance to acknowledge that something was wrong and that the gayness or lesbianism was an issue. Attempting to deal with the situation three different strategies were at work: *keeping quiet*, when the heterosexual was unaware of their spouse's changing sexual identity; *kissing and telling*, when both partners became aware of why something was wrong; *keeping up a pretence*, a variation of the former where both spouses spent some time pretending that they were not aware of the sexuality.

Keeping quiet

Some gay men reconsidered their sexuality after becoming husbands and fathers and began to lead a double life. Although aware that something unusual was happening they did not reveal this to their wives but instead employed the strategy of 'keeping quiet'. Richard's wife, Ruth, was unaware that he was questioning his sexuality and who he was seeing during his lunch hour, so for her 'nothing unusual was happening'. As Richard explained:

> During those early years I was aware that I wanted relationships with men. . . . I didn't have any desire to give up the marriage and be gay . . . I used to read *Gay News* and answered some ads and met a guy. . . . I used to have lunch with him and gradually learnt what being gay was about. . . . I was very conscious of the deceit so far as Ruth was concerned.

Chris, a wife who was not aware of her husband's pre-marital doubts about his sexuality became suspicious that 'something unusual was happening' when her husband was spending more time than usual with a male friend. Yet she neutralized this and shifted to a stance of 'nothing unusual is happening'. As she said: 'I remember saying, "if I didn't know you better I'd think that you had 'a little bit' somewhere". This was a joke and the idea quite preposterous to think about!'.

The gay men had some awareness of why something was happening because they had questioned their sexuality before marriage. But this was not so for lesbians, like Cathy, who said:

> When I had my son I got very depressed. . . . I went to a psychiatrist about the depression. I remember talking to him about a friend. . . . . This guy said did I think I was possibly attracted to her, I thought, yes, I probably am. And somehow everything seemed to make sense. . . . Initially, I didn't think I had to do anything about it.

Although Robert was aware that his lesbian wife, Sandra, was depressed and unhappy, he took a stance of 'nothing unusual is happening', saying 'I just carried on going to work coming home, playing golf, so you see, everything was all right from my point of view'.

Kissing and telling

Some gay men and lesbians opted to kiss and tell their spouses why something was wrong in their marriages. Yet both spouses were reluctant to acknowledge that the shift in sexuality was the source of their marital difficulties. Many blamed other issues including financial problems and the children. Consequently, they maintained that it was 'nothing unusual'.

Joan, who was aware of her husband's gayness before they married said:

Occasionally he would tell me that he was looking at men in a way that he shouldn't if he was straight. He would get upset and we'd talk about it . . . we were both naive enough to think that it was just a phase he was going through.

Harry's lesbian wife, Janice, did 'kiss and tell' him that she had questioned her sexuality before marriage and again afterwards. Harry said that he assumed that once married they would lead a conventional married life. However, after the disclosure when married, Harry maintained that they were fairly happy, although, he added, like other couples they had financial problems with two young children.

Keeping up a pretence

Other couples, although aware of the shift in sexuality, employed various strategies by keeping up a pretence that nothing unusual was happening. Ted had told his wife before their marriage that he had doubted his sexual identity. However, it was some time after the wedding that these doubts arose again. Yet, Ted denied that his sexuality was a problem, saying:

I've always felt that there were problems not with the homosexuality but the marriage in fact. She felt that she was left with the children too much whilst I was away on courses. . . . Whenever we had rows I began to feel resentment towards the children in a way.

Like others, Ted's wife, Caroline, had not expected the pre-marital disclosure to be a problem after their wedding. Yet, when the gayness was disclosed during their marrige she responded by 'keeping up a pretence' that their problems and conflicts were due to other factors, saying:

91

We had our ups and downs but over the last couple of years something seemed to be wrong. I think that you look at all sorts of things and wonder why we seemed to be disliking each other and so on, why have we gone off each other? . . . But then it was so wrapped up in other things. . . . Our sexual relationship was normal at that stage, whatever is normal, then we moved house and got snarled up with extensions and mess. . . . However, we made it all seem logical and quite natural.

Sarah, a lesbian wife, and her husband decided to have sexual counselling after her disclosure. Because they had had sexual problems since they married, Sarah thought that she was frigid. They discussed her lesbian concerns with the counsellor. However, he laughed and dismissed this, telling her that she would also laugh at the idea six months hence. She assumed that as a professional had told her this she must be wrong and she and her husband maintained the pretence that nothing unusual was happening.

However, Sarah and the others were to confront the issue later and yet again employ further strategies.

COMING OUT

This turning point was a very painful and distressing experience for all the couples because this was the event when the gay or lesbian sexuality was revealed and confirmed. Whether either partner had been aware of the gayness or lesbianism before they married, they had assumed that they would be living in a 'real' heterosexual marriage and family. But now they faced a totally unexpected situation – that they or their partner was gay or lesbian.

Like the other turning points that these couples had confronted 'coming out' was characterized by a diversity of experiences with various responses and strategies.[2] I found that there was no single way of 'coming out' but at least three: *wanting more time*, when one partner disclosed their sexuality to their spouse because they wanted to spend more time exploring their sexuality in the gay/lesbian world; *finding suspicious clues*, when the heterosexual spouse found clues which aroused suspicion about their partner's sexuality (some challenged their partner's behaviour after finding a gay magazine in their home, a few became concerned about their spouse's declining sexual interest, others questioned the increasing time spent with a same-sex friend); *being caught in the act*, when the spouse disclosed the sexuality because of an impending police prosecution for 'cottaging' or medical confirmation of venereal disease.

Even though conventional wisdom would assume that the disclosure would be immediately followed by marital separation, this was not so. Surprisingly, the couples employed diverse strategies to deny that their marital difficulties were due to the gayness or lesbianism.

They did so in four main ways: through a *denial of responsibility*, when many other issues were blamed before the gayness or lesbianism, including financial difficulties, working long hours, a new baby; *condemning the other*, when the gay or lesbian condemned the actions of their partner, the heterosexual wife blamed herself, the heterosexual condemned the lover of their spouse; *appealing to experts*, when either or both partners sought professional advice or read literature in an attempt to neutralize the sexual 'deviance' and/or the deviant marriage; if this did not prove fruitful there was the fourth strategy – *seeking confirmation*, by joining the gay community, a lesbian group, or a self-help group where they could neutralize the 'deviant' behaviour and/or the marriage in interaction with others in a similar situation.

Gay men and their wives

Does your wife know? This question is commonly asked of married gays. Should he tell or not? This was a question many of the married gay men asked themselves. A wife's reaction to such a disclosure is largely unpredictable. He may be happily married and a contented and involved father. The revelation could mean the loss of both even though he may feel a sense of relief after 'coming out'.

When the wives became aware of their husbands' gayness their responses ranged from wanting him to leave the home to a willingness to renegotiate their marriage contract to ignoring the issue entirely. A few did not know what gayness was. Some blamed themselves and felt guilty and most experienced a sense of isolation. Several assumed that their husbands were sick and/or in need of professional help. For others it was confirmation of suspicion or an explanation of why previously something 'odd' was sensed as happening. All in all, most wives experienced a mingling of resentment, anger, disbelief, and shock. Whether they had been aware of the gayness before the wedding some believed that 'love conquers all' and all felt that marriage was confirmation of the husband's heterosexual identity.

Lesbians and their husbands

In contrast to the gay men, the lesbians were not aware of their sexuality before they married. Consequently, 'coming out' for them was very complex because they were negotiating a shift in their sexual identity, not only for the first time but also as married women and for some as mothers. The risks involved in disclosing their sexuality to their husbands could include losing their home, marriage, and, if they were mothers, their children. They could, of course, opt for total secrecy and the decision of whether to tell was agonizing. Like the wives of the gay men the lesbians' husbands' reaction to the disclosure was unpredictable.

For some husbands the revelation was confirmation of suspicion. Others responded by refusing to believe it or regarded it with apparent disinterest. Some lesbians were surprised and mystified when they did not receive an expected negative reaction to their news. This often led to feelings of guilt and confusion. On the other hand, some husbands responded with hostility and/or tried to persuade their wives to stabilize their heterosexual identity. In some instances, where there were children, they were used as a lever by the husbands who threatened to try to deprive the wife of any contact with the children if she opted for a divorce. However, as will become evident, divorce was just one response to the disclosure as couples adjusted their life-style when 'negotiating a new life'.

NEGOTIATING A NEW LIFE

Throughout their relationships these couples had been employing various strategies to cope with the emergent changes. And now they were in the process of 'negotiating a new life' and creating new life-styles with or without their marital partners. At this turning point there were three different types of adjustment: *open marriage*, when the couple maintained a mutually acceptable relationship, yet, at the same time, both were involved in extra-marital affairs; *just good friends*, when the couple maintained a friendly, non-sexual relationship, with one or other involved in an extra-marital relationship; *parting of the ways*, when one spouse opted for a separation or divorce. However, separation did not necessarily presage divorce. For some it was a 'breathing space' leading to another adjustment.

Open marriage

Tim 'came out' in the context of 'being caught in the act' when he was awaiting an impending police conviction for 'cottaging'. Following this he and his wife renegotiated their marriage contract and opted for an open marriage. In this negotiating process Tim ceased 'cottaging' and developed a specific gay relationship yet maintained his commitment to and his love for his wife. As he said: 'There was never any question about being in love with Rosie, I still am. I never expected to go back to any homosexual practice when we married. Tim's wife, Rosie, had married on the assumption that he was heterosexual and had gone through various stages of change and adjustment throughout her marriage. Her identity had shifted from a heterosexual wife married to a heterosexual to a wife married to a gay man. Then after developing a woman-to-woman relationship her identity shifted to a lesbian married to a gay. Yet, as she explained, she felt that these changes had enhanced their lives, saying:

94

We have learnt a lot about each other; also it's added a great deal of knowledge and colour to our sex life. I think in this respect we are lucky because there are a number of couples living together happily . . . but not a good sexual relationship . . . he enjoys his sex life with me . . . he enjoys his sexual encounters with his fellers . . . I can at least understand that it is perfectly possible to love someone of the same sex and the opposite sex . . . one can do both, the two are very different.

Just good friends

Others renegotiated their marriage contract by adjusting to being 'just good friends'. Although they abandoned their marital sexual relationship they maintained the marriage because they enjoyed the companionship of their partner and the sharing of family responsibilities. Jack 'came out' in the context of 'finding suspicious clues', then he and his wife Val adjusted to being good friends. After this his role as husband and father had altered, as he said:

> It has changed in that I do take more part in the family life than before I came out, far more, and it has grown. At the same time the relationship between myself and everybody is much more of a relationship between Jack or me rather than husband and father . . . It's a much more flexible role that I think I am able to play.

Some time after Jack's disclosure Val met Philip with whom she formed a sexual relationship. This relationship was very important to Val for, like many other wives on becoming aware of their husbands' gay activities, she had suffered a blow to her self-esteem and confidence. As she said: 'I think it's important when you reach the point that I did that you find somebody or just get out . . . what I give to Philip I cannot give to Jack because he doesn't want it.'

Parting of the ways

Within the context of 'parting of the ways' there are two sub-contexts: separation and divorce. Separation is not final but is another type of adjustment which may shift to divorce or another mode of adjustment. Although divorce is final in legal terms many couples still provided financial, emotional, and practical support.

The gay men did not choose divorce or separation. It was their wives who opted for this form of adjustment. The husbands would have preferred to remain married and continue to pursue their gay activities.

Ted, who came out in the context of 'wanting more time', described his preferences, saying:

> I never understood why she wanted a divorce . . . I would have liked a loose arrangement, my cake and eat it. A separate part of the house or buy a house round the corner or next door.

Of course, some couples did adjust in such a way but this type of arrangement was not satisfactory for Ted's wife, Caroline, who said:

> I thought, can one live with this? I was thinking about the children and everything, as one does. I was becoming crosser and crosser and when he came home late I would be lying in bed absolutely livid and eventually I said, 'you either stop it or move out'. . . . I petitioned for unreasonable behaviour. It is unreasonable in my eyes. . . . I think that if our marriage had continued I would have been very dishonest with myself and to the world in general. You know, you masquerade as a happily married woman and it gets you down after a while.

Trying to maintain her identity as a heterosexually married woman was also stressful for Cathy, a lesbian, who came out in the context of 'wanting more time'. As she explained: 'I told James I wanted to leave after careful consideration for weeks. I told him I decided that I needed to be me. . . . I just couldn't cope with the guilt any more.'

Whereas most of Caroline's dissatisfaction was with her husband's sexual behaviour, for Cathy it was more the inequalities of the division of labour in the home within the ideology of heterosexual marriage. As she described it:

> However sharing James was, I was still lumbered with the housework, the cooking, the organizing of all the social life, the dinner parties, the baby sitters and all that. . . . That's something I enjoy about a close friendship with a woman. We really share things. There's tremendous equality that I like. . . . With a woman it's much more shared and much more comfortable, suits me much more.

Although there was a difference in the sexualities of Caroline and Cathy, both of their accounts of this stage reflect social attitudes surrounding marriage and sexuality. Furthermore, Caroline's husband did not question her ability to raise their children as a divorcée. Whereas Cathy's husband raised some concern about the type of household that their son would be exposed to if he lived with his mother after she had shifted her sexual identity from heterosexual to lesbian. Yet, in none of the modes of adjustments in this stage did the heterosexual wives perceive their husbands' gayness as a cause for concern in their role as fathers.

CONCLUSION

The changes in the relationships and identities reveal that marriage is neither inevitably heterosexual nor a validation of heterosexual identity. Moreover, this chapter has shown that marriage and sexual identity are not static but socially constructed: their meanings are constantly changing.

Moral rhetoric and political legislation attempt to regulate sexual behaviour by promulgating heterosexual marriages and families as the 'norm' and reacting with hostility towards gays and lesbians and their relationships. It was because of these attitudes and the prevailing ideology that the couples I met employed the strategies illustrated in my chapter, I found that their loves, sexualities, and marriages were socially constructed as they attempted to make sense of their own reality as they passed through four stages: 'Starting Together', 'Something's Happening', 'Coming Out', and 'Negotiating a New Life'.

Their experiences reflect the difficulties faced by many other couples across the world who live in societies that continue to discriminate against and oppress gay men and lesbians because of their sexuality. The couples I spoke to in the 1980s told of their struggles and adjustments in their efforts to make sense of their lives. They employed diverse strategies in their resistance to labelling themselves, their loved ones, and their family arrangements as abnormal.

Unless there is some ideological shift, I am sure that these types of situations and stories will continue in the lives of others into the 1990s, not least now because of the moral assumptions and condemnation of relationships and life-styles which are not heterosexual and monogamous, since the onset of AIDS. All this is exacerbated and fuelled by the legal system and political statements, including Section 28, condemning couples who live in 'pretended' families and are perceived to be a political threat in a heterosexist society.

NOTES

1 See Emerson (1970) for further analysis of this concept.
2 For further discussion of the coming-out process see the chapter by Peter Davies.

8

DARING TO PRETEND?

Motherhood and lesbianism

Pat Romans

'But you can't be a lesbian and a mother – can you?' The terms 'lesbian' and 'mother' carry many stereotyped and deeply influential implications for women. Lesbianism is stigmatized and ridiculed – a process which generally takes the form of reducing a total life experience to certain types of sexual behaviour which are then labelled deviant.

> A lesbian is conceived as a hard, sophisticated female who indis-criminately seduces innocent girls or women into the mysteries of some 'perversion' they know little or nothing about.
>
> (Martin and Lyon 1972)

Motherhood on the other hand is regarded in idealized images and persists through a dense mythology as the state all 'normal' women naturally wish to attain (Rich 1976; Oakley 1979). A somewhat ironical contradic-tion absorbed within the ideology of motherhood is that this 'natural maternal desire' should become active only within a stable, monogamous, heterosexual relationship (MacIntyre 1976). An obvious muddle exists here between biologically determined factors and social constructs that have been built around motherhood.

Public opinion holds that lesbianism and motherhood represent an unacceptable combination (SCPR 1988/9). Lesbian mothers are the 'least appropriate' of a three-tiered motherhood hierarchy constructed by the social values attributed to sexual orientations and family forms (DiLapi 1989). The most appropriate category is that of married, heterosexual mothers, while included as 'marginally appropriate' are single mothers, teenage mothers, and foster mothers. These values are underpinned politically in the UK at the present time by legislation such as Section 28 of the local Government Act 1988 prohibiting the promotion of homosexuality as a pretend family relationship; by parliamentary efforts to exclude lesbian women from AID services at officially recognized clinics; and the hostile reactions of some local councillors and the media to an increased number of applications to foster and adopt by openly lesbian women. These examples of institutionalized heterosexism legitimate prejudice and

98

discrimination against the lesbian mother who can accept no incompatibility between her desire to relate sexually to other women and her ability to rear her children successfully.

THE EMERGENCE OF 'THE LESBIAN MOTHER'

The lesbian mother presents a threat: she challenges the dominant ideologies of gender, motherhood, and family which together are felt to contribute significantly towards the stability of society. The ideology of gender persuades women to strive towards femininity and to become mothers helps to clarify their position. To appear in public with children is to invoke automatically the presumption of heterosexuality (Rich 1980). The ideology of the family helps to define women's roles as mothers within familial structures – a set of ideas carrying enormous implications for women, both personally and politically, in terms of how they experience their lives. Because women who are lesbian and mothers pose a threat to the status quo by turning many of these ideological frameworks upside down, measures are adopted to minimize this threat. Institutional barriers like the relegation to the position of 'pretend family' assist in invalidating the lesbian-headed household as a legitimate family form.

Yet during the 1980s in the UK, and indeed throughout much of the Western world, a significant change occurred within the lesbian community as many hitherto secretive lesbian mothers began to identify and articulate the oppression they were experiencing. Assisted by the support networks established by the women's and gay liberation movements of the 1970s, they began to question their assigned position of 'inappropriate mothers'. A distinct shift occurred: from a position of almost silent apology to a positive and confident assertion that lesbian motherhood was a valid, alternative life-style in which to raise children. The new 'lesbian mother' was born.

This can be seen as part of a wider change in the family in Western society. The proportion of people living in a traditional family, i.e. a married couple with dependent children, now makes up only 42 per cent of the total in the UK (1991). Increased divorce statistics and the growth in single-parent families, usually headed by a woman, facilitate the lesbian mother's efforts to create her alternative family structure.

In addition to these demographic trends, lesbians in the UK received a higher media profile in the late 1970s (Hemmings 1980). Coverage referring specifically to lesbian mothers, e.g. lesbians becoming mothers through artificial insemination and contested lesbian custody cases, helped lesbian mothers' growing awareness of a need for more obvious solidarity. Support systems like the Rights of Women Lesbian Custody Group[2] began to form. This type of central organization, assisted by a growing network of local groups, had never existed before and indicates how far lesbian mothers have become established as a social category in their own right.

Local and national networks of contact have in turn become strengthened by support at an international level. Dialogue with lesbian women in Europe, the USA, and Australia particularly has been facilitated by conferences during the past decade.[3] International discourse encourages both research and the flow of information – as the present volume indicates. Lesbian mothers are benefiting from this wider field of debate in which their unique position within the lesbian community is acknowledged and which enables them to develop a wider persepctive to include women from other countries and cultures.

Current UK trends

During the 1980s the rights of gays and lesbians to become parents have been raised against a backdrop of growing discriminatory attitudes. A campaign to emphasize the importance of traditional patterns of family life has persisted throughout the present Government's period in office. The lesbian life-style is one of the biggest threats to this image of the traditional family, for here can be found individuals living happy, effective lives outside the recognized norms. The lesbian, with her ability to achieve a good life without a man, is of particular significance. The lesbian mother transgresses even further by undertaking motherhood as a gay parent rather than within the confines of a traditionally acceptable nuclear family. Lesbian mothers go beyond: in rearing children they create new familial patterns and new living arrangements which push the boundaries of present family forms into new areas of potential.

POSITIVE LIFE-STYLES IN A HOMOPHOBIC SOCIETY

In 1987 I conducted some research into the life-styles of lesbian mothers living in the UK in order to fill an obvious gap in the recently growing Western literature on lesbianism (e.g. Ponse 1978; Moses 1978; Tanner 1978; Wolf 1979; Ettore 1980). A sample of forty-eight women were interviewed. Although I tried to meet as diverse a group as possible, there were gaps. Missing from the samples are women from ethnic minorities, disabled women, and only a very few were working-class.[4] Excluded too of course are the really 'secret' lesbian mothers who will never be part of any research (Darty and Potter 1984). The research does claim to have achieved a reasonable age range, the youngest woman interviewed being 22 years and the oldest 65 years, and they were resident throughout England and Wales in both rural and urban situations. A number of women had not discussed their lesbianism with anyone before, some requiring considerable persuasion to do so on this occasion, and therefore the sample avoided being comprised of uniformly 'out' lesbian women or members of specific, established groups.

The main focus of the research was to consider the different life-styles and family structures of lesbian mothers in the UK of the late 1980s. Successful management of such a life-style is a complicated procedure requiring constant modification and negotiation in daily interactions with others (Hart and Richardson 1981). The life-styles adopted ranged widely from those women almost totally denying their lesbianism, to a small group who had decided to prioritize this aspect of themselves over and above everything else – including their role as mothers. It was possible to develop a typology which encompassed this wide variety of life-styles quite effectively.

Concealers

Women in this category, while acknowledging and accepting their lesbianism, had made decisions which meant that their motherhood role remained consistently more central to them than the expression of their own sexuality. Eight respondents were identified as concealers. Six of them, despite the discovery of their lesbian identity, had opted to remain within their heterosexual marriages, at least for the time being. (Of the remaining two, one was widowed and the other divorced.) This group of women were anxious to represent themselves as conventional married women, as much for their husbands' sake as their own. They were overwhelmingly middle-class and were managing this difficult combination of life-styles with varying degrees of success.

Hazel, a journalist in her 40s with three children, is well able to speak for the group. Of her marriage she said:

> It's very warm and it's very good and I cannot imagine life without him. The way I look at it is I made my decision to get married and to have children and I don't think I either want to throw it up or have the right to.

Her husband is aware and has accepted her sexual need for women but Hazel has allowed him to believe she is bisexual although she knows this not to be true. When talking of the possibility of leading a more 'open' life-style in her village she said 'certainly here it would be death because they couldn't begin to understand'.

Her inevitable inability to fulfil her lesbian sexual needs, apart from occasional meetings with partners that familial responsibilities allow, is an ongoing source of pain – 'At the moment I am celibate and it hurts'.

The position of these lesbian women remaining in their heterosexual marriages is not a wholly tenable one. While there from the best of motives, they were engaged in various forms of deceit, necessary to protect the feelings of their hubands, and they experienced considerable frustration in the constant coping with a situation so difficult to maintain. They felt

101

themselves to be a tiny minority marginalized by their decision to remain within their heterosexual marriages.

Confronters

At the opposite end of the spectrum were seven women who were prepared to take on society over their lesbianism and in some situations to risk their motherhood role rather than compromising their position as lesbians. A major factor which tended to set this group apart from many of the others in the sample was the methods by which they used dress and appearance as a form of expression of their sexuality. What people choose to wear often tells as much about them as what they choose to say. These women were acutely aware of the impression that their general appearance gave to others and of the political function that could result from this. The fact that 'confronting' lesbian mothers tend to fulfil popularly held stereotyped views of lesbians was a source of irritation to the more conforming women in the sample who saw the dangers of being part of a potentially 'discreditable' minority population (Goffman 1970).

Barbara, a 22-year-old mother of two, who finds coping satisfactorily with her children difficult, said:

I look like a transvestite when I've got a skirt on. I like to look like a dyke myself – I feel I want to be identified.

This respondent was not alone in expressing frustration about the way in which being a mother inhibits their full commitment to the lesbian life-style of their choice. Eve, for example, in her late 20s and married and divorced twice, had only two of her four children living with her but would happily have placed them in some form of alternative care to allow her to develop her lesbian life-style more fully. And Nancy, a 43-year-old lecturer still giving a home to her teenage son, had decided to ask him to find alternative accommodation rather than allowing his presence to curb her lesbian activities in any way.

The confronters in the sample were impatient of other lesbian mothers not prepared to make a similar stand over the validity of their life-style. Eve spoke for them all:

We never make a pretence that we are not lesbians. It would be helpful if everybody was out because there would be so many of us.

Compromisers

By far the largest number of women, exactly half the total sample in fact, were placed in this category. They were to varying degrees open about their position as lesbian mothers, but were prepared in certain circumstances to compromise this position for the sake of expediency. For the most part these circumstances would involve the well-being of their children. It is the existence of her children of course which renders the lesbian mother that much more vulnerable than the majority of the homosexual population. She is anxious on two counts. First, there is the anxiety, often well founded, that she might lose care and control of her children if her ability to fulfil her motherhood role was ever legally contested. A second, ongoing concern is that her chosen life-style might lead to her children being ridiculed and abused in situations where she would be in no position to defend them.

Compromises may well be made where the children's education is involved. Typical of comments here were – 'I have a dress that I wheel out for certain occasions, when it's a school play or something' and 'When my son has things at school it costs me absolutely nothing to wear a bra, put on make-up and wear a dress and all the rest of it'.

The problem of whether they should fully explain the home background to the school staff was a topic repeatedly raised by mothers of school and pre-school-age children. The idea was almost totally rejected on two main counts. First, there was anxiety expressed over written reports in school records. Aligned to this was the feeling that any information provided would encourage teachers to see lesbianism as 'the cause' of any problems which might arise and the latter possibly being enlarged or indeed manufactured in a form of self-fulfilling prophecy.

The reasons behind the decision about whether to come out or not in the school or any other situation were generally based on sound common-sense principles of expediency. As Dawn, a 44-year-old historian and mother of two daughters, said:

> I just wouldn't come out to all and sundry. I think it's a question
> of practicalities in a lot of ways, that if there's going to be an adverse
> result, then it's stupid to come out for no reason.

Co-ordinators

From the total sample, nine women were identified as having achieved co-ordinator status, having brought the heterosexual and lesbian aspects of their life-styles into successful relation one to the other. This group were completely at ease with their identities as lesbians and mothers and they had achieved a complete integration of both roles so that one never tended to take precedence over the other. In this way they were able to present their whole selves to society with a natural openness and from knowledge that their life-style is a totally valid alternative to the more traditional family forms. Definitions of the final stage of self-identification as gay – 'stabilization'

(Plummer 1975), 'identity synthesis' (Cass 1979), and 'integration' (Coleman 1982) – are positive terms all having relevance to the way in which this particular group of women were living their lives. Co-ordinators were confident and secure enough to manage their life-styles in a consistently able way. Lesbianism for them had become ordinary rather than unusual and they had carved themselves a position within mainstream society as ordinary and not unusual too. The difficulties in attaining such a level of stability are necessarily acknowledged but it must also be recognized that anything short of this goal leaves the lesbian mother marginalized and thus vulnerable. Total integration brings confidence in the private as well as public spheres: Smalley (1987) notes that women with integrated identities find it easier to develop successful relationships. It leads to a positive presentation of the lesbian mother life-style as opposed to an apology at not quite measuring up to the ideal.

Betwixt and between

Of all members of the gay community it is the lesbian mother who most obviously experiences the necessity to be part of both the heterosexual and homosexual worlds. She is aware that it is the polarization of these two worlds which forms a barrier to the integration of her two identities and thus to an uncompromised life-style. Because of her children she is propelled towards all those institutions in society which emphasize and endorse mainstream ideologies of motherhood. Ante-natal clinics, mother and toddler clubs via play groups through to PTAs are all sites of her struggle for integration. As Rowena, an established lesbian before conceiving her little boy by a private AID arrangement, said:

I feel right out of place [at playgroup]. All they seem to talk about is what they're going to give the old man for tea and knitting patterns. I can't knit and I haven't got an old man.

To nurture and express the lesbian aspects of her identity however, the lesbian mother needs to turn to the lesbian community and here she may meet as much disapproval of her dual identity as she does from society at large. The lesbian community can so often label her a 'pretend' lesbian; in fulfilling her wish to have children she finds it necessary to defend her position as a tenable one in the face of adamant criticism from other lesbians. As Wyn, a 41-year-old writer, said:

Lesbians are disapproving because they say if you are a real lesbian you won't go messing about dealing with children and men and semen and such things.

Shulman (1986) argues that the decision of many lesbians to remain childless was a primary weapon in the fight for change. She goes on:

104

I was very angry and felt deeply betrayed when suddenly, all around me, many women, most of them lesbian feminists of one sort or another, all in their late twenties to early thirties, are either trying to become pregnant or having babies, most of them by self insemination.

In addition to these political and ideological clashes, a number of women in the sample felt very let down in terms of day-to-day practical support from the lesbian community. This was most obvious in the lack of offers to share child care and for such support most of them had turned to other lesbian mothers. Censorious reactions to her life-style from the lesbian community were particularly devastating and one woman talked of feeling herself 'a minority of a minority'. But it is pressures such as this which help to encourage the growth and maintenance of various support groups aimed specifically at the needs of lesbian mothers. While these services are still patchy, there now exists a solidarity among lesbian mothers which prior to the 1980s was not in evidence at all.

PEOPLE OF THE FUTURE

Despite repression, an international network of communication now exists for lesbian mothers which would be very difficult to dislodge because, to quote Wyn:

We all feel strengthened in our identities simply by knowing it's not just me or it's not just an abstract figure or women but real women you can actually find and meet.

Concern was expressed that ways should be found of initiating and upholding support services to provide help and protection for all lesbians. One woman talked of a 'kind of childishness in a lot of lesbian identity' which is hard to combat and yet must be dealt with if the lesbian community is not to remain subject to the whims of various governments. It needs to grow and accept responsibility for its own future well-being.

Goodman (1977) talks of lesbian mothers being responsible for raising 'people of the future'. Here there is no compromise, no apology for the type of parenting offered by lesbian mothers. The more confident women interviewed claimed that they can do if anything a better job than many heterosexual parents in helping to break down the barriers that the ideology of gender has helped to erect. This is to be achieved by raising children more aware of their full potential as human beings, free of the restrictions created by socially constructed ideas of what constitutes femininity and masculinity.

Such positive ideas are currently being tested by growing numbers of lesbians and gay men anxious to deal effectively with the erroneous connections made between their sexual identity and their ability to parent. In her motherhood hierarchy model, DiLapi (1989) describes lesbian mothers as being considered 'inappropriate' and as such deprived of access to services which assist more 'acceptable' women to achieve motherhood. Certainly, in the UK, artificial insemination for lesbian women at officially recognized clinics is currently subject to political review. There is evidence[5] still that mothers applying openly as lesbians for custody of their children may encounter judicial prejudice which, if not actually depriving them of their right to motherhood, will involve restrictive clauses in the custody agreement which would be considered totally unacceptable to heterosexual litigants. Lesbians who are making official applications to foster and adopt are causing many local authorities to review their policy towards such applicants. Faced with the casualties of child abuse, both physical and sexual that can occur within the traditional family if it fails to live up to its revered ideal, local authority officials are beginning to consider alternative family forms.[6]

There are huge obstacles still to overcome. The prejudice against the many forms of family which do not conform to the traditional nuclear family remains. Lesbian mothers currently making a stand against this particular brand of heterosexism tend to be white, articulate, and middle-class. The position of black lesbian mothers for example is as yet undefined.

Lesbian mothers, along with other members of the gay community, are beginning to make a firm stand against the prejudice which states that they cannot make good parental figures if they happen also to be gay or lesbian. Not only can we succeed in raising our own children as 'people of the future' but we might also be able to repair damage caused within traditional family life in the atmosphere created by an alternative family structure. Children raised thus are likely to be accepting of the validity of gay lifestyles and this constitutes real change.

NOTES

1 In 1978 two reporters from the London *Evening News* infiltrated a self-help group, posing as a lesbian couple seeking AID. The subsequent sensationalized coverage by their newspaper was both vicious and ill informed. It increased prejudice and exposed the women involved to much suffering and expense in their unsuccessful attempts to get the story suppressed – the Press Council eventually ruled that the *Evening News* acted justifiably and in the public interest.

2 The Rights of Women Lesbian Custody Group, 52–4, Featherstone Street, London EC1 8RT, was formed in 1982. It is comprised of lesbian mothers and feminist workers offering advice and information on issues relating to lesbian mothers and child custody. Similar groups exist around the world.

3 In 1989 an international conference was held at the University of Utrecht, Holland, the only European university with a full lesbian and gay studies programme. A similar conference took place at the University of Essex, UK, in July 1991.

4   The failure to achieve a sample representative of social class was a serious concern. The researcher was able to make what were considered quite valid subjective assessments of differences between respondents but when checked against recognized scales based upon occupation the middle-class bias was obvious. Working-class women are not sufficiently represented here.

5   A recent Rights of Women Briefing Paper (1990) discusses 'the backlash against lesbian parents'. A member of staff confirmed that in a case heard early in 1991 a lesbian mother lost custody to a man who is not the biological father of her children.

6   A controversial sentence has been deleted from the Children's Act 1990 guidelines on fostering. 'Equal Rights and Gay Rights policies have no place in fostering services' has been dropped. But a Department of Health spokesman said (April 1991) that the guidance still reflected the view that a child's welfare is best served by having a foster mother and father.

9

THAT'S WHAT FRIENDS ARE FOR

Friends as family in the gay and lesbian community[1]

Peter M. Nardi

What is the good of friendship if one cannot say exactly what one means.

(Oscar Wilde)

In his collection of stories, *Buddies*, Ethan Mordden (1986: 189) tells the story of a reunion between two old friends, one of whom is now married with children:

> He asked me how I could live without a family and I said my family is all the guys I was telling him about. Isn't it? But he didn't get that. He said no – a family like playing with them and learning from each other and living with them inseparably, and I said that's what we do. And finally he sort of got it, that my family is my buddies.

Mordden (1986: 175) also observes: 'What unites us, all of us, surely, is brotherhood, a sense that our friendships are historic, designed to hold Stonewall together. . . . It is friendship that sustained us, supported our survival'. Not only are friends a form of family for gay men and lesbians, but friendships are also a political statement. And unlike most heterosexual friendships, gay friendships have a sexual dimension that calls into question not just the meanings of sexuality in society but also the constructions of gender roles in a culture. How friendship among gay men and lesbians affects the political, sexual, and familial dimensions of society is the focus of this chapter.

THE COMPONENTS OF FRIENDSHIP

Friendship is typically seen as a voluntary, egalitarian relationship, involving personal choice and providing individuals with a variety of psychological, social, and material support. Yet, patterned variations in how friendships are formed and maintained point to important social structural components. The opportunities to meet others and initiate friendships, the content of the relationships, and the frequency of interactions are all a function of the limitations and freedom imposed by the nature and number of social roles people must enact (see Hess 1972).

Issues related to social psychological definitions of self and identity also motivate individuals to initiate and maintain friendships. Rubin (1985: 13) points to the role friendship plays in reinforcing and shaping the self:

[I]t is friends who provide a reference outside the family against which to measure and judge ourselves; who help us during passages that require our separation and individuation; who support us as we adapt to new roles and new rules; who heal the hurts and make good the deficits of other relationships in our lives; who offer the place and encouragement for the development of parts of self that, for whatever reason, are inaccessible in the family context. It's with friends that we test our sense of self-in-the-world, that our often inchoate, intuitive, unarticulated vision of the possibilities of a self-yet-to-become finds expression.

These ideas of personal choice, social structural constraints, and the emerging self are clearly illustrated in an analysis of the role of friendship in the lives of gay men and lesbians. In particular, they are evident when focusing on the *political, familial, and sexual* aspects of gay people's friendships. How gay men and lesbians socially construct friendship and what the impact of these friendships is on identity and society are examined in more detail in this chapter. Some of the discussion is based on data collected in a survey of gay men and lesbians (see Sherrod and Nardi 1988; Nardi 1992) and some is based on interpretations of and speculations about other studies on the role of friendship in people's lives.

THE FAMILIAL

As Mordden's quote illustrated, for many gay people, friends are frequently viewed as family. Certainly, in the past century with the rise of bureaucracies and the mobility of much of contemporary industrial and post-industrial society, modified extended families have become more important. Friendship groups fall structurally between the face-to-face contact of neighbours and the permanency of kinship groups (Litwak and Szelenyi 1969). Friendships provide 'alternative ways for doing things when the formal structure of society is clearly inadequate . . . when the normative rules of society have come to appear especially artificial and fragile' (Suttles 1970: 135).

This is particularly so when the social institutions exclude certain kinds of interpersonal relationships. For gay men and lesbians, social approval of intimate relationships is typically absent or limited by legal, religious, and cultural norms. For some, their families of origin (parents, siblings, and other close relatives) may not acknowledge or legitimize gay people's friendships and relationships. In the context of these social constraints and the need to sustain a sense of self, friendship takes on the roles typically provided by heterosexual families (see Weston 1991). As Altman (1982a: 190) wrote 'what many gay lives miss in terms of permanent relationships is more than compensated for by friendship networks, which often become de facto families'.

One 30-year-old male illustrated the pull between family and friends at holiday time, such as Thanksgiving or Christmas. He said that he wants to spend time with both and often does, but that 'I still go to my friends first'. As one 42-year-old male in our survey stated: 'Friends to me are family. When people ask if my best friend and I are lovers, I say "No – we're much closer than that"'.

Rubin (1985: 17) similarly notes that 'when people wanted to impress upon me the importance of their friendships and the quality of closeness, they invoked the metaphor of the family'. However, for gay people, it is more than a metaphor. The 'friends as family' model, in which friends actually provide the kinds of emotional, social, and psychological support families often do, makes sense in light of Allan's (1989) argument that the more extensive and personal the help required, the greater tendency there is to use primary kin for assistance. For gay people, friends often provide the role of maintaining physical and emotional well-being, especially when difficulties arise when soliciting social support from their families and other kin (see Kiecolt-Glaser and Glaser 1988; Warren 1980). In fact, Kurdek and Schmitt (1987: 65) found this to be the case only for the homosexuals in their study who 'saw friends as more prominent providers of emotional support than family'.

In short, as a gay man in his 30s said:

Friends become part of my extended family. A lot of us are estranged from our families because we're gay and our parents don't understand or don't want to understand. That's a separation there. I can't talk to them about my relationships. I don't go to them; I've finally learned my lesson: family is out. Now I've got a close circle of good friends that I can sit and talk to about anything, I learned to do without the family.

The search for social support from friends rather than from family is also given some credence when looking at the ways men in particular socially construct their friendships. Typically, men (when categorically compared to women) are less intimate with same-sex friends, less satisfied with their friendships, and perceive less social support from their friends (Sherrod 1987). In part, this is related to men's position in the social structure which encourages 'the formation of sociable relationships with others, but, at the same time . . . restrict(s) the extent to which the self is revealed within them' (Allan 1989: 71). It is also related in part to the patterns of socialization which tend to encourage a limit on self-expression and emotional intimacy between men.

110

As a result, men often turn to women friends for emotional well-being and social support, while women seek such intimacy more often through same-sex friends (O'Meara 1989; Rubin 1985). For most heterosexual men, that woman is often a wife or a female romantic partner. The traditional family – or, at the least, the ideology of the family – is the major source of emotional support for most heterosexual men, not same-sex friends. Ironically, this was not always the case. For centuries, 'the image of male friendship closely parallels that of romantic love. Both idealize a dyadic relationship and set expectations of undying loyalty, devotion, and intense emotional gratification' (Hammond and Jabow 1987: 242). But this idea of male friendship has since given way to one in which 'men and women seek fulfillment of their emotional needs in the family. It is here that the most intense relationships exist, and friendship plays a secondary role' (Hammond and Jabow 1987: 256).

However, how gender influences friendship depends on the interaction with other factors that shape people's sociability (Allan 1989). In particular, sexual orientation may play a salient role in mediating such gender differences in friendship. Whereas the gender differences in heterosexual friendship patterns illustrated the importance for men in obtaining social support from within the family context of female spouse or partner, gay men and lesbians equally seek emotional support from same-sex friendships (Sherrod and Nardi 1988).

A 35-year-old male said this about his very supportive friends:

My best friends and some of my close friends provide an outlet for my need to share my life and concerns with others. I also have a strong need to express affection, warmth, laughter, support and ideas with my friends.

This expression of intimacy and emotional support between men appears to be more typical of gay men than heterosexual men. Gay men and lesbians are equally disclosing, equally seeking of social support, and equally engaging in activities with their mostly same-sex friends (Sherrod and Nardi 1988). For gay men, expressive and instrumental support, as well as self-disclosing feelings and emotions, come from their friendships with other men, unlike what traditional male norms about friendship suggest.

The remarks of a 29-year-old male provide another good example of the importance of gay friendship as a primary source of intimacy and identity. He illustrates the transition from traditional learned male behaviour of being non-expressive to one of more intimacy, once he dealt with his gay identity and found other gay men to be open with:

Up till two to three years ago, I had great difficulty getting emotionally intimately close to friends of both sexes because I was thoroughly unsure of how to handle my sexuality. . . . I learned to cultivate

111

and to appreciate casual friendships, but did not often go much further. Since I started to accept myself and to bring more honesty and intimacy into my trusted friendships, my ability to deepen the friendships in my life has steadily improved and I am far more happy today than before about the reality of friendship in my life. . . . I have great difficulty in making close friends among non-gay people and especially non-gay males. I am fairly open . . . but that openness doesn't always evolve into close friendships and in the case of non-gays, rarely does.

In addition to providing opportunities for expressions of intimacy and identity, friendships for gay men and lesbians serve as sources for various kinds of social support (ranging from the monetary to health care) and provide them with a network of people with whom they can share celebrations, holidays, and other transitional rituals (see Sherrod and Nardi 1988). In addition, an emerging global connection has developed, as gay subcultures, political and social, appear in many countries and cities around the world. Interconnected by a network of customs (clothing styles, for example), social institutions (such as bars and AIDS organizations), and even language (the word 'gay' is used in many langauges), the globalization of gay subculture has resulted in an international family of friends who provide travellers with places to stay, eat, and socialize. It's as if one is visiting members of the family from the 'old world' or who have moved away.

THE SEXUAL

The sexual component in friendships typically emerges when discussing cross-sex friendships among heterosexuals. As Harry said to Sally in the movie *When Harry Met Sally*, 'Men can never be friends with women. The sex thing always gets in the way'. O'Meara (1989) argues that cross-sex friendship is an ambiguous relationship in our culture since it must continuously resolve the tension created by the 'sex thing' as well as the absence of roles, rituals, and terminology in a context which often treats such friendships as deviant or threatening.

When a sexual relationship does occur, 'the basis of the solidarity of the friendship is altered and usually it is difficult to revert to the previous state once the sexual relationship ends' (Allan 1989: 83). O'Meara (1989: 534) similarly reports that for many men sexuality in friendship often destroys the friendship and, thus, passion and sexual attraction must be 'continually monitored, contended with, and regulated through negotiation'.

An interesting test case of the role of sexuality and sexual attraction in friendship is available when studying the friendships among gay men and among lesbians. Rubin (1985: 179–80) argues that 'most friends come together out of some combination of attraction to the other and their internal psychological needs and desires'. Yet, O'Meara (1989: 529) states (without much supporting evidence) that 'this factor of sexual attraction appears nonexistent in friendships among gays'. But given the sociological argument that 'different "boundaries" are constructed around friendships' in part due to personal choice and the socio-cultural context (Allan 1989: 15), the friendships of gay men and lesbians might have a very different sexual component to them than cross-gender heterosexual friendships.

Sonenschein (1968), in an early ethnography of a gay male community, developed a typology of relationships based on duration and level of sexuality. Essentially, he argues that first-order friendships (best and really close friends) and second-order friendships (good friends but not permanent) were entirely non-sexual. Extended encounters (sexual affairs) were often unstable and not characterized by strongly committed social support, while brief encounters were typically non-permanent sexual relationships. Permanent partners (lovers) are sociosexual relationships akin to heterosexual marriages in terms of commitment and stability (see Blumstein and Schwartz 1983). For the most part, Sonenschein (1968) concludes, gay men tend to keep those people who serve their social needs separated from those who serve their sexual needs.

A gay man in his 20s told us:

> I will not and have never had sex with any friend. I've either dated the person or became friends with them. Once I went out with this guy for two months and there was no physical relationship yet. We had agreed to take it slowly. But one day I realized I didn't want to sleep with him, so we talked about it. He's now my closest friend in the city.

Although some individuals were acquaintances first and then became sexual partners, people were clearly distinguished as sexual partners or social partners, rarely both. Sonenschein (1968: 72) speculates as to whether the category of 'friends' is 'really a residual category of individuals who did not work out as sexual partners or whether there are differential expectations through which individuals are initially screened to become either "friends" or "partners"'. The evidence from his observations and from our own data indicates that both processes operate: many gay men and lesbians have had sex with their best friends, but more have been sexually attracted without sex taking place.

One 34-year-old male said:

> The best close friends I had were from when I was sexually active. . . .
> I would date for a few weeks and when they got too 'amorous', I was very good at stopping the sex and turning it into a friendship. . . .
> It upsets me to realize that I cannot make new friends unless I work with them or have sex with them.

In our study of 161 gay men and 122 lesbians, we asked if they were sexually attracted, sexually involved, or in love with their best friend, either in the past or currently. (Best friend does not include one's lover.) It is important to establish first that the majority (82 per cent) of gay men have a gay or bisexual male best friend and the majority (76 per cent) of lesbians have a lesbian or bisexual best friend.

Of those who have a best friend who is of the same gender and sexual orientation, 79 per cent of the men and 77 per cent of the women had been at some point in the past at least minimally sexually attracted to their best friend. Currently, 52 per cent of the men and 31 per cent of the women say they still are sexually attracted to their best friend.

In the past, 59 per cent of the men and 59 per cent of the women had sex at least once with their best friend. Currently 20 per cent of the men and 19 per cent of the women are sexually involved with their best friend.

In the past, 57 per cent of the men and 54 per cent of the women were in love with their best friend. Currently 48 per cent of the gay men and 28 per cent of the lesbians say they are at least somewhat in love with their best friend. Remember that best friend excludes current lover.

Clearly, the data indicate that sexual attraction has played a role in the friendships of gay men and lesbians. Sexual activity and love were also important elements in the early stages of their friendships. Although attraction and love are still strong emotions in their current friendships, a decline in sexual activity with friends is more evident, perhaps suggesting the emergence of an 'incest taboo' among the family of friends. One other interesting finding is that for lesbians, 45 per cent said their best friend is a former lover, while only 19 per cent of the men said so. (For additional findings from this study, see Sherrod and Nardi 1988; Nardi 1992; and the report in *Out/Look*, Spring 1990, Number 8.)

These findings tie into traditional gender-role research which emphasizes the more instrumental view men have about intimacy and sexuality and the more expressive view women have about them. For many women, intimacy is achieved first, then sexuality evolves from that. For men, intimacy is often achieved through sexuality. When the sex ends, often the intimate relationship does also. For women, when the sex ends, the intimacy is still there. Gay men and lesbians appear to reinforce some of these traditional gender differences as can be seen by the greater percentage of women who continue to see their ex-lover as their best friend. Yet, unlike cross-gender heterosexual friendships, sexuality among gay people does not appear to be an impediment to the formation of friendships with potential partners. And gay men seem to continue with an intimate friendship even after the sexual relationship has ended.

Such findings raise additional issues about the dialectical role of friendship, sex, and attraction in gay people's lives. White (1983: 16) discusses the role of sex and friendship in his essay about gay men in the 1980s by comparing it to Japanese court life of the tenth century:

Friendship . . . intertwines with sexual adventure and almost always outlasts it; a casual encounter can lead to a life-long, romantic but sexless friendship. . . . [S]ex, love and friendship may overlap but are by no means wholly congruent. In this society, moreover, it is friendship that provides the emotional and social continuity, whereas sexuality is not more and no less than an occasion for gallantry.

Another approach is to consider what the role of sexual attraction might be in the formation of all friendships, not just those involving potential sexual partners. Seiden and Bart (1975: 220) have speculated that 'There is probably an erotic component in most close friendships . . . but this appears to be disturbing to many people and is denied or repressed'. Rubin (1985: 179) similarly argues:

More than others, best friends are drawn together in much the same way as lovers – by something ineffable, something to which, most people say, it is almost impossible to give words. . . . [P]eople often talk as if something happened to them in the same way they 'happened' to fall in love and marry.

Although Rubin (1985: 180) also says that in friendship 'the explicitly sexual is muted, if not fully out of consciousness', she does acknowledge the 'appeal of the physical' in the process of friendship initiation and development. The data from gay men and lesbians, on the other hand, point to the powerful role sexual attraction and sex itself have in the structuring of friendships. Sex is often the way to achieve casual and close friends, especially for gay men, but once friendship is established, the sexual no longer remains the main organizing activity among best friends. But even if sex did not occur between best friends, sexual attraction is an even greater and more lasting dimension to the initiation and development of that friendship.

THE POLITICAL

Mordden's notion of 'friends is survival' (quoted in the beginning of the article) has a political dimension that becomes all the more salient in contemporary society where the political, legal, religious, economic, and health concerns of gay people are routinely threatened by the social order. In part, gay friendship can be seen as a political statement, since at the core of the concept of friendship is the idea of 'being oneself' in a cultural context that may not approve of that self. For many people, the need to belong with others in dissent and out of the mainstream is central to the maintenance of self and identity (Rubin 1985). The friendships formed by a shared marginal identity, thus take on powerful political dimensions as they organize around a stigmatized status to confront the dominant culture in solidarity. Raymond (1986: 8–9) makes a strong argument for the political power of female friendships, or what she terms 'Gyn/affection', that is, the 'personal and political movement of women toward each other.... The best feminist politics proceeds from a shared friendship'. Jerome (1984: 698) also believes that friendships have economic and political implications, since friendship is best defined as 'the cement which binds together people with interests to conserve'.

Suttles argues that

> The very basic assumption friends must make about one another is that each is going beyond a mere presentation of self in compliance with 'social dictates'. Inevitably, this makes friendship a somewhat deviant relationship because the surest test of personal disclosure is a violation of the rules of public propriety.
>
> (Suttles 1970: 116)

Friendship, according to Suttles (1970), has its own internal order, albeit maintained by the cultural images and situational elements that structure the definitions of friendship. In friendship, people can depart from the routine and display a portion of the self not affected by social control. That is, friendships allow people to go beyond the basic structures of their cultural institutions into an involuntary and uncontrollable exposure of self – to deviate from public propriety (Suttles 1970).

Little (1989) similarly argues that friendship is an escape from the rules and pieties of social life. It's about identity: who one is rather than one's roles and statuses. And the idealism of friendship 'lies in its detachment from these [roles and statuses], its creative and spiritual transcendence, its fundamental skepticism as a platform from which to survey the givens of society and culture' (Little 1989: 145). For gay men and lesbians, these descriptions of friendship illustrate the political meaning friendship can have in their lives, in their society, and in a global context. They also illustrate how powerfully gay friendships can restructure the social forces that seem to constrain the nature of friendships for many men in our culture. And, through friendships, women can 'affect, move, stir, and arouse each other to full power' (Raymond 1986: 229).

The political dimension of friendship is summed up best by Little:

> the larger formations of social life – kinship, the law, the economy – must be different where there is, in addition to solidarity and dutiful role-performance, a willingness and capacity for friendship's surprising one-to-one relations, and this difference may be enough to transform social and political life.... Perhaps, finally, it is true that progress in democracy depends on a new generation that will increasingly locate itself in identity-shaping, social, yet personally liberating, friendships.
>
> (Little 1989: 154–5)

116

The traditional, nuclear family has been the dominant model for political relations and has structured much of the legal and social norms of our culture. Raymond (1986: 11) argues that this is especially the case for women: 'we live in a hetero-relational society where most of women's personal, social, political, professional and economic relations are defined by the ideology that woman is for man'. People have often been judged by their family ties and history. But as the family becomes transformed into other arrangements, so do the other political and social institutions of society, including friendship and romantic relationships. For example, the emerging concept of 'domestic partnerships' has affected a variety of organizations, including insurance companies, city governments, private industry, and religious institutions (see Task Force on Family Diversity Final Report 1988, and Henning Bech's article elsewhere in this book).

For many gay people, the 'friends as family' model is a political statement, going beyond the practicality of developing a surrogate family in times of needed social support. It is also a way of refocusing the economic and political agenda to include non-traditional family structures composed of both romantic and non-romantic non-kin relationships.

In part, this refocusing has happened by framing the discussions in terms of gender roles. The women's movement and the emerging men's movement have highlighted the negative political implications of defining gender roles according to traditional cultural norms or limiting them to biological realities. The gay movement, in turn, has often been one source for redefining traditional gender roles and sexuality. So, for example, when gay men exhibit more disclosing and emotional interactions with other men (see Sherrod and Nardi 1988), it demonstrates the limitations of male gender roles typically enacted among many heterosexual male friends. By calling attention to the impact of homophobia on heterosexual men's lives, gay men's friendships illustrate the potentiality for expressive intimacy among all men.

The assumptions that biology and/or socialization have inevitably constrained men from having the kinds of relationships and intimacies women often typically have can readily be challenged. The questioning of the dominant construction of gender roles is in itself a socio-political act with major implications for the legal, religious, and economic order.

White also sees how gay people's lives can lead to new modes of behaviour in society at large:

> In the case of gays, our childlessness, our minimal responsibilities, the fact that our unions are not consecrated, even our very retreat into gay ghettos for protection and freedom: all of these objective conditions have fostered a style in which we may be exploring, even in spite of our conscious intentions, things as they will someday be for the heterosexual majority. In that world (as in the gay world

already), love will be built on esteem rather than passion or convention, sex will be more playful or fantastic or artistic than marital –
and friendship will be elevated into the supreme consolation for this
continuing tragedy, human existence.

(White 1983: 16)

If, as White and others have argued (see Plummer 1988), gay culture
in the post-Stonewall, sexual liberation years of the 1970s was characterized by continuous fluidity among what constituted a friend, a sexual partner,
and a lover, then we need to acknowledge the AIDS decade of the 1980s
as a source for the restructuring of gay culture and the reorganization of
sexuality and friendship. If indeed gay people (and men in particular) have
focused attention on developing monogamous sexual partnerships, what
then becomes of the role of sexuality in the initiation and development of
casual or close friendships? Clearly, gay culture is not a static phenomenon,
unaffected by the larger social order. Certainly, as the moral order in the
AIDS years encourages the re-establishment of more traditional relationships, the implications for the ways sexuality and friendships are organized
similarly change.

Friends become more salient as primary sources of social and emotional
support when illness strikes; friendship becomes institutionally organized
as 'brunch buddies' dating services or 'AIDS buddies' assistance groups;
and self-help groups emerge centring on how to make and keep new friends
without having 'compulsive sex'. While AIDS may have transformed some
of the meanings and role of friendship in gay men's lives from the politicalization of sexuality and friendship during the post-Stonewall 1970s, the newer
meanings of gay friendships, in turn, may be having some effect on the
culture's definitions of friendships.

Interestingly, the mythical images of friendships were historically more
male-dominated: bravery, loyalty, duty, and heroism (Hammond and
Jablow 1987; Sapadin 1988). This partly explained why women were
typically seen as not being capable of true friendships. But today, the images
of true friendship are often expressed in terms of women's traits: intimacy,
trust, caring, and nurturing, thereby excluding the more traditional men
from true friendship. However, as discussed above, gay men appear to be
at the forefront of establishing the possibility of men overcoming their male
socialization stereotypes and restructuring their friendships in terms of the
more contemporary ('female') attributes of emotional intimacy.

To do this at a wider cultural level involves major socio-political shifts
in how men's roles are structured and organized. Friendships between men
in terms of intimacy and emotional support inevitably introduce questions
about homosexuality. As Rubin (1985: 103) found in her interviews with
men: 'The association of friendship with homosexuality is so common among
men.' For women, there is a much longer history of close connections

with other women, so that the separation of the emotional from the erotic is more easily made. However, women need to be liberated from a world view that places women's existence primarily in relation to men; they need to create a feminist politics through friendship with other women (Raymond 1986).

Lehne (1989) has argued that homophobia has limited the discussion of loving male relationships and has led to the denial by men of the real importance of their friendships with other men. In addition, 'the open expression of emotion and affection by men is limited by homophobia. . . . The expression of more tender emotions among men is thought to be characteristic only of homosexuals' (Lehne 1989: 426). So men are raised in a culture with a mixed message: strive for healthy, emotionally intimate friendships, but if you appear too intimate with another man you might be negatively labelled homosexual.

This certainly wasn't always the case. As a good illustration of the social construction of masculinity, friendship, and sexuality, one need only look to the changing definitions and concepts surrounding same-sex friendship during the nineteenth century (see Richards 1987; Rotundo 1989; Smith-Rosenberg 1975). Romantic friendships could be erotic but not sexual, since sex was linked to reproduction. Because reproduction was not possible between two women or two men, the close relationship was not interpreted as being a sexual one: 'Until the 1880s, most romantic friendships were thought to be devoid of sexual content. Thus a woman or man could write of affectionate desire for a loved one of the same gender without causing an eyebrow to be raised' (D'Emilio and Freedman 1988: 121).

However, as same-sex relationships became medicalized and stigmatized in the late nineteenth century, 'the labels "congenital inversion" and "perversion" were applied not only to male sexual acts, but to sexual or romantic unions between women, as well as those between men' (D'Emilio and Freedman 1988: 122). Thus, the twentieth century is an anomaly in its promotion of female equality, the encouragement of male-female friend-ships, and its suspicion of intense emotional friendships between men (Richards 1987). Yet, in Ancient Greece and the medieval days of chivalry, comradeship, virtue, patriotism, and heroism were all associated with close male friendship. Manly love, as it was often called, was a central part of the definition of masculinity (Richards 1987), just as Whitman has written in his poem, 'A Song', about the 'love of comrades . . . the manly love of comrades'.

It is through the gay, women's and men's movements that these twentieth-century constructions of gender are being questioned. And at the core is the association of close male friendships with negative images of homo-sexuality. Thus, how gay men structure their emotional lives and friendships can affect the social and emotional lives of all men and women. This is the political power and potential of gay friendships.

119

CONCLUSIONS

Emerson wrote in his essay on friendship that 'A friend is a person with whom I may be sincere. Before him I may think aloud'. This characterization is clearly one that describes the role of friendship in the lives of gay men and lesbians. In search of a context that contributes to and maintains identity, gay people have elevated friendship to an importance perhaps not matched by any other group. Friends are family; friends are like the romantic friendships of nineteenth-century Britain and America; and friends are a political force redefining gender and sexual roles on an international scale.

As Whitman wrote in 'A Song':

Come, I will make the continent indissoluble;
I will make the most splendid race the sun ever yet shone upon;
I will make divine magnetic lands,
With the love of comrades,
With the life-long love of comrades....
I will make inseparable cities, with their arms about each other's necks;
By the love of comrades,
By the manly love of comrades.

NOTE

1 This paper would not have been possible without the suggestions and assistance of Drury Sherrod. His help in designing our original research, our many conversations, and our friendship are a major part of this article.

10

A COCKTAIL OF ALARM
Same-sex couples and migration to Australia 1985–90

John Hart

I would rather sell my household furniture which will amount to about six or eight Pounds. This sum I will most willingly give to Government to lessen their expences of sending me out to Sidney, provided they would be graciously pleased to send me by the first Ship.

(Hughes 1988: 133)

I am begging you Sir to act immediately in our case. We are a victim of circumstances wherein we are deeply committed to building our lives together but not able to continue to do so because the immigration laws between two countries will in a few days separate us. I submit with this letter for your consideration documents which will prove the commitment of our relationship.

These two applications are separated by one hundred and sixty years. The first was from a wife of a transported man and written in 1830. The second comes from a letter to the Minister for Immigration and Ethnic Affairs sent in 1987 from the Philippines by a male Australian citizen aged 23 and a male Filipino citizen aged 22. Both these applications resulted in the authorities granting the applicants' requests to live as couples in Sydney, Australia.

Australia is a land of migrants, and is still a country of migration. Because of the tyranny of distance and early gender imbalance, there has long been an opportunity for male residents to be joined by a life partner to share a country about twenty-five times larger than Britain and Ireland. By 1990 the population reached only 17 million. Over the past two hundred years of European colonization there has existed a tradition of allowing the, initially reluctant, male settlers a partner of their own, and the government's, choice. I emphasize the latter element as until 1973 an official 'White Australia' policy ensured that such partners could not be Asian, Black, or otherwise visibly demonstrate non-Caucasian features. In this chapter I will argue that same-sex migration can be understood as part of this ambivalent tradition in Australia.

The chapter describes an arrangement made between a pressure group, the Gay and Lesbian Task Force (see Table 10.1), and the Australian Government which enabled some 500 couples to live together in Australia during the late 1980s when one partner was neither an Australian citizen nor resident. My research[1] looked at this arrangement, and the adjustment of the couples, both to the rules of government and to each other. The couples

Table 10.1 Chronology of major events during the arrangement

1983	Hawke Labour Government elected. First Immigration Minister, Stewart West, receives applications from same-sex couples, makes no decisions.
1984	Second Immigration Minister, Chris Hurford. Pressure group formed to achieve equality in the Australian immigration system for gay and lesbian couples – The Gay and Lesbian Immigration Task Force.
1985	Minister agrees to meet Task Force. An arrangement is made in which the Minister will personally use his discretion under the Migration Act 1958 to decide on applications on a case by case basis. A four-year duration of relationship requirement is placed on same-sex relationships.
1987	The next Minister for Immigration, Mick Young, appears reluctant to make case decisions.
1988	Minister is again changed and the new incumbent, Clyde Holding, faces hostile questioning in Parliament. Same-sex migration (again) linked with AIDS in Parliament and the media.
1989	The fifth Minister of the Labour Government, Robert Ray, takes over and announces his determination to restrict Ministerial discretion under the Act. September: Duration requirement reduced to thirty months. December: Migration Act amended. Restrictions on Ministerial discretion aimed at removing abuses of the general migration programme have the effect of stopping the use of Ministerial discretion to enable same-sex couples to be 'quietly' approved by the Minister.
1990	Transitional arrangements made awaiting the decision of yet another new Minister, Gerry Hand. Same-sex applicants can apply for extensions of their temporary entry visas when in Australia. Immigration Department confirms that there is 'no class of visa for homosexual partners of Australian citizens or residents'.
1991	April 15, the Federal Government introduces a new regulation for Non-Familial Relationships of Emotional Interdependency which provides a new visa and permit category which could be used by same-sex partners to achieve residency. A six-month length of relationship is required before an application which could be only for conditional residency. A two-year waiting period for permanent residency is still demanded and the Minister remains the primary decision maker. The Task Force views this as a major victory, although their aim of a migrant entry category similar to heterosexual couples for same gay and lesbian partners has not been created.

were male and female and the non-resident partners came from both developed countries and those of the developing world surrounding Australia. These men and women were therefore a unique group – both in terms of previous research on gay and lesbian couples and from the perspective of cross-cultural relationships. The 'officially sanctioned' aspect of their homosexual relationships is also unique in gay and lesbian experience.

Australia would not, at first glance, appear to be a likely site of such provision. A similarly hostile environment relating to gay and lesbian rights to that which pertains in the United Kingdom might be expected. In the United States (Lundy 1986; Carro 1989) no possibility exists for same-sex couple migration. The potential in Europe is indicated by Bech in his chapter in this volume on the Danish experience. In Australia a high rate of HIV positivity in the main metropolitan areas, the fears of Asian migration, and anxieties about same-sex relationships resulted in continual tension during the life of the arrangement achieved with government. It was, indeed, a 'cocktail of alarm'. A brief history of this arrangement is described in Table 10.1.

A GENUINE AND MONOGAMOUS RELATIONSHIP: A PASSPORT TO AUSTRALIA

The origins of the ruling

When the first Labor Government of Bob Hawke came to power, self-help groups saw this as an opportunity after eight years of conservative rule – the Liberal Government of Malcolm Fraser – to press for social change measures, such as homosexual law reform in some states. In New South Wales same-sex acts between men were decriminalized in 1984, just in time before an AIDS panic hit Sydney. At the pivotal meeting with the Minister, the Gay (later, and Lesbian) Immigration Task Force records noted:

> Mr Hurford had begun by stating that he would not consider granting Australians the right to sponsor their same-sex partners under the Family Reunion Category of the migration programme. He then quickly went on to say what he would offer. The Minister conceded that applications for change of status on Compassionate and Humanitarian Grounds could be made solely on the existence of a same sex relationship. This was a development of previous policy where there had to be additional compassionate factors. The Minister then stated that, 'Our relationships must pass stringent tests of stability and genuineness. Thus he will not approve residency until the relationship is of four years duration (much longer than heterosexual

couples are required to demonstrate). But he agreed to issue change-of-status applicants with temporary entry permits and work permits so that there is no structural impediment to reaching the required four years duration.'

Under this arrangement partners had to enter Australia, or remain as visitors, telling what the Minister described as 'little white lies' about their intentions to apply for change of visitor status to resident while in Australia. The Minister would then use the considerable personal discretion available to him under the Migration Act to approve their applications. The Minister judged this procedure as the only one which would avoid a 'public outcry' about the issue. So it was that the Labour government became locked into an arrangement with a gay and lesbian political pressure group involving some deceit. Over 90 per cent of applications were approved for residence in Australia. The political judgement made by Chris Hurford proved to be enduringly accurate. For example, in May 1988, the then Minister Clyde Holding was faced with hostile questioning in Parliament, what the *Sydney Morning Herald* headlined: ' ''No poofters'' lobby queries gay immigration' (25 May 1988). The Minister was able to issue a news release (24 May 1988) which pointed out the separateness of this procedure from the Family Reunion Programme. Before noting the full knowledge of the Opposition about the applications, the press release stated:

> Homosexual applicants must satisfy the minister that they have a genuine *and monogamous* relationship of at least four years standing with an Australian citizen or resident. (my italics)

To claim that persons could not apply as homosexual migrants under the Family Reunion Programme was true. The arrangement, however, enabled people to leave their countries of residence with migration solely in mind. The five hundred same-sex couples represent less than one in a thousand of those persons who were granted residence visas for settlement in Australia during the period 1985 to 1989. Each of the applications however was dealt with on a case by case basis using the then available personal discretion of the Minister for Immigration. Minister Chris Hurford assured me, in an interview in 1987, that he personally scrutinized the applications of each couple when they were placed on his desk for a decision. This numerically small number of persons thus caused a disproportionate amount of political and personal *angst*. In order to understand the tensions we should review the way in which the same sex couples were characterized.

The model of the ideal couple

Until the 1970s couples were assumed to be heterosexual. Homosexuals were regarded as solitary, usually male creatures who inhabited parks and

woodlands at night, only emerging during the day in captivity or treatment! Over the past twenty years, however, access to non-clinical populations
alongside the space rented by personal and political liberation movements,
has enabled researchers to discover that homosexual couples exist (Plummer
1978) in relatively large numbers as part of diverse family forms. Large-
scale surveys (Bell and Weinberg 1978) established the varieties of gay and
lesbian experience which included long-term couple relationships. In the
1980s the academic debate shifted to the values and health of these newly
discovered homosexual couples (see the summary of research by Peplau
1988). To account for their longevity a stage model was proposed which
accounted for the development of *the relationship* from a period of two to
over twenty years (McWhirter and Mattison 1984). Generally the conclusion was that same-sex couples were healthy, if not monogamous. In
comparison with heterosexuals, homosexual couples were observed as being
more like other men and women than each other (Duffy and Rusbult 1986).
'Post AIDS', the research emphasis continued on the common emotional
and behavioural experience of couples in general. As those in relationships
all seemed reluctant to roll on the condoms, this hinted that the values
espoused in relationships still seemed to centre around emotional equalling
sexual trust (Carr 1989).

The ideal model – in practice

The Gay and Lesbian Immigration Task Force proved to be very successful
in acting as a processing arm of the Australian Government's Immigration Department during the period. The majority of applicants were
voluntary clients of this self-help group and the complex documentation
of the application was made through the group. Legal declarations were
required of an approved standard, evidencing committed, publicly known
about, homosexual couple relationships. Declarations from relatives of the
couple were encouraged, as was evidence of joint bills, telephone accounts,
wills, and photographs. Most important of all were the personal stories of
each partner: a prescribed narrative involving loneliness, then meeting and
complete happiness, with the threat of enormous deprivation for the
Australian partner if they were then deprived of this relationship. Hence
the deceit involved in gaining entrance to Australia had to be combined
with unusual openness about the sexual nature of the relationships. Mere
companions, good friends, or lovers who were neither cohabiting nor
exclusive were not allowed under the arrangement. The Department
required a four-year duration period for the relationship which later was
reduced to thirty months.

When the values imposed on the couple are specified, the quality of
monogamy rears its head. This was probably insisted upon by the Minister
to allay fears about HIV infection. In married relationships values approved

of could be assumed; in other unions they had to be tested, and more stringently. In the case of the same-sex couples this was by annual review. The homosexual partners were required to demonstrate a *genuine* relationship at the time of application and then, because of ongoing policing by the Department of Immigration, they also had to prove these genuine relationships to be *successful* over a specified time. No such requirements were made for heterosexual couples in the migration programme. The reasons for this discrimination are clearly implied in this excerpt from a departmental document produced prior to the beginning of the arrangement:

2. The importance of family definition is that the spouse and children of the application are exempted from many of the normal immigration processes and get what amounts to concessional entry.

3. The objective behind the family unit definition is to facilitiate the migration of a particular type of family unit which successive governments have believed to be beneficial to Australia. There are other units (eg extended families in the Asian sense, polygamous and under age marriages, and homosexual relationships) that governments have not included in the definition.

4. A homosexual relationship is not regarded as a family unit for migration purposes. This policy does not single out homosexuals for special treatment. There are many types of relationships ranging from friends, cousins, aunts, etc. that are not regarded as families for the purpose of granting concessional migration entry. Sometimes these relationships can be stronger than those recognised for migration purposes.

(Department of Immigration and Ethnic Affairs 1983)

In making the arrangement the Australian Government was reliant on the Task Force to ensure that *genuine and monogamous relationships* were presented by the couples. In turn the Task Force was dependent on the good will of the individual Minister using his discretion to approve the applications.

COUPLES AT RISK:
THE WORKINGS OF GAY AND LESBIAN
RELATIONSHIPS

It is possible to see the arrangement, so hard fought for and requiring much political manoeuvring by pressure groups and politicians, as being bound to cause stress for all the principal actors involved. It can retrospectively be seen as politically fragile. Homosexual partnerships without the societal supports of the dominant culture would be unlikely to 'do as well' in terms of dominant relationship models of success and failure. The arrangement ensured that the dominance of traditional heterosexual relationships

126

models in the immigration programme would not be threatened. The Family Migration Programme was already potentially controversial enough, for example the 'Asian brides' of heterosexual men. The amendments to ministerial discretion made late in 1989 were aimed at preventing the abuse of migration provisions for heterosexual relationships. It was an unintended consequence of this policy change which resulted in the end of the arrangement for same-sex couples. Homosexual migration was not going to be invited to contribute a chapter in Australia's ongoing conflictual immigration history. Homosexual men and women were, as in the wider society, to remain in the margin. We need to ask what were the consequences for those who did participate in the arrangement, so uniquely sanctioned and marginalized by the State?

The Minister, Mr Hurford, had introduced our discussion in 1987 by saying how much he wanted to read what I eventually found out about the homosexual couples staying together. I asked, 'What do you think that I will find?' Mr Hurford answered, 'My intuition is that about half of them will stay together over the four years – but that result would not change the decision I made. After all, look at the divorce rate'.

WAS THE MINISTER RIGHT?
THE ANSWER DEPENDS ON WHO IS ASKING

The government perspective

From the Department's perspective there is, almost, a 100 per cent success rate over the duration period, as they do not usually hear of the 'failures'. This is not entirely accurate as they have access now to information about HIV status and the Minister then responsible was in 1989–90, according to the Task Force, rejecting all applicants who tested positive to the antibody. This provided a 'natural brake' on the number of male applicants under the arrangement.

From the perspective of the relationships and the Department's laid-down criteria of committed, ongoing, sexually monogamous cohabiting, my research revealed a failure rate of something over 20 per cent in the outcomes. These 'failures' are not known about by the Department or openly discussed by the Task Force. I have assessed that this failure rate may rise significantly when departmental reporting requirements are removed. As the Department went over to a thirty-month duration test for applications already lodged this may be especially pronounced in the two years beginning in 1990. The Government can however be reassured by my research that the majority of relationships were *genuine*, even if the reasons for them being created were a combination of economic, avoidance of oppression, and certain, variable, feelings about the Australian partner. Such motivations do not differ from those of heterosexual partners who are similarly motivated to leave their countries of origin to enjoy what has been labelled the Lucky Country – Australia (see, for example, Department of Immigration and Ethnic Affairs 1984). In terms of success or failure of the relationships – at the point of the research – these are not in excess of those of hetero-sexual migrant partnerships. The differentials in terms of age and other status differences may result in developments for the overseas partners which inevitably mean the relationships will not continue in the intimate way they were demanded to have begun. These differentials are not dissimilar to those of Australian men and brides from South-East Asia. The partners in the study have however been tied for only up to four years. This emphasizes the necessity of not assuming that the couples in this study were any different from heterosexual couples in their mixed reasons for being in Australia. All migrants are 'pushed' from their overseas country; there is sometimes only a desperate wish to leave behind poverty and op-pression to join a recently met friend in Australia. Additionally for some same-sex couples there was stress in not being able to migrate as a joint primary partner.

The partners' perspective

The current Western literature on modern couples stresses the need for equal attachment. Initially all of the couples in this study are unequal in that only one has the right of residence in Australia. Gender differences were especially apparent in two additional areas involving structural inequality: the country of origin of the overseas partners and the ages of the partners. The lesbians chose partners who usually were from Western Europe or North America while the male partners came from Europe, North and South America, and South-East Asia. Gender also accounted for some age differences. The women usually chose partners of the same age, while for the men large gaps were common. The oldest woman in my survey group was 45. The oldest male partner was 67. At the other end of the age range of the group were two women partners who were both aged 20.

Some examples of 'failed' relationships in departmental terms will emphasize the effect of structural factors on the couples. In the first there is a relationship still involving cohabitation, but the quality has changed, according to the participants. An Australian/Thai relationship consists of an Australian man, Bob in his 50s, and a Thai, Prasit, in his mid-20s. This was one of the couples who had significant differences in age, education, Australian language ability, and income. The form of the relationship had already ceased fulfilling departmental critera by the time of my first questionnaire. However, one year later the couple are still together as a business partnership. Prasit is very happy in Australia. Bob sees the relationship apparently more negatively as time goes on. Prasit responded by writing that the relationship changes were, for him, 'Some good, some bad'.

Is this an example of a failed relationship in terms of the two people involved or the type of unit the Australian Government should accept for concessionary migration? The young Thai is now a different sort of partner for the Australian who is a successful businessman in Australia and Thailand. It is possible Bob will seek out other young men to fulfil his sexual and emotional 'needs'. 'Minor wives' in Thailand are an accepted part of social relationships. A similar duration test applied to Western heterosexual couples might also reveal that partnerships move from being emotional and sexually exclusive relationships to business or breeding partnerships. The Australian partner has chosen not to report the ending of their relationship under the arrangement. He can be said thereby to be exercising his right for intimate companionship in Australia.

What of those relationships which only conform for a limited time? The Australian partners appear from the study to be providing an environment where the overseas partner was given accommodation, financial assistance, and socialization to the Australian way of life. Cameron, the Australian partner of Daniel, an Israeli man, wrote this after the relationship had changed within the official duration period. Their relationship was not sexually exclusive and they lived in separate homes:

He is almost completely independent of me now. He is capable of looking for and usually finding work by himself. He is developing his own friendships and ideas and now lives in a different house. I feel less emotionally dependent on him.

Daniel:

There were arguments. Not feeling close all the time. . . . Australia feels a lot like home, I have a lot to do with this country. I feel more comfortable, with freedom to do things.

Daniel has avoided being called up into the Israeli army, which was one of his motivations for staying in Australia.

For some women the structure required by the arrangement was too much like heterosexual coupledom to be creative: Doreen and her Australian partner Dawn met in the UK in 1985. After nine years of marriage Doreen was applying for a divorce from her husband when in 1988 she made an application in Australia under the arrangement. Dawn wrote:

I feel I've been expected to be involved in a relationship likened to marriage whereas I'd like to break that mould for a better sort of relationship that has room for growth and individuality.

Doreen commented:

I feel the Dept. of Immigration is basing the elements of a relationship on heterosexual standards and is trying to validate and contain lesbian and gay relationships on the same pattern, e.g. Living together, Lifelong commitment. Sharing bank accounts, etc., loss of individuality. Does it have to be like this to be genuine?

One year later Doreen left to be with another woman.

My research has suggested that the Government requirements are encouraging the formation of relationships and indeed keeping some couples together, just as perhaps marriage vows or other social pressures do for heterosexual partners. Those couples who develop outside of the model do so quietly. Beyond Government requirements, the quality of relationships will determine their longevity. For many couples a period of a few years will be either a quality or a necessary time. They may then feel able to move on to other relationships in the partner's new country. These partners have to some extent established themselves in Australia and may be seen as qualifying for consideration to stay in their own right.

A question raised by the research is about the forms of relationship which, beyond the dependency imposed by migration, do not apparently exibit the dominant Western ideology of equality in relationships. In the male study group relationships that are unequal in terms of age, education, and financial status may have been entered into precisely because of these factors. This applies to both Australian resident and overseas partner.

It is my impression that the desire for a partner, combined with attraction to younger men, socialisation in the old patron–protégé system, and the economic advantages of North Americans over Third World peoples, all combine to lead a disproportionate number of older homosexual men to seek a partner from the populations of those Third world countries where youth is still socialized to respect and defer to elders. These young men are less affected by the generational watershed of gay liberation which has profoundly altered the homosexual populations of North America and Europe.

(Lee 1987)

In their answers to my initial questionnaire some partners spelled out their situation in terms which appear to be influenced by a narrative of economic rationality, rather than different socialization. As one partner, Michael, put it in a telephone interview:

If a man like myself in his 40s goes into a gay bar in Australia no heads are going to turn. There are a few young Asian men and a lot of Rice Queens. In Thailand the position is reversed and the Caucasian man can choose.

In response to my asking about why an overseas partner was chosen, another Australian, James, responded thus:

130

If falling in love is 'choosing' then that is the reason. Why did I gravitate to Asians? Because some are lithe, cheeky yet humble, smooth skinned and sexy and cuddly.

Generally, with the exception of the two students in the group, or those who were illegally resident, it is overseas that male Australians meet their Asian partners. This is despite the large number of students in Australia from mainland China, Hong Kong, and other South-East Asian countries where pockets of wealth allow Asian parents to send their children overseas to be educated. Despite the mythology about the veneration of age, Asian men in Australia, if able to make the choice, appear to wish to make relationships with Australian men of their own age. This is also a pattern which is developing among Filipino women who are choosing men nearer their own ages, having been introduced by friends rather than by mail order. It is possible that decreasing racism among younger Australian men is changing patterns of erotic interest and partnerships of equality will become more possible between younger Asian and Australian men.

There is still left the question of whether some initially unequal relationships will endure in a culture which will increasingly expose the partners to beliefs about the rightness of apparently equal relationships. Is equal *emotional* attachment involving complementary qualities possible beyond continuing structural inequalities? An example from the East/West group will balance any implied negative stance to such possibilities. The overseas partner, Razak, was an illegal migrant from Indonesia. Twenty-four years separated their ages. Both Razak and his partner Greg have high anxiety levels amounting to clinical stress states and required a great deal of reassurance during their application process. The Australian's answer to the question about why choose an overseas partner was this:

No thought of choosing overseas partner. Rather the person for his warmth – good heart – and loving caring nature. The best person I've ever known.

TRUE CONFESSIONS:
TELLING TALES OF COUPLEDOM

As I was writing up the research I received a telephone call from a Task Force member; the Australian partner Bruce said: 'I hope you have found that people apply under the arrangement because they cannot bear to be living away from their partners'.

The fact that Task Force members had to believe in a 'purer' motivational force is possibly because of their marginalized position in the Family Reunion programme. Equally the Task Force's public commitment to monogamy and lookalike heterosexual relationships can be seen as being a defence against negative judgements about the quality of their relationships. This is also related to direct associations made publicly between the spread of the HIV and the multiple partners of gay men. Successful relationships, however, require the negotiating of space for emotional growth with emotional security, whether or not people are closed or open in their sexual arrangements. My research has indicated there are differing *stories of relationships* produced for each audience: government, Task Force, the folks back home (who may not know how their son or daughter has qualified for migration to the Lucky Country). Sometimes different stories were also produced for each other, giving, for example, different stories of why they migrated or of their sexual exclusivity. The research process itself also created stories about the relationship for these men and women. In this chapter I have claimed that the couples researched were unique in the literature. The results of this study imply that all couples are unique: in the stories they produce for a particular research process, in the form that the stories take, and the way the stories are produced with a particular audience in mind.

Rather than a search for the truth we can observe the process of story telling involving tellers, prompters, and an audience (Plummer 1990). The stories which are available to tell come from a local context of personal experience and a wider repertoire of cultural attitudes to same-sex behaviour. The European colonization of Australia and the relationships in the Colony of gender and race have made attitudes to sexuality deeply ambiguous. Perhaps this provides a key to understanding why Australia, so notoriously male homophobic and contemporaneously homosocial *quietly* developed the arrangement for same-sex migration and then measured relationships against the traditional family form of a primary and a dependent migrant pair. That these unions were achieved with varying degrees of stress is, in essence, explicable by the impact on the men and women of the need to present both a genuine and successful relationship to a Government and to a society which appeared to assume the opposite and then provided temporary and discretionary opportunities for the couple's existence in Australia. Those individuals like Razak and Greg who are most conforming to a story of themselves as part of a couple appear from my research to suffer the most stress. For others the impact on their lives of their time as same-sex migrants has been less important than the increased opportunities for economic or life-style choice in a developed country. They will already be, or will soon become, aware that the efforts to *create a story of a genuine relationship* for public consumption do not then guarantee a successful private outcome as couples for each of the two individuals in Australia.

The research has unearthed a group not previously accounted for: same-sex couples in formalized relationships where there are structural differences, either personally chosen or imposed by the migration experience including government processing. The success or failure of such units has been seen to be both independent of and dependent on the sanctions imposed by Government requirements. 'Success' and 'failure' have also been seen to be meaningful in a particular time and value context. In this investigation the diverse patterns of same-sex couple relationship have been revealed against a backdrop of assumptions made and formally adhered to which clearly relate to lifelong heterosexual married unions of a dependent and primary migrant unit. The result has been a story presented to an audience with power to control the futures of the individuals as non-residents in Australia. Their future adjustment as couples has been a separate question. As a gay men's magazine devoted to promoting East/West relationships put it in 1990, 'All you need is love and the paper work'. For some, the stress they suffered was the result of believing in such modern fairy tales.

The perspectives here revealed may make future investigations less dependent on linear developmental models of relationships and more open to hearing of the adaptations of men and women who are together for varying periods of time and with emotional and physical commitment which cannot be taken for granted. This research, centred around uniquely socially sanctioned homosexual and lesbian relationships has, ironically, made it possible to suggest that the lifelong or even long-term heterosexual monogamous emotionally committed model is not necessarily a base for measuring the success or failure of couple relationships. Economic, social, and emotional advantage are part of the reasons that men and women enter into such unions: the achievement of these does not have to be the story of a lifetime.

NOTE

1   Hart, John (1990) PhD thesis, *A Genuine Relationship? An Investigation Into some Results of the Use Between 1983–1989 of Ministerial Discretion and the Migration Act 1958*, University of Sydney Library.

The research involved contacting over ninety of the 500 couples. Thirty couples were personally interviewed on two occasions: first in 1988 and then in 1989. The others returned postal questionnaires on both occasions. Just over 15 per cent were women.

11

REPORT FROM A ROTTEN STATE

'Marriage' and 'homosexuality' in 'Denmark'

Henning Bech

On the 28th of June 1990, two men left the Town Hall in Copenhagen, having been there on perfectly lawful business. While there, they had held hands. On leaving, they were met by ten policemen.

The two – a jurist at the Ministry of Social Affairs and a policeman – had contracted a *'registered partnership'*; and the ten policemen at the gate formed a guard of honour for their colleague and the newly registered couple. The contract was made in accordance with the Danish law on 'registered partnerships' between two persons of the same sex, in force since 1 October 1989. The ceremony was carried out by the same officials and in the same surroundings as those used at civil marriages and with an equivalent wording.

In a 'registered partnership' two people of the same sex obtain the same rights and obligations as a man and a woman do in marriage (except for the rights of adoption and church wedding). Up to the end of March 1991, 789 couples have contracted this sort of union. Some of them have subsequently had their partnership blessed by a vicar.[1]

In such ceremonies we meet many of the agents so well known in the regulation of same-sex sexuality in the modern West – but appearing in a curiously inverse order. What sort of 'society' is this where these constellations are possible, what sort of 'homosexuality' are we witnessing here, and what are the relations between such a society and such a homosexuality? In order to illuminate these matters I will start by examining the arguments put forth in the debate surrounding the legislation.[2]

THE DEBATE OVER 'REGISTERED PARTNERSHIPS'

Not surprisingly, many of the arguments of the Danish debate were familiar ones, well rehearsed in countless controversies over 'homosexuality and society'. There were, however, some significant shifts of emphasis, and some of the old assertions, though industriously repeated, turned out to have lost their power.

The case against: God and Nature, Family and Society

For the *opponents* one series of arguments referred to the authorities of *Bible* or *Nature*. Homosexuality was sin and heathenism, inborn defect or perversity. Consequently, homosexual relations should not be officially recognized by society. Such views, expressed by Christian and conservative groups, constitute the major part of the printed public argument, not only in the (narrowly circulated) Christian newspaper, but also in the press as a whole.

Another series of arguments against the law centred on notions of a *dissolution of marriage, family, morality, culture, and society*. Again, there were various versions, more or less intertwined. Marriage would be devalued and ridiculed, families broken, children harmed, and youngsters bewildered. Homosexuality would spread, as would crime, drugs, and disease in its wake; and the gates would be opened for further decay: child adoption by homosexuals, church weddings of homosexuals, bigamy. Such assertions, especially those stressing marriage and family, were the most weighty arguments of opponents, in the sense that they were common ground for various groups and were presented also by respectable and influential conservatives (editors of newspapers, members of Parliament) not particularly associated with religious fundamentalism.

A third cluster of arguments might be termed *juridico-technical*. There was no need for such legislation. Very few persons would care or dare to make use of it. It would imply changes in hundreds of other laws, and endanger Denmark's relationship to the rest of the world, since 'registered partnerships' would not be accepted elsewhere. It might cause a new influx of refugees, since contracting a registered partnership with a Dane would be one way of gaining access to the kingdom. The common denominator of these arguments seems to be: too much juridical-administrative trouble for too little or no gain. They were widely present in the statements of opponents, sometimes as main points, but usually combined with other arguments. Precisely because of their technical character, they may easily appear in need of more substantial reasons to lean on.

Other subsidiary arguments concerned the *status of Denmark in the world*. If such a bill was passed, Denmark would lose its reputation, become an object of ridicule, get into lots of trouble with other nations, be flooded by immigrants, and maybe even cease to exist like other civilizations – Sodom, Rome – under similar circumstances. Such assertions are easily linked to the other arguments, and they were frequently set forth as major supplementary reasons.

Equal value, difference, and otherness

So far, all the arguments against the law presupposed that homosexual relationships in themselves are not of the same value as heterosexual ones. Others raised objections from the opposite point of view, arguing that the law did not acknowledge the fundamentally equal value of homosexuals, but instead *perpetuated discrimination and oppression*.[3] Again, there were various versions of such criticism.

By omitting the rights of adoption and church wedding, the law cemented the status of homosexuals as second-rate citizens. It opposed or did not take into account the specific experiences, possibilities, and problems of women, e.g. in relation to adoption, bearing, and rearing of children. By favouring relationships similar to heterosexual marriage, it would induce women – or homosexuals in general – to form such relationships, and thus place them in economic dependency, social isolation, emotional stagnation, physical violence, and repressed conflicts. Furthermore, partners in these couples would not be regarded as individuals. The law discriminated against traditions of life-style among homosexuals, such as non-permanent relationships and the primacy of friendship networks. In suggesting a common model for the life-style of homosexuals and heterosexuals alike, it discouraged an acceptance of homosexuals in their difference and otherness.

Such 'radical' views were, however, rare in the total amount of public debate, and were mainly put forward by a few lesbians and gay men.

The case for: Liberty, Equality, and Justice

Most arguments of *proponents* centred round the principle of *equality*. Homosexuals would now gain (with a few exceptions) the *right to an equal freedom of choice* as had heterosexuals, in relation to privileges and obligations of couple building.

Among the gains mentioned by proponents were the opportunity for greater emotional and financial security in relationships, as well as for increased seriousness and responsibility in feelings and actions. In this connection, a few homosexuals also referred to the emotional and public-symbolic value of contracting a partnership – as an act wherein partners could solemnly declare their feelings for and dedication to take care of one another, in front of each other, their family and friends, and society at large. Generally, however, the depiction of the various possible benefits of living in 'registered partnerships' was not a main theme. The emphasis lay on the *principles* of equality, freedom, and justice.

The realization of these principles was often presented as a value in itself, not least in relation to the situation of minorities. Furthermore, it was frequently added, legal equality implied a formal and official, societal acknowledgement of the *equal value* of homosexual and heterosexual relations. This would have a positive impact on the attitudes of homosexuals to themselves, as well as on the attitudes and reactions of others in relation to them. A similar positive effect would occur as the knowledge and practice of registered partnership would increase the visibility of homosexuals.

These were the main arguments of proponents. They included, among others, politicians from left and centre parties, the national organization of gays and lesbians, and some editors.

A particular, 'moralistic' version of such arguments held that formal equality and official approval would *strengthen long-term monogamous relationships* among homosexuals since they would no longer have to meet and live under dark and dubious circumstances and since partners would be encouraged to take on a responsibility in relation to one another. Thus, it was sometimes added, the law might also help prevent the spread of AIDS. Further, it would improve the public image of homosexuals. Some of these arguments were mentioned in the notes to the Bill, but primarily as supplementary, not main reasons. Apart from that, they were presented only by a few male homosexuals in newspaper articles.

Of greater significance was a series of arguments concerning the *status of Denmark in the world*. Denmark was seen as traditionally being in the forefront of civilization, in relation to tolerance and equal rights. Consequently, it had an obligation to lead the way for other nations also in this matter.

In summary

The main argument of opponents was the *dissolution of marriage and family* argument, often bolstered by the religious and technical ones. The main arguments of proponents were those on *equality* and *equal value*. For both parties the *status of Denmark in the world* was a major supplementary theme. There were, of course, also many arguments that were attempts at directly refuting those of the opposite party. Basically, however, the debate consisted in the assertion of two fundamentally opposed sets of principles and values: 'traditionalist' ones on God, nature, and family, versus 'modern' ones on liberty, equality, and justice.[4]

The arguments of opponents constituted the majority of printed debate, and were also the most widely circulated. This was mainly due to the zeal of Christian groups, who invested much energy in arranging meetings and writing petitions to Parliament and the press. The small Christian party, participating in government at the time of the proposition of the Bill, declared it a major theme of their (also nationwide televised) election campaign in the spring of 1988, made its withdrawal a condition for their further participation in government after the election, and threatened to organize a referendum if it was passed.

All to no avail. The Christian party lost ground in the election (from 2.4 per cent of the votes to 2 per cent), was not included in the government (though no doubt primarily for other reasons than their opposition to 'registered partnerships'), and was far from able to produce the parliamentary support necessary to issue the writs for a referendum after the law was passed on 26 May 1989. This final result was in accordance with the will of the majority of the Danes, according to opinion polls in 1988 and 1989.

The introduction of 'registered partnerships' in Denmark, then, shows a society where traditionalist principles and values have increasingly lost their power, and where the homosexual no longer inhabits the place of absolute evil in the general symbolic system. Does this amount to the realization of the 'modern project' of a society governed by the rational arguments of freedom, equality, and justice? And does it signify that homosexuals have become fully accepted by the majority? To help clarify this, I will turn to look at the wider context of the Danish events.

MODERNITY AND HOMOSEXUALITY AS A FORM OF EXISTENCE

During the past few decades, scholars have argued extensively that *the homosexual* is a specifically modern construct, produced in (North)Western societies since the second half of the nineteenth century (McIntosh 1968; Plummer 1975, 1981a; Foucault 1979; Weeks 1977, 1981b; Faderman 1981; Katz 1983; and so on). Consequently, this special creation may disappear again in the course of history.

Elsewhere, I have criticized such 'constructionist' scholarship for attaching, *in general* and *in theory*, too much weight to matters of consciousness – expectations, attitudes, ideas, perceptions, discourses, labels, roles, and identities (Bech 1987, 1989c). Because of this emphasis, constructionists have had some difficulty in perceiving that 'being homosexual' is not merely a matter of ideas and identities, but a way of *being*, a *form of existence*. And, consequently, they have also had some difficulty discovering a number of the *conditions of life* that make up the essential background to this form of existence. Indeed, when trying to identify the particular characteristics and 'causes' of the modern homosexual, the appropriate primary object of one's study might be neither genes, hormones, and chromosomes, *nor* categories, labels, and roles, but railway stations, opera houses, discotheques and consulting rooms. Below, I shall concentrate on the *male* homosexual, but I am confident that an analogous analysis can be made in relation to the lesbian.

As a form of existence, the modern homosexual comprises a number of particular characteristics.[5] These include certain basic *moods and recognitions* – e.g. of existential uneasiness and freedom, of injury and of feeling watched, as well as of a certain distance from one's own masculinity and potential femininity. There are also particular *ways of experiencing* – such as sexualization, aestheticization, camp, and sensitivity; particular *dreams and longings* – eg. of another country; and particular *forms of behaviour and*

138

expression – such as stylings and stagings, travels and breaks, signals and gaze. Further, there is a specific *social world* – including brief encounters, changing relationships with partners, pornography, couples with institutionalized infidelity, as well as organizations and friendship networks. Finally, and fundamentally, there are particular *life spaces*, such as streets, parks, bars, and consulting rooms.

The *background* to this form of existence are the modern conditions and problems of life. This includes the city; the collapse of absolute norms; the absence of stable and pre-given community and of identities to identify with completely; the problematization of gender; the institutions of art, the visual media, and professional design; the idea and practice of liberal democracy; the police and the apparatus of self-analysis (psychiatry, psychology, etc.). The homosexual form of existence is an outcome of these conditions and problems of life, bearing their immediate mark as well as being an answer to them.

Such conditions of life are, of course, increasingly universal in modern societies. To the extent that the homosexual form of existence differs from that of the majority, this is largely because the homosexual has been living in longer and closer contact with these specifically modern conditions. One example must suffice here: when the (future) homosexual left his family, or his work, he came out – in *the city*. The 'heterosexual' returned to family.[6]

The idea of a homosexual form of existence does not, of course, imply the assertion that all actual 'homosexuals' are identical and have been so since the end of the nineteenth century. However, in realizing certain erotic preferences – *wherever they come from* (Bech 1989a) – one cannot avoid becoming involved to some extent in this form of existence. This is partly because such realization leads one into close contact with the very same conditions of which the homosexual form of life is a result and to which it is an answer, and partly because one will also encounter this form of existence as something which is already there, since it *has*, as a matter of fact, become established as the dominant model for living under such circumstances (Bech and Lützen 1986; Bech 1987).

The modern homosexual, then, is a conglomerate, (cor)responding to a particular conglomerate of socio-cultural conditions. It may be noted that such an approach solves a number of problems involved in the constructionist–essentialist debate, since all of the factors in these conglomerates have differential histories and some of them might thus be found at other points in world history.

Incidentally, and by the same means, it does away with some of the problems in the debates on the when and what of modernity and post-modernity. Only in the latter part of the nineteenth century did the particular multiplicity of factors mentioned above come together in the conglomerates of 'the homosexual' and 'modernity'; and only in so far as these change radically may we speak of the end of the homosexual and the beginning of postmodernity. The two may not necessarily coincide, however. Whether or not a society has truly become modernized can no doubt be determined by the presence of the homosexual; but his and her end may signify the culmination of modernity rather than its termination.[7]

Common changes

The approach presented above allows us to specify the circumstances under which the homosexual might disappear. This would come about in so far as the conditions of his/her form of existence change radically, *or* in so far as they become actual, close, and constant realities for everyone.

The latter seems to be precisely what is going on in (North)Western societies. Marriage and family, once the buffer against the realities of modern conditions of life, are in a process of steady dissolution. Living in the city – in 'a world of strangers'[8] – has become a reality for more and more people; and visual media and everyday design permeate life, suggesting ways of conduct and experience such as aestheticization, staging, camp, and kitsch. For most, not much seems pre-given or eternally secure and stable in relation to work, social intercourse, and personal identity – even gender has generally grown into a role and a problem. The institutions of high art, transformed and democratized as film, video, and rock music, help promote sensitivity in everyone. The theory and practice of liberal democracy increasingly become a lived reality, as each identity is from the outset conceived in terms of relative oppression and the right to improvements. With changes in life space, direct social control from family and neighbours gives way to anonymous, potential supervision and control for everyone and the corresponding attention and awareness of the possibility of being watched. The ideologies and institutions of self-analysis are ever expanding, leaving practically no one without some idea that they have an inner self and sexuality, precious, but hidden and dangerous, always in potential need of therapy.

That such processes of *modernization* are going on in the West has been documented by numerous scholars since the nineteenth century. It is also well known that the changes are connected with developments in symbolic universes, from 'traditionalist' to 'modern' principles and values.[9] And, according to the theory presented above, the fate and situation of the 'modern homosexual' is related to all of these processes and changes.

With this background, I will take a closer look at what is going on in Denmark, where men are coupled with men, and women with women, under the auspices of public authorities.

THE STATE OF DENMARK

Have the modern changes in conditions and forms of life been particularly profound in Denmark? Relevant data (on the spread of *camp* experiences, psychotherapy, etc.) have not been systematically collected and examined, but the issue may well be worth pursuing, for Denmark could be leading in such important matters as changes in gender relations (Nordic 1988; Prondzynski 1989). Further, the way in which the modernization of existence is experienced – as pleasure or danger, compulsion or opportunity – is no doubt coloured by other factors, primarily the quantity and distribution of economic affluence and state-provided social security. In these respects, Denmark has been in the forefront since the 1960s. Thus, there is no longer any particular need to experience and represent the homosexual as the incarnation of the threats of modernity.[10] However, I see no reason to assume that the level and 'tone' of modernization are *significantly* different in Denmark than in other (North)Western societies.[11]

There are also some indications in the debates and events surrounding the introduction of 'registered partnerships' which would support such a conclusion. What was accepted for homosexuals was in fact a *restricted form of marriage*. Both aspects are important. It was *marriage*, in so far as legislation on that traditionally most highly esteemed form of life was extended to homosexuals and not abolished (as some radicals preferred, demanding that no particular form of life be given special societal privileging). But it was marriage in a *restricted form*: the rights of adoption and church wedding were left out. When trying to counter the 'dissolution-of-marriage-and-society' argument, proponents sometimes became involved in a confused debate, claiming that equal rights were not given to homosexuals, that registered partnership was not equivalent to marriage, and that marriage was strengthened and not threatened when being extended to more people. The traditional *aura* of marriage still seems so strong that one may want to profit by it and simultaneously must fear to violate it.

What has been discussed so far may also help throw some critical light on the apparent progressiveness of the Danes in relation to an acceptance of homosexuals. True, the majority did not base their opinion of 'registered partnerships' on the 'against-God/against-nature' arguments nor on those of 'dissolution-of-marriage-and-society'. But from this we may not conclude that they considered homosexuals to be of *equal value* to heterosexuals – or even that they did not consider them 'unnatural' and the like. All that can be safely concluded is that they thought homosexuals should be given (more of) the same *rights* that heterosexuals had. This was also the central argument of proponents, and was what the majority actually endorsed in their answers to opinion polls, where questions were asked in terms of equal rights.

It may be objected that, by accepting legal equality, the majority must by implication have accepted also a societal recognition of *equal value*. In so far as this is the case, it does not necessarily indicate that they considered homosexuals to be of equal value. Viewed in the context presented above, it is more likely that they merely thought homosexuals should be treated *as if* of equal value – precisely because they did not consider them to be so. The mainspring may as well have been a sense of pity as of respect. The fact that homosexuals were not given full marriage rights points towards this interpretation, which is also supported by other available evidence (Lützen 1988; Bech 1989b).

Modern values and principles, then, have not simply overcome 'traditionalist' ones in Denmark. Rather, the two symbolic systems entered into a specific alliance. This situation testifies to a society not particularly advanced, but somewhere in the middle of the sort of transformation sketched above, in relation to forms of life as well as to the end of the homosexual.[12]

Fairyland

The fact remains, nevertheless, that a (kind of) equality in relation to 'marriage' was first realized in Denmark. Why?

Some facts directly related to the status of homosexuality in Denmark seem relevant here. The tradition of legal equalization is fairly old. Homosexual relations between consenting adults over 18 were decriminalized in 1933; and, although regulations were tightened in 1960, decriminalization continued from the mid-1960s, with the result that since 1981 there has been no discrimination against homosexuality in relation to criminal law (Comm. Rep. 1988). Adherents of sickness ideas have no authority to cling to; the leading medical and psychiatric authority in the field of sexology has publicly and unmistakably declared that homosexuality is not an illness (Hertoft 1985). There is a well-established national organization of gays and lesbians (founded in 1948), which has close contacts with influential politicians from various parties (Axgil and Fogedgaard 1985). Homosexuality and homosexuals have become increasingly visible in the media since the 1970s, and in less stereotyped or negative ways (Mikkelsen 1984; Lützen 1988; Bech 1989b). Large-scale public campaigns for the prevention of HIV and AIDS, directed by the health authorities, have been conducted in a way that on the whole seems not to have provoked hostility towards homosexuals and sexual activity (*condom use* being the main message) (Bech 1989b). But, again, one must ask why such developments have managed to succeed in Denmark?

Searching for an answer, we may once again return to the debate surrounding the legislation of 'registered partnerships'. One issue was of considerable concern to opponents and proponents alike: the status of Denmark in the world. It appeared that the evaluation of this status was directly correlated to the other arguments of each party. Opponents would speak of the impending dissolution of Denmark since the legislation was against God, nature, or society. Proponents would talk of the progressiveness and moral obligation of Denmark in relation to the rest of the world. This was *the* country of *frisind* – broad-mindedness, tolerance, and social responsibility in securing real equal opportunity for everyone.[13] By thus being at the front edge of civilization, it had an obligation to lead the way for the rest of the world.

Such cultural rhetoric has played an important role in Danish national identity since the mid-nineteenth century (Lunde 1988; Østergaard 1989); and pioneering *frisind* has actually, to some extent, been a reality in social, legal and political life. (Thus, Denmark was the first country to legalize pornography, in 1967 and 1969 (cf. Kutchinsky forthcoming).) As a rhetoric, it is no doubt accentuated at the present time when Denmark is economically in trouble and politically in the process of disappearing as an independent unity. The national cultural symbol then adds weight to an argument, and ideology becomes reality.

Thus, an essential part of the answer to the question of *why Denmark* is – *because of 'Denmark'*. Notably, this is the one argument that could not be used in any other country.

'The rest of the world'

As stated above, however, conditions and forms of life in Denmark are not basically different from those in the rest of the (North)Western world. Thus, it is likely that a debate on 'homosexual marriage' will proceed in other countries in much the same way as in Denmark. Opponents will mobilize 'God', 'nature', 'family', and 'society'; proponents will (have to) rely on the special mixture of 'traditional' and 'modern' values and principles: the continuation as well as the decline of respect for marriage; ideas of rights as well as a sense of pity. And the outcome may very well depend upon whether proponents manage to mobilize supplementary support for their cause, in the form of powerful national cultural traditions and symbols.

In Norway, the situation seems not unlike that of Denmark. Religious and other traditional values do play a more prominent part, as Norwegian society was, for geographical and economic reasons, more resistant to modernization. But here, too, proponents of homosexual partnerships may associate with symbols of, if not *frisind*, then freedom, autonomy, and solidarity. Sweden, on the other hand, has different, strong traditions and ideologies of social welfare in the form of direct state intervention in people's lives. By way of a mixture of prohibitions and support, social authorities are supposed to secure not only the *conditions* of citizens' well-being, but their actual well-being. The latter is defined in terms of material comfort, education, health, cleanliness, and order (Hirdman 1990; Henriksson

1991). In this context, a type of argument that obtained conspicuously little emphasis in the Danish debate may gain supremacy – the assertion that societal acceptance of homosexual partnerships will lead homosexuals to engage in steady, monogamous relationships and consequently to lead 'cleaner' lives. Such purity may not be a plausible prediction, in view of the traditional variety of life-styles within the homosexual community and the general trend in changes of modern conditions and forms of life (Bech 1987). But its assertion may be good tactics, on the way to the disappearance of the 'modern homosexual' as a specific socio-cultural phenomenon, liable to particular treatment and concern.

In some countries, certain arguments *against* 'registered partnerships' appear to play a more prominent part than they did or do in Scandinavia. This seems to be the case with arguments centring on notions of *marriage as a repressive institution* and of a *radical difference and otherness* of homosexuals in relation to heterosexuals. One version of such views holds that 'registered partnerships' will make gays and lesbians '*integrated*' and '*bourgeoisified*', so that they will lose their oppositional or revolutionary power – as outsiders fighting or negating the established order and as symbols of 'liberated', 'alternative', and more pleasurable ways of life. In this way, it is sometimes added, gays and lesbians will become subjected to updated, more *sophisticated forms of social control*.

One may ask why such arguments were all but absent in the Danish debate. A possible answer, of course, might be that the vast majority of Danish gays and lesbians were already 'bourgeoisified' and frantically mad to get married. The comparatively small number of 'registered partnerships' set up since the legislation, however, does not support such a thesis. It is also worth remembering that the main emphasis of proponents was not on the possible blessings of 'registered partnerships', but on principles of human rights: equal opportunity and equal value. There are some indications, in the debate as well as in the number of registrations, that lesbians generally may have been more reserved towards the legislation than were gay men.[14] But the overall state of the debate makes it reasonable to assume that the majority of both gays and lesbians simply considered it an extension of their possibilities of choice and social acceptance. Therefore, they saw no reason to argue against 'registered partnerships', even if they themselves had no plans of giving up their own particular way of life in favour of it. Besides, arguments on the radical 'difference' and 'otherness' of *the homosexuals* may not appear too convincing, as 'the heterosexuals' are becoming increasingly like them.

NOTES

1 *Some details concerning the legislation.* Apart from the rights of church wedding and adoption (including the right of custody of partner's children), the law on

'registered partnerships' also differed from legislation on marriage in demanding that at least one of the partners must be a Danish citizen and domiciled in Denmark. A month after the law had come into force, and after complaints from Christian groups, a unanimous Parliament voted that, in case of impending divorce, partners in 'registered partnerships' (unlike marriages) had no right to obtain conciliatory counselling by a vicar. The reason adduced for this provision was the regard for the conflicts of conscience to which vicars might be exposed. (Blessing by a vicar is performed on a private basis in private homes, and tolerated by some bishops though not by others.) The Bill was introduced in Parliament in January 1988, by parties of the social liberal centre and left wing, in close co-operation with the National Danish Organization for Gays and Lesbians. Various forms of legislation on homosexual partnership had been discussed and proposed by some of the same parties since the late 1960s, but the proposals never reached passage in Parliament (Comm. Rep. 1988). The present legislation (with minor changes identical with the Bill introduced in January 1988) was passed with the support or lack of opposition (i.e. abstention from voting) also of some members of right-wing parties, among others the majority of the ultraliberalist 'Fremskridtsparti'.

2   The presentation of the *discourse* and other events in connection with the introduction of 'registered partnerships' is based on an interpretation of material from the following sources: *Parliamentary and legal documents, press reports and debates*, and *opinion polls*. I have intended a total coverage of relevant material from these sources for the period from December 1987 through February 1990. (A detailed list of source material is available from the author.) December 1987 is the month when the planned introduction of the Bill on 'registered partnerships' was first announced. From November 1989, and particularly from January 1990, public media interest in homosexual matters shifted its focus to another topic (see below, note 12). Since then, and until the time of finishing the present article (June 1991), public debate on 'registered partnerships' has been very sparse. It was, however, rather extensive in 1988 and 1989. In an opinion poll of November 1989, 94 per cent of the respondents had heard of the new legislation.

    Remarks (at the end of the article) on conditions in Norway and Sweden are based on a selection of press material as well as the author's interviews with leading figures from the homosexual movement in these countries.

3   'Equal value' (in Danish: *ligeværd*) is a matter of human worth and dignity, whereas 'equality' (Danish: *lighed*) refers to social and legal rights and opportunities.

4   Cf. also Bech 1991, where I have reviewed the Danish debate in the context of a history of justifications.

5   The theory of a homosexual form of existence and its relation to modernity, which I can summarize only briefly in this article, is elaborated in detail in Bech 1987. I do not, of course, deny that very many researchers (including the ones I have mentioned above) in the field of homosexuality have been aware of other elements than roles and labels, medicine and law. Indeed, I have made extensive use of the results of others in my own work. But I do think that constructionism in general has been somewhat hampered by too narrow a theoretical framework.

6   As I am here illustrating my points by referring to the *male* homosexual, I would like to emphasize that the theoretical framework I am presenting basically implies not *one* homosexual form of existence, but *two*: one male and one female. The difference is connected with the different positions of men and women

145

in relation to the various modern conditions of life. For purposes of illustration, however, and when stressing the formal features of the concept, one may be justified in speaking of 'the' homosexual form of existence. (Both forms – the male *and* the female – are, of course, connected with a variety of homosexual life-styles, life courses, etc. (cf. Bech 1989b).) I have dated the birth of the 'modern homosexual' to the second half of the nineteenth century. I do not, however, deny that this rupture is related to another – and maybe larger – one around 1700 (see Trumbach 1977; Meer 1988).

7   I do not, of course, deny that the world is changing – sometimes in very impressive ways. I stick to the term 'modernity', however, for two reasons. (1) Most of what is generally associated with 'postmodernity' – such as visual media, city life, and gender games – was there from the start of modernity. (2) I do not see that the ideas of 'postmodernity' contain any radical break with 'modern' notions of history or cultural hierarchy. On the contrary, 'postmodern' thinking is very much about phenomena that could come into existence only at a certain stage and place in world history. Indeed, one might argue that 'postmodernism' = 'evolutionism' when thought through.

8   In the felicitous phrase of Lyn Lofland (Lofland 1973).

9   A detailed list of references could go on endlessly. I have to limit myself to a few 'modern classics', with fairly different emphases and interpretative frames: Benjamin 1973, 1982; Berman 1982; Foucault 1977, 1979; Habermas 1984/1989, 1989; Sontag 1966, 1977 (cf. Bech, 1987). Excellent recent works (preferring the term 'postmodern' instead of 'modern') are Fiske 1987; Featherstone 1991.

10   In an opinion poll of 1947, 61 per cent of the respondents rated homosexuality as the worst or second worst 'crime' on the following list: murder, rape on adult woman, burglary, forgery, drunk driving, hunting outside the hunting season, and homosexuality (reported in Havelin 1968: 73). In an opinion poll of 1985, 50.7 per cent of the respondents found that society in general did not show sufficient understanding of the conditions of the homosexuals. It is also worth noticing that in the debate over 'registered partnerships' very many of the opponents of the law expressed some sympathy or pity for the homosexuals, and said that their opposition to the law should not be misinterpreted in terms of a persecution.

11   By the phrase '(North)Western societies' I refer primarily to Australia, New Zealand, Canada, the USA, and countries in Europe *west* of the former Iron Curtain and *north* of Greece, Southern Italy, Southern Spain, Portugal, and Ireland. When speaking of a considerable degree of state-provided social security and of distribution of affluence, one must, of course, also exclude the UK and parts of the USA.

12   *A test case: antidiscrimination.* As mentioned in note 2, public media interest in homosexual matters shifted its focus very soon after the law on 'registered partnerships' had become effective. In the context of the present article, this new topic of interest deserves brief comment: a law suit, brought to court by the Public Prosecutor at the request of the National Organization for Gays and Lesbians against the writer of a reader's letter. Invoking the Bible, the woman in question had described homosexuality as the most loathsome form of adultery, and the homosexual as a sort of thief who steals his neighbour's honour and perhaps his life, by inflicting AIDS upon him. She was sued according to the law on antidiscrimination, which since June 1987 includes the provision that a group of people may not be publicly defamed because of its sexual orientation. The case can be treated in no detail here; its result

- it was finally lost – does not contradict the conclusions of the present article.

13   The Danish word *frisind* literally means 'free mind' or 'free spirit'. Like other idioms of national peculiarities – such as the German *Anständigkeit*, the French *gloire*, and the Swedish *folkhem* – it is not easily translated into other languages. In its idealized form, it does not simply denote permissiveness, but enlightened tolerance in matters of personal belief and moral conduct, combined with a social commitment to establish the conditions for individuals to think and live as they prefer.

14   Of the 789 partnerships registered up to the end of March 1991, 191 were set up by women.

This article was made possible by the financial support of the Danish Social Research Council.

Part V

TRANSCENDING AIDS
Models of love, support, and activism

No late twentieth-century writing on same-sex experience can neglect AIDS and HIV. Both as disease and symbol it has played a powerful part in the reshaping of gay and lesbian communities throughout the 1980s. The articles here are clearly concerned with the tragic nature of the disease: with the death and grief that have touched so many lives. But they go well beyond this. For predictions of 'holocausts' and the 'end of the homosexual' have been transcended. Instead, these articles demonstrate the growth of new communities of support, care, and activism.

12

THE AIDS DIALECTICS

Awareness, identity, death, and sexual politics

Tim Edwards

The fact that it was used in that way, as if it was uniquely a gay plague once again, I mean, it's quite frightening that people can use those type of things and there will be lots of followers with them. I got the sense that when those posters were plastered around everywhere, that everywhere I went, you know, on my way to work, that every time I came out of my property that people were watching me and thinking 'Oh yeah, he's the one with AIDS'.

(Clive)

AIDS is, in a signficant sense, 'a gay disease'. It is a medical condition and a symbolic phenomenon, and in each of these respects the gay community is often over-represented in relation to its proportion within the population of Western society as a whole. First, in Western advanced industrial societies, where the gay community is a recognized group, it forms statistically anywhere from 30 to 90 per cent of the population of people with AIDS and in other societies, where the gay community is not a recognized group, the denial of AIDS often goes hand in glove with the denial of gay sexuality (Chirimuuta and Chirimuuta 1989; Panos Institute 1990; Sabatier 1988). Second, and more importantly, the gay community has felt the full force of a stigmatization process of media stereotypes, persecution, and phenomenal mistreatment on all levels from personal paranoia through to the implementation of national policy (Watney 1987). Consequently, it is crucially necessary to separate the metaphorical conceptually from the medical aspects of AIDS, and this calls for an inquiry into the effects of the impact of AIDS as a myriad of metaphorical, as opposed to medical, meanings upon the gay community. Thus, when I started to study AIDS in the UK in 1988, my intention was to investigate the social-psychological, as opposed to the medical-epidemiological, aspects of AIDS, particularly through the use of in-depth interviews, group discussions, and questionnaires. Consequently, as the study progressed, four themes emerged in importance: first, the theme of Awareness; second, the development of Identity;

third, the theme of Death or mortality; and, fourth, the importance of Sexual Politics. On top of this, the underlying principle that underpinned these four themes was that of the AIDS dialectics, or the primarily interactive impact of AIDS, or the impact of Awareness, Identity, Death and Sexual Politics upon AIDS and the impact of AIDS on Awareness, Identity, Death, and Sexual Politics. This chapter is thus structured according to a consideration of these four themes, using, selectively, the data derived from my conversations with gay men.[1]

THE AWARENESS DIALECTIC

I thought it was just a sensationalist piece of media journalism.

(Dominic)

The most common and simple conception of the impact of AIDS is that, as a sexually transmitted and mostly terminal medical condition laden with meaning, it must have an overwhelmingly important and overridingly significant effect. However, practically without exception, the people I spoke to perceived AIDS as insignificant at first. For example, Mark, a 30-year-old man living in London, said: 'I suppose at first it didn't really affect me.' Yet he later added:

I suppose I knew it was coming . . . I used to have nightmares . . . I knew people that were HIV positive and that really hit home and especially when a friend of ours died last year, that really brought it home.

(Mark)

This factor of friends dying was far and away the most important in forming a consciousness of AIDS as personally significant. Consequently, this then raises a question of contexts of significance or a model of AIDS related to a process of personal distancing or closeness. Thus, when someone knows of no one else with AIDS other than in America, it remains over there; once cases are heard of in their own country, it comes over here; once an acquaintance suffers or dies, it comes down the road; once a friend dies or falls ill, it comes to the front door; and once a lover or very significant other suffers, it comes into the home. Moreover, this then raises the curious question of the American connection, or the initial perception of AIDS as a primarily American epidemic due to America's simultaneously primary and super-powerfully influential position in this respect. A particularly important factor in forming the in/significance of AIDS is mis/information interconnected with the American connection, as initial information concerning AIDS in the UK often came in the form of reports from the USA, and particularly in a series of Horizon programme documentaries including *Killer in the Village*, a lurid documentary contrasting colourful images of glamorous gay men in sexualized disco scenarios with hideous skulls cocooned in hospital hygiene:

> *T*: How did you first become aware of AIDS?
> Er, I think through the gay press, and then television, I remember watching, before then though, I think early eighty-four when I was with the other guy I'd seen *Killer in the Village* and I'd found that absolutely horrifying.
>
> (Jonathan)

Most of the people I spoke to were clearly moved by the emotive imagery of the programme though mostly missed some of the more constructive information. Information is of course often seen as playing a primarily important part in the prevention of the spread of AIDS and HIV. However, a very clear distinction arises contrasting media *mis*information in the form of, for example, 'sex equals death', 'the AIDS virus', and 'promiscuity causes AIDS', and more constructive information, for example, 'certain activities are considered risky' or 'risk is reduced through the use of condoms'. The former tends to lead to reactions of fear, terror, and fatalism that are ultimately not very preventive in practice; while the latter tends to lead to a cooler consideration and weighing of pros and cons that are potentially preventive in practice. The important point on top of this though is that information, or misinformation, is, first, individually *perceived* through a process of personal interpretation and, second, *negotiated* in a process of individual and/or collective action. Consequently, in particular, this includes attitudes towards sexuality, self-definitions, and conceptions of 'promiscuity'. For example, a perception of oneself as not promiscuous, a very context-dependent concept, potentially leads to a false sense of security –

> In a way I s'pose I didn't see myself as being quite as much at risk, simply because I'd been in a, w-what I knew to be a monogamous relationship.
>
> (Terry)

– whilst risk is negotiated in a process of weighing pros and cons, of pleasure *versus* danger, in the practice of sexuality: 'It's Russian roulette really' (Clive).

Given this array of factors affecting the significance of AIDS what one necessarily needs to consider are the contexts of awareness affecting the significance of AIDS, illustrating a dialectic of awareness and AIDS, particularly at the levels of the interactions of the personal and the political, and the interaction of the past and the present. The key factor here is life history and at the crux of this is identity.

THE IDENTITY DIALECTIC

It was like living in a shell really, thinking I was the only person that was gay. No sort of terminology or anything else until I met somebody else who was gay and that was the greater process of coming out.

(Clive)

Identity is not a fixed entity. It is a complex, interactive, and developmental process of self-definition in interaction with the wider social, economic, and political context. Consequently, definitions of identity have tended to alter over the last century and particularly since the political development of a positive 'gay', as opposed to 'homosexual', identity in many Western societies. Over the past twenty years or so, politics of identity have developed, and identity, like the personal, is now political. A key factor in this process of development was the production of the concept of 'coming out', of publicly proclaiming one's sexuality, and the linked concept of 'coming together', implying political activism, community, and positive sexuality. Consequently, coming out is commonly seen as some form of unitary phenomenon when it is more importantly a developmental process that operates on several levels: first, telling oneself that one is gay; second, telling others within the confines of a safe, homosexually exclusive place; and, third, telling the wider and usually 'straight' society of family, friends, and workplace. It is primarily a messy, complex, and developmental process. For example, Mark said: 'I mean, I didn't sort of announce it, other than to my younger brother, just sort of accepted it over the years.' However, for others, the effects are occasionally more dramatic, a case of 'caught in the act'. The impact of AIDS upon this process is equally complex, contradictory, and developmental, as AIDS undoubtedly adds ammunition to the problems and difficulties of coming out in the potential stigmatization of sexuality or ostracism, but for others AIDS has consolidated, particularly politically, identity to the point of an intentional no return:

So again, I mean it was like not, degrees of coming out, that's why I say it's a process that's gone on through AIDS, so it's, I would say AIDS actually had finally completed my coming out to the point of something I will never hide again.

(Martin)

There is little doubt though that the AIDS epidemic can still inhibit the coming out process in some cases. For example:

I think it's made me even more reticent to enter into relationships, to want to have sex which I've never been that keen on anyway, and it's made me even more withdrawn and isolated within myself and, it's made me opt out more and more I think, it's almost pushed me

154

back to the point where I was at 21 when I was just not interested in living any more really, I just existed.

(Colin)

Consequently, coming out is a complex process interactive with other factors of cultural situation and individual development; not a simple step impacted upon as the AIDS epidemic spreads.

On top of this, the definition of identity stands in dialectical relation to AIDS as sexual identity is often defined as 'naturalistic' or 'constructed', according to the degree of individual or cultural learning involved in the definition. For example, the first person I spoke to said: 'It's just always there, it's like this [grins and gestures] *irresistible urge*' (Clive), while his partner pointed out: 'It's a sort of, stupid macho sort of thing, they sort of have to prove themselves' (Mark). The former definition is 'naturalistic', centred on a notion of sexuality as a sort of innate force or drive, while the latter definition is 'constructed', highlighting a question of masculine socialization. The implications of these different situations in relation to the AIDS epidemic are quite significant as the former tends to lead towards a fatalistic and fixed lack of control model of sexuality, while the latter is implicitly more open or plastic. This constructionist factor also applies to the practice of safer sex, as the incorporation of practicalities it involves impact upon sexual activity and, indeed, identity:

I mean, I felt AIDS affect my sense of virility,
T: mmn, in what sense?
Well, I mean because I practise safer sex so, I mean it's very very different to put a condom on as a contraceptive and to put one on because there's a risk of, infection, and, that affects your sense of, your sexual sense of your self, your sexuality, and the technology of it is more messy, it introduces more breaks, more barriers, more, more likelihood for performance failure – to lose your erection which then impacts back on your sense of yourself as – it's quite, it's not easy, and I think that's an unspoken part of safer sex educators.

(Martin)

The point put simply though is that the more dominant cultural emphasis is still overwhelmingly naturalistic and difficult to resist (Epstein 1988).

THE DEATH DIALECTIC

I don't think it would have changed very much if AIDS wasn't a disease that killed people.

(David)

One of the most striking factors concerning the sociological literature surrounding AIDS is its essential denial of it. Writers, researchers,

155

polemicists, and academics alike are, mostly and implicitly at least, at pains to point out that AIDS is not 'the gay plague', that it is not 'the killer disease of the century', it does not necessarily even kill at all, that HIV infection is not necessarily even related to it, that testing is part of conservative control, that the media misinform, distort, and alarm: in short, that AIDS is just another medical condition surrounded with a myriad of wholly unnecessary meanings and significance. Thus, in a sense, AIDS does not exist over, above, or beyond the level of constructed discourse. There is, of course, a vast array of evidence and analysis to support this perspective (Boffin and Gupta 1990; Carter and Watney 1989; Crimp 1988). However, when speaking to people in interviews, at the level of their individual practices and experiences, it seems AIDS does still arouse very real fears surrounding dying, loss, and sexuality. First, in connection with the contexts of awareness cited earlier, there is a consideration of AIDS as a cause of death and a negotiation of this situation. This negotiation varies from defensive fatalism in the form of semi-suicidal kamikaze risk taking to displacement of personal impact in the form of concern for friends rather than oneself, from: 'I think it's made me more kamikaze in a way, more, I think pre-AIDS I was more responsible' (Clive), to:

I s'pose that, it makes you more worried about other people that you do know, more people that you've known even slightly that have died, the more you're concerned about the people you know, you know better still.

(Julian)

Furthermore, this defensiveness or displacement is premised upon a perception of AIDS as a particularly painful illness, fuelling fears of suffering and stigmatization: 'I think it's the awful, (h...) the deteriorating and debilitating effects of it, you know, which sort of drain your energy and drain you of everything, every dignity' (Colin). Second, this then feeds into the actual handling of death or mortality when finally confronted with it in some way:

One of the interesting things I feel obliged to explain is that medical knowledge for people in my situation has only been available retrospectively whereas instead we had symptoms that didn't exist, we had conditions that only latterly have been diagnosed, and we had a fear which was [half laughs] not considered serious, I mean AIDS has only become a popular and medically careerist issue since 1985.

(Martin)

This highlights the dialectic of AIDS and death at the level of the interaction of life history with wider social history. Significantly, the question is also raised as to the interaction of individual personality and the development of the AIDS epidemic as, for example, some of the people I spoke

156

to who had AIDS or AIDS-related conditions themselves reacted very differently to fairly similar medical conditions, varying from: 'I found a strength in me that, I've never known before' (Dominic), to: 'Well, it's a devastating effect, it's really very unpleasant, I'd rather be in Philadelphia, I mean it's that sort of, feeling or approach' (Martin). In particular, conditions such as AIDS-Related Complex and HIV positivity produce even more violent reactions due to an added question of uncertainty. Similarly, perceptions of the impact of AIDS upon people or society varied from the apocalyptic: 'Without reason I'd just be caught in this horrible, horrible world of my friends dying, and maybe myself dying and it's just, just unthinkable' (Martin), to the profoundly ordinary: 'I don't regard it as any more serious than a disease such as leukaemia or some cancers' (Richard), and it is at this point that the politics of AIDS are particularly apparent.

THE SEXUAL–POLITICAL DIALECTIC

The perception of the political impact of the AIDS epidemic is particularly contradictory and dialectical, centred on contrasting perceptions of the past, the present, and the future. For example, some saw the AIDS epidemic as an imposition, particularly politically or sexually: 'The on-going effect of AIDS on the gay community I think is the most dreadful, imposition, and restricter of quite acceptable and normal activities in the gay world' (Mike); while others saw it positively as providing a sense of community and consolidation: 'I think it's brought a lot of people closer, and the gay community is, or gay people, I think have got a lot more tolerance, of each other, I think it's given a sense of er, togetherness' (Dominic).

In addition, this highlights a dialectic of differing sexual and political perspectives, according to an emphasis placed more on the sexual or the political. On top of this, international comparisons are critical, as the UK was often seen as particularly sexually oppressive compared with certain parts of America and Europe, usually seen as more open or pluralistic in their approaches to and practices of sexuality: 'I find it very exciting, they seem to have a lot more openness and the gay life is a lot more, obvious, more part of the society than what it is here' (Richard). Ultimately, the question centres on the potential impact of the AIDS epidemic or, more particularly, pessimistic or optimistic perceptions of the outcome, from 'a flowering of the gay community' (Chris) to 'more AIDS, more death, more friends . . . a bit unpleasant' (Martin), which ultimately remains unknown, though increasingly pervasive as part of life:

It's there, it's here, and it's just something we're going to have to get used to, it's, I've never said this to other gay friends of mine, whether we like it or not it's changed our lives, and it's gonna continue to change our lives, some to a greater or lesser extent, you know, I think I'd challenge any gay man who was doing anything before AIDS to say it hasn't changed his life.

(David)

CONCLUSION

On intending to study the impact of AIDS upon the gay community, the unintended and unexpected impact was the impact of the gay community upon AIDS. This more particularly applied to the impact of the personal upon the political, the present upon the past; as opposed to or as well as the previous conception of the impact of the political upon the personal, the past upon the present. In addition, this then set up a dialectic of these factors reflected in the four parts of this chapter as awareness, identity, death, and sexual politics in dialectical relation to AIDS. AIDS does, of course, have an impact: first, at the time of completing this chapter over two thousand people have died from AIDS-related diseases in the UK and statistics run into the tens and hundreds of thousands internationally; second, in the UK the number of sero-positive people is estimated at well into the tens of thousands and into millions internationally; and, third, on top of all this, there are of course the full effects felt throughout society at the levels of loss, caring, and financial costs, and across an *international* canvas. Nevertheless, it remains true to say that this chapter has constantly illustrated that the impact of AIDS is consistently *opposed*, *resisted*, and *undermined* through a series of personal, political, and social factors. This depends partly of course on the distinction of AIDS as a medical condition from AIDS as a social phenomenon. As the medical impact of AIDS perpetually increases, the social, economic, and political impact of the epidemic remains essentially a contested terrain of information, meaning, and outcome. This terrain is contested on four levels in this chapter: first, at the level of an Awareness context; second, at the level of identity and life history; third, at the level of the denial of Death and mortality; and, fourth, at the level of Society and sexual politics. There are, of course, many other areas and themes dialectically related to AIDS, including, for example, racism and sexism; and, ultimately, the impact of AIDS is unknown as a series of ripple effects throughout society. Consequently, the conclusion is, in one sense, a non-conclusion as AIDS has no linear development, no cause and effect impact, no importance *per se*, as separate from the social, economic, and political phenomena it taps into or encompasses. Its importance is essentially in process, as AIDS develops as part of life itself, no more and certainly no less.

NOTE

1 The research I conducted included twenty-two in-depth interviews with gay men living in Southern England and, in addition, two group discussions and twenty-one questionnaires. The quotations in this chapter come from the interviews. However, names are, of course, false.

13

LESBIAN POLITICS AND AIDS WORK[1]

Beth E. Schneider

I'm going to show them what a real live lesbian looks like. Nobody in the AIDS bureaucracy seems to think we exist, let alone are affected by AIDS. Their ignorance kills women, gay and straight, and we don't know how many because the CDC doesn't keep *those* numbers.
(*Gay Community News*, 9–15 October 1988: 5)

In the United States, the early identification of AIDS among gay men affected the initial social organization of the response and the politicized nature of the discourse surrounding AIDS (Patton 1985; Altman 1986). With nearly obsessive public attention to the sexual practices of gay men, lesbians were largely ignored as sexual beings and as members of the lesbian and gay community. Later, when it became clear that intravenous drug users were particularly vulnerable, lesbians were largely ignored. When sexual partners of gay or bisexual men or IV drug users were considered, once again, lesbians were ignored. And, when lesbians were not ignored, they were medically certified as the group least likely to be infected, except, of course, for cloistered nuns.

In the mid-1980s, most lesbians, if they thought about AIDS at all, were acutely aware of this characterization, and many were unselfconsciously proud of it. For example, when I told a lesbian friend of mine, a 50-year-old mother of three adult children, very active in the feminist community, that I was writing an article on lesbians and AIDS she looked at me oddly and said:

Why in the world are you doing that? I can't think of any group of people who are less likely to contract AIDS than lesbians, because they are the only people who do not have sexual relationships with men, and they do not seem to transfer the virus through their own sexual activity. If I wanted a blood transfusion, I would want to get it from a lesbian.

In 1986, this was a typical comment. None of the lesbians I spoke with that summer actually had thought much about women getting AIDS, let alone lesbians. With the exception of a few women active in health and AIDS circles in cities with the largest AIDS caseloads, access to information about women with AIDS in the United States was meagre.

Nevertheless, in the first writing of this article in 1986, I identified five domains of lesbians' lives (the social, the sexual, the reproductive, the economic, and the political) in which the potential or actual impact on lesbians of this crisis could be observed, and I demonstrated very tentatively how lesbians thought they were affected by AIDS. Today, with four years more of my own experience, observations, and reading, many of the patterns I identified are much more obvious, and some new issues have emerged.[2]

In what follows I discuss *six* domains – the social, medical, sexual, reproductive, economic, and political. The section on the political domain, by far the most lengthy, reflects the most volatile, complicated, and challenging arena over the long run for lesbians and our communities. The political, broadly construed, seeps into the discussion in the other domains as well.

But, a simple observation before proceeding. Lesbians and our communities in the US are not monolithic. Individually, we differ by age, racial and cultural identification, our feminism and other political commitments, and our sexual histories and interests. Our communities vary widely in size, resources, and organizational infrastructures. This diversity suggests not one, but many potential responses to AIDS among lesbians. It is my hope to reveal complexity and contradictoriness in lesbians' thinking about AIDS, considerable variability in lesbians' identification with AIDS as a community issue, and an untidy, historically contingent and shifting story for individual lesbians and for our communities.

THE SIX DOMAINS

Social: lesbians as friends and colleagues of homosexual men

Lesbians, more so than most heterosexuals, have direct contact with persons who are living with AIDS and those who are most concerned about the spread of this disease. Many lesbians have important relationships with gay men, as friends, co-workers, or political colleagues.

As early as 1986, lesbians whose friends included gay men were typically telling tales of great loss, *losses experienced by the men*: 'I know one man who has lost twenty-five friends'; 'I have one friend who has died from it, and other friends of mine have had friends who have died'; 'I have a good friend who lost his best friend and his lover in the same week, and that's really upsetting'. Even those less emotionally close with gay men knew someone who knew someone who had died.

Some lesbians were and are incredibly impressed with the ways gay men were handling AIDS. They marvelled at their resourcefulness and their new approach to living and dying. And they found that they, too, were forced to confront in themselves, albeit at some distance, the nature of their personal and political commitments and concerns.

Linda, who in 1986 had got involved in gay Alcoholics Anonymous, described her view of the gay men she met there and their relationship to AIDS:

> They are more in touch with their day to day lives and what they want to be doing to make their lives better, and so maybe there's a little bit more, spiritual presence. . . . Emotionally, they are much less frantic. I just talked to a man who was extremely promiscuous, and he says that he might have AIDS and he won't have regrets because he's *lived*. I've heard a lot of gay men talk that way.

In the last few years, other lesbians have become aware of how limited their acquaintance with gay men has been, noting that they rarely talk about health or sex or politics.

Whatever the depth of the relationship to gay men, lesbians have been deeply affected by and talk often about the frequent denial of sexual identity and denial of lovers in obituaries of men who had died of complications of AIDS. The lesbians, many too young to worry about serious illness and death, are forced to confront their own relationships with family and friends and the extent to which they are out as lesbians. Numerous lesbians are concerned for the first time with the arrangements they want when they die as well as with wills, powers of attorney, and other legal means to legitimate their partnerships.

By the end of the decade, it was not unusual to find lesbians talking and writing *about their own personal loss*. For example, Barbara Smith, publisher of Kitchen Table: Women of Color Press, quoted in an article/obituary of her friend Joseph Beam:

> I used to refer to Joe as a spiritual brother of mine. He did such a huge amount in the short time he was here. I will miss him for the rest of my life. I also felt he was such an incredible ally for me – we were trying to do such similar kinds of work. His work was actually more similar to mine than any Black woman I know. It is very rare to have such a relationship.
>
> (*Gay Community News* 1989)

Likewise, Mab Segrest writes about her friend Carl's death and its effect on her personal and political views:

> Neither Carl nor we could stop AIDS from killing him. But nothing stopped Carl from dying on his own terms. In dying this way, he left

me with two great gifts: he lessened my fear of my own death and taught me I could trust men to be my teachers. It was a faith I had lost a decade before in the initial anger and exhilaration of lesbian-feminism.

(Segrest 1989)

We read names of those who have died during local AIDS Awareness Weeks and when the Names Project/AIDS Quilt comes to town, and some of those names are our friends. I find my feelings about the gay men I now work with and meet alternate wildly between sadness, fear, anger, and love, as I try to figure how much investment to make in them emotionally when they may die soon and abandon me with my feelings and unending political work.

It seems that the more contact lesbians have with gay men as colleagues and friends, the greater is their medical knowlege about AIDS, the more detailed is their awareness of the emotional turmoil AIDS creates, and the clearer is their sense of the political ramifications of the disease. While some have not been materially, emotionally, or politically affected by AIDS, many others have become friends with gay men, often for the first time, and put increased time, money and attention into political activity around AIDS-related issues in their communities.

Medical: lesbians with AIDS and other serious illnesses

In December 1986, 7 per cent of the US diagnosed cases of AIDS were women; in 1991, it is 10 per cent. These figures were, and are still, underestimates since the US Centers for Disease Control has not added the gynaecological infections women with HIV infection suffer to its list of opportunistic infections and women have been consistently misdiagnosed. Most of the women with AIDS were and are intravenous drug users or women who had sex with an infected male; two-thirds were, and still are, women of colour.

The women with HIV infections do not constitute a self-conscious, politically active community. The women of colour were not well connected to organized political groups of any sort. With a few important exceptions, even the more informed feminist and lesbian public was largely unaware of these women until the last years of the 1980s (Schneider 1992).

Estimates of the number of lesbians in the US who are HIV-infected in 1991 hover between 100 and 200. But in 1986, there were no substantiated cases of AIDS *sexually transmitted* from one lesbian to another though there were several unsubstantiated reports of lesbians with AIDS and several substantiated reports of lesbians who contracted it through transfusions or IV drug use (Shaw and Paleo 1986). This information was not generally known to the vast majority of lesbians. Transmission of HIV through most lesbian sexual practice seemed very remote; it still seems that way to most lesbians.

163

For the most part, the lesbians with AIDS were not very public or linked to lesbian communities; some chose to keep their health status secret. Certainly, at mid-decade, conversations about lesbians having sex with men (though certainly many were engaged sexually with men in the previous seven to ten years) and using IV drugs were relatively taboo and talk about high-risk sexual practice was fraught with controversy. Even so, in most AIDS-prevention materials targeting lesbians, sharing needles and other paraphernalia when using IV drugs is identified as the most important risk factor, and precautions during sex are clearly listed. In 1991, most viable communities have experienced the death of at least one known lesbian, and most have workshops on safe sex. Still, many lesbians only begrudgingly acknowledge that HIV transmission may be a problem for lesbians.

The financial and political energy directed towards gay men around AIDS has generated a heightened interest in lesbian health, particularly in the problem of breast cancer, and considerable resentment has surfaced. Concern for breast cancer has increased in light of the estimate that 20–25 per cent of 44,000 women in the US who died of breast cancer in 1990 were possibly lesbians. But, with the exception of a few health activists, awareness about lesbian health has been minimal. They point out that the community is well educated about AIDS but few people, and only a handful of gay men, know anything about breast cancer as a health matter of lesbians. One noted that 'No one takes care of women or lesbians except women or lesbians' (Winnow 1989). Some of the most effective fighters in the AIDS epidemic have been lesbians, while health issues that profoundly affect them have had virtually no attention from the media, the medical community, the gay and lesbian community. For example, while there are remarkable resources to support people with AIDS (like food banks, buddies, home health care), support networks for lesbians with breast cancer are absent in virtually every community.

Sexual: lesbians, the sex debates, and AIDS

In the early 1980s, many lesbians were actively engaged in the heated feminist dialogue and debate about the definitions of, and the means to, pleasurable sex (Vance 1984; Snitow *et al.* 1983). Ironically, the feminist and lesbian debate about sex occurred at the same time that AIDS was being identified as a problem among the gay men. While gay men were rethinking the 1970s male ideology of sex, turning stigmatized sexual practices into safe ones, and discussing issues of commitment, monogamy, and intimacy in relationships, lesbians were becoming more public about the varieties of their sexual practice, revealing significant conflict among lesbians about sex (Califia 1979; Linden *et al.* 1982).

The actual impact of publicity about AIDS and the advocacy of safe-sex practices on the behaviour of lesbians is necessarily unclear. It was only towards the end of 1986 that safe-sex guidelines designed exclusively for women at risk and lesbians at risk were disseminated (Gage 1986). In 1986, none of the lesbians I interviewed reported changing any specific sexual practice, though one, Margaret, determined to stop having a relationship with a woman who also had sex with a drug-using, bisexual man. Interestingly, in all guidelines for women, sado-masochism is included, despite the considerable controversy about these practices over the last decade. In recent years, safe-sex workshops for lesbians have been offered throughout the United States, not simply in California, at women's music festivals and lesbian and gay centres. The very popular books written by sex therapist Joanne Loulan, and her speaking engagements, now incorporate discussions of safe sex. Given the dearth of information about transmission and the small numbers of infected lesbians, in 1991 controversy continues about what the safe-sex message to lesbians ought to be.

While the impact of AIDS on actual sexual practices was not on the minds of most lesbians in 1986, 'promiscuity' was. The link of AIDS to 'promiscuity', fuelled in the first years of this epidemic by medical people, the media, religious fundamentalists and the writings of many gay men, was reproduced among lesbians in a number of ways. Some were critical of how much sex gay men had. Others, like Sharon, simply focus on differences between these two groups.

> I think of lesbians as being women and gay men as being men.... I don't think women as a group are as promiscuous as men, and I don't think lesbians are very promiscuous; I don't think it's because they are gay men but because they are men. And what makes men less promiscuous are women. So if you take women out of that environment you run the risk of having more promiscuity.

While this explicit comparison minimizes lesbian 'promiscuity', other lesbians admitted to and named 'promiscuity' in their own past sexual behaviour, particularly in their previous heterosexual histories. Some reviewed their heterosexual experience, noting that it was long enough ago that the incubation period for HIV would be long over and they felt safe now. They are grateful they do not have to contemplate seriously the sexual histories of the men, frequently many of them, with whom they had sex. But other lesbians face their heterosexual histories as recent events and, in 1986, virtually anything prompted them to wonder about those encounters, and the chain of connection to them. One observed:

> Just recently is the first time I felt any concern at all after reading this week's latest *Newsweek* about a woman who had AIDS after a sexual relationship with a man, an intravenous drug user, that was seven years ago.... Reading about this specific case made me nervous for the first time ... I thought, my God, I don't know about that

165

long ago; I certainly slept with plenty of men in the past. I am not worried at all about the women I've been involved with, most of the women I have been with never had sex with men, so that's comforting.

While this woman totally dismissed the possibility of an HIV-infected lesbian, others had many sexual relationships with women. They, too, review what they know about some of those women especially if their partners were active drug users or sexually involved with many men. They wondered, when prompted, whether they could get AIDS. Mary observes: 'I had a lover three years ago who had a lot of relationships with men. She thinks she is a lesbian but does have sex with men, especially bisexual men. And it crossed my mind that it could have been a problem for me.'

The issue of 'promiscuity', along with a clear and multifaceted resentment of gay men, has not completely faded in the last five years. Responding to a woman writer's article about her reaction to the Names Project/ Quilt, another lesbian submitted a letter to *Gay Community News* and generated a flood of mail in the autumn of 1988 about the characterization of the men's sexuality. The letter read, in part:

I, too, have a hard time mourning men whose own sexual and lifestyle excesses brought them to where they are now. The notion of 'honey, wasn't it fabulous' to mourn a life points out the shallowness of both much of the gay male community and the NAMES Project itself.... When the lives of women – women who are killed, battered and abused every day with no one to mourn them – are so little matter to the world, the Quilt looks pretty silly indeed.

Similarly, dialogue between some lesbians and gay men about AIDS continues to generate sparks. Gay men often resent anyone telling them what to do about sexuality, whether these moral entrepreneurs are right-wingers advocating monogamy or lesbians urging a search for 'female energy'.

In the mid-1980s, Patton (1985) argued that if lesbians are able to confront internalized homophobia and erotophobia, both heightened by this medical crisis, the exploration of a broader vision of sexuality can continue. The dialogue about sexuality, begun with the 'sex debates' and further fuelled by AIDS, has generated more explicit discussion of sexual practices, preferences, and fantasies and greater consideration of sexual histories. The definition and meaning of lesbian is less collective than it was in the 1970s and early 1980s.

Reproductive: lesbians as mothers

In the 1980s, many lesbians chose to be mothers, and often relied on artificial insemination using sperm from sperm banks, from male friends, or from anonymous donors (Pies 1985; Wolf 1984). Some unknown, but seemingly significant, portion of the donors in past years have been gay or bisexual men. But, in 1986, few lesbians who were mothers or those contemplating motherhood considered the AIDS epidemic a major deterrent to their desire for, or lives with, children. This was so despite several relevant and troubling occurrences: violence and hostility towards children with AIDS in the public schools; fear of contagion and explicit rejection of lesbians or their children by heterosexual acquaintances who knew they conceived through artificial insemination; danger of increased chances of developing AIDS during pregnancy for HIV-infected women.

In 1986, those lesbians who had already inseminated and were currently pregnant, and those who delivered children through insemination in the recent past had reason to fear that they themselves or their children had been exposed to HIV. In San Francisco, a lesbian insemination research project began whose aim was to determine through antibody testing whether lesbians who had inseminated since 1979 with semen from heterosexual, bisexual, and homosexual donors had been exposed to HIV. The onset of this project created controversy among lesbians who differed over the use of scarce resources in this particular way and over the value of HIV testing at that time. But issues of prevention and the desire for information among women who used donors fuelled interest in the project. Many women who were considering a second child through artificial insemination also felt the desire to know. None of the 200 women who were tested was HIV positive despite several donors subsequently found to be positive.

At the first writing, it was unclear how, if at all, decisions had changed about who the donor/father should be and with what consequences to lesbians' plans. Currently, support groups for lesbians thinking about having children consider at length the impact of AIDS. It certainly seems that lesbians seeking donors now have fewer choices than they did in the past, since many are forced to reconsider gay men as potential partners or donors. On the other hand, sperm banks routinely do screening for AIDS, and many lesbians typically now make use of their services. Parenting books for lesbians (Pies 1985), AIDS projects, and lesbian mother groups throughout the country now follow the lead of the San Francisco and Los Angeles women's AIDS projects by publishing lists of practical suggestions for women using donors and/or artificial insemination.

Aside from the problem of reduced numbers of potential donors, other aspects of the lives of these lesbians are affected. In a wonderfully sensitive article written by a lesbian mother who got pregnant through insemination (Jones 1985), the loss of some special connection with gay men is described:

> The donor/donee relationship and the opportunity for gay men and lesbians to parent together seemed like the closest I'd ever felt to a primary link between our communities. We were talking with each other and participating in something very major together. Further,

167

my own process of getting pregnant had loosened my judgements and opened my mind. I was beginning to feel maybe there *were* some ways we were a community together. And now, I feel a paranoia creeping into that relationship, making things perhaps worse than they had been before. For me, it was a very disappointing development on many levels, aside from being terrifying and tragic.

Of all the ways in which gay and lesbian kinship networks and patterns have been affected by AIDS, this seems to be the aspect least often articulated.

Economic: lesbians as paid workers and unpaid caregivers

The most heterosexually orientated context in which lesbians find ourselves daily is our workplaces. With the exception of the few businesses and services which cater primarily or exclusively to the lesbian or gay population, lesbians are forced to consider how open to be, and many are relatively closeted (Schneider 1984). The AIDS crisis has created a series of dilemmas for many lesbians, enhancing homophobia and consequently fear about the revelation of sexual identity at work, while simultaneously generating situations in which the defence of gay men and homosexuality generally is much more likely.

The impact of AIDS on lesbians' employment situation means consideration of those workplaces in which discussion of AIDS or direct work with AIDS patients is necessary or highly possible, and all the other contexts. An unknown portion of the lesbian population is engaged in health, human services, and educational institutions. In the health field, lesbians may have direct contact with people with AIDS, many having chosen to get involved with AIDS patients at their hospitals, especially when confronted with the hysterical or homophobic reaction of many of their co-workers. In schools, controversies about gay male teachers transmitting the disease may affect their own employability or debates about the admission of HIV-infected children can force them to take sides in heated discussions about who is an 'innocent victim'.

In addition, lesbians are caregivers involved in all aspects and levels of AIDS work from paid directors of agencies to support staff to office volunteers and PWA buddies. Over the course of the last five years, the number of women has increased; in many locations, women are approximately 50 per cent of all staff and volunteers. Other women, many lesbians, are public health officers, researchers, lawyers, doctors, and psychologists, affiliated on ad hoc or permanent bases with AIDS-related projects in the larger cities.

Conferences such as 'Lesbian Caregivers and AIDS', held in San Francisco in January 1989, generate personal and political support for women involved in this work. While delighted to be together with time to talk, a great many questions were raised in often heated debate: How do lesbians deal with grief, and with death as a routine occurrence? How has the work affected relations with friends and lovers? How is it possible to deal with the racism, sexism, and class privilege of many of the white gay men with whom they work? What about the health problems of lesbians that go unattended? For many involved in AIDS work, heterosexual fear and stigmatization have provided a new impetus to organize, creating a more open gay presence, as seems particularly the case in the medical profession (Altman 1986). Some lesbians have been grateful for work situations in which they can at least 'come out', and for some that is one of the major reasons for taking a job with an AIDS organization.

In other work environments, everyday life for lesbians is more often affected by talking and joking around about sexuality, gay men, sexually transmitted diseases, and AIDS. In most work environments, the talk is typically not neutral. While some of it is sympathetic, the rest, particularly at mid-decade, was decidedly hostile and homophobic. Usually, the comments required a response.

For example, when AIDS was first publicized, it was the subject of a great many jokes in Mary's university office. But as she explains, the joking was short-lived.

First, the man I work for has a gay son, and it wasn't something he thought was fair game for jokes. I am very critical of those kinds of comments. And there is an awareness in our office that there are at last three gay workers there, and I think the straight people know that. Once people got beyond their horror and initial reaction, the seriousness of it for the people who suffered and the fact that many of the people in our office have had friends who have died from it or are sick has also tempered joking about it.

On the other hand, in some work situations, the homophobia is blatant. Teresa who works in the building and construction business, often the only woman in an environment with 100 men, described the AIDS talk on one particular project.

At least once a week at lunch, there would be some kind of conversation about AIDS.... I was shocked, the attitudes were archaic, brutal and uninformed.... There was all this insanity about catching it. They didn't trust any of the medical work that was being done and thought doctors were only trying to protect homosexuals. They sounded like crazy Klan members.... Well, they think it is the gay men's fault, and I couldn't tell them anything else. At the yard, the men say things like 'If we had gotten together and killed all the fags in college like we planned to, we wouldn't have these problems'.

169

What is clear in these and other accounts as well as in public opinion polls on attitudes to homosexuality in the United States is the mixed, inconsistent response to AIDS among heterosexuals, sometimes hostile, sometimes tolerant and kind. For lesbians in most workplaces, judicious decisions are needed about when, what, and with whom to communicate about gay men, sexuality, and AIDS as well as if and when to come out.

Political: lesbians, oppression, and community

Through the 1970s and early 1980s, the gay rights movement argued with some success for the recognition of our community and acceptance of lesbians and gay men as a visible social, political, and cultural minority (Adam 1987). During that period, lesbians and gay men frequently came together in crisis, often moving apart again to work on separate issues in less extreme times. This fluctuation reflected the differences between lesbians and gay men around sexuality, economic condition, legal status, and reproduction and familial issues. In addition, these relationships were necessarily contradictory since the very dynamics of developing identity, solidarity, and commitment to one's sex made co-operation very difficult to attain and maintain. Finally, many lesbians found the women's movement a more congenial arena than the gay liberation movement for political work (Weitz 1984); most gay men were uninterested in feminism and lesbians' issues, and many lesbians were hostile to much of the gay male movement's political agenda.

But both women and sexual minorities were threatened by the emergence of the New Right whose political agenda linked issues of civil rights and resource allocation to limits on sexual privacy, critiques of alternative domestic arrangements, and arguments for restrictions on sex education. The AIDS epidemic coincided with the politicization of this religious fundamentalism which is, as Altman so aptly puts it, 'recycling medieval language to explain AIDS' (1986: 10) and, in so doing, attributing AIDS to God's punishment for a homosexual life-style.

Lesbians were often subsumed in the right-wing analysis of AIDS. For example, Phyllis Schafly linked abortion, lesbianism, the draft, and AIDS under the banner of her anti-Equal Rights Amendment organizing. In this argument, all homosexuals are high-risk, a view taken as well by two-thirds of the undergraduates at a major California university who believed that lesbians are at higher risk of AIDS than male or female heterosexuals, because 'they're homosexuals' or 'because homosexuality causes AIDS' (Japenga 1986).

Virtually all of the lesbians with whom I spoke in 1986 mentioned increased homophobia in the society as the single main way in which they were affected by AIDS; while many admitted to heightened stress in their lives, most claimed no other immediate effects. They argued that AIDS

170

was used to justify the local rejection of anti-discrimination ordinances, the callous and discriminatory 1986 US Supreme Court ruling on sodomy, the LaRouche 1986 Initiative in California (supporting quarantine of HIV-infected people), and the defeat of civil rights and domestic partners legislation throughout the country. While most lesbians resent being deprived of a political existence through inclusion as a female version of male homosexuality (Rich 1980), lesbians, aware of the right-wing literature on AIDS at mid-decade and these legal and political decisions, began to recognize more common cause with gay men.

In my 1986 interviews and reading, I looked for evidence of changes in lesbians' political activity as a result of AIDS. What I found reflects a complex interplay of historical conditions, cultural differences, and personal circumstances that affect lesbian participation in AIDS-related politics. This is equally true in 1991. AIDS both increases a sense of community and sharpens gender divisions. Many lesbians have responded to the crisis with energy, time, and money. But many lesbians (sometimes the same ones) resent that gay men, who rarely showed any interest in women's health, now expect total commitment from lesbians. The history of support has not been reciprocal, and politically this poses an obstacle to easy unity (Winnow 1989). Even around AIDS, the fear remains strong among many lesbians that gay men can achieve most of what they want without any real effect on the position of women.

Early in the crisis, few feminist communities, the most likely locale for such work, had embraced the AIDS issue, though nationally, in 1986, the National Organization for Women adopted a resolution, presented by lesbian members, calling for more AIDS research and opposing any civil rights violations of persons with AIDS. The pull to engage in political work on AIDS evolved primarily out of ongoing social and political networks. Lesbians who had no contact with gay men, who did not belong to mixed gay groups, or who were not part of local feminist health communities were not likely to be politically involved around AIDS. If a lesbian was going to get involved, it was most likely when she was confronted directly in some way with its full implications for herself, other women, or her specific community.

For example, the Women's AIDS Network was established in 1983 in San Francisco with a membership composed of women who work in AIDS services, in the medical, mental health, and social services, and community activists and policy advocates. Its aim was to share information, support each other's work, and develop strategies for AIDS services and education towards women. In 1986, there was some work by lesbians for lesbians. The Southern California Women for Understanding, an 800-member organization, began a kind of defensive action, outreach to the hetero-sexual community to counter misunderstandings about lesbians and AIDS, despite the potential for fostering division rather than unity between gay men and lesbians. The group encouraged lesbians to come out and to speak against repressive legislation (Japenga 1986). And in smaller cities or more rural areas, though lesbians had the sense that they were less directly affected, some began to get involved in work on local AIDS task forces and in local political campaigns around civil rights that drew on their skills in either community organizing or health delivery.

Five years later, the ways in which AIDS has affected lesbians' political work have multiplied and the community has been transformed in the process. Most dramatically, lesbians are very actively involved in lesbian and gay community centres and organizations, both locally and nationally as well as throughout the AIDS services system. In fact, lesbians are now, as they once were not, in the leadership of many of the groups once dominated by men, using skills developed in the feminist movement. In the gay press, lesbians are implicated in all the losses and gains of gay rights measures and of the anti-violence legislation. Lesbians have been acknowledged as active participants, if not leaders, in the National Gay and Lesbian March for Rights in Washington, DC, in 1987 and as pivotal persons in the national organizing efforts of lesbian and gay people of colour. For many lesbians, this is the first time they are working with gay men.

This responsibility for the community is taken very seriously and not taken for granted by the lesbians. An advertisement for a recent panel discussion entitled 'Lesbian Leadership in the Age of AIDS', attended by the most visible lesbian leaders in Los Angeles, read: 'What are our roles and responsibilities as human beings, women, lesbians, and members of the lesbian/gay community in the shadow of AIDS?' Such questions emerge from a struggle among lesbians, carried on in letters to the editors of gay newspapers and magazines, about the degree of energy given to AIDS rather than to the feminist or lesbian community. The debate has become quite heated, with lots of name-calling: 'man-defenders', on one side, 'traitors to the lesbian/gay community' on the other. Feminist activists like Sonia Johnson have claimed that working against AIDS 'sidetracks' lesbians and 'infantilizes' gay men. Others simply do not believe any woman's energy should go to men, no matter who they are; they see the lesbians working in gay and lesbian organizations as 'delusionary' and 'politically incorrect'. Some of the criticism is more limited and situation-specific: questions about the shape of an organization when all the money donated goes to AIDS, concerns that no one is providing educational programmes for lesbians, anger that some AIDS programmes do not have programmes for women, concern for the negligence of the health of lesbians.

All the rifts between lesbians and gay men have not been resolved. In a recent editorial in *Out/Look* magazine, Escoffier, writing for the editors, asserts:

A new cooperation between lesbians and gay men has seemed to emerge spontaneously from the lesbian response to the AIDS Crisis.

But outside the AIDS arena, forging new links hasn't always been easy or successful. The recent movement at some universities to establish lesbian and gay studies programs has not achieved gender parity. Nor have recent efforts to organize the lesbian and gay presence in the publishing industry.

(Escoffier 1989:1)

Additionally, conflict exists between lesbians and gay men in the AIDS groupings about resources and the politics of AIDS organizations. The caregiving and leadership around AIDS have not resulted in consistent substantive support from gay men for women's issues. In my experience, broken promises are particularly frustrating and horrifying to the women who have been working on AIDS. Venetia Porter, serving at the New York Division of the Office of AIDS Discrimination, chastised the shortsightedness of a gay and lesbian newspaper for its coverage of the Presidential Commission on HIV:

[C]ommunity voices of noted experts continue to be men.... Your recent analysis did mention the problems women PWAs face yet no women involved in the AIDS movement, women's health care movement or Black gay/lesbian rights were apparently available for comment. What the hell is the matter with this picture.... We are AIDS activitists and experts, and we are definitely pissed off. Until the day someone else notices that lots of other people besides white gay men are dying, I think your report and analysis will remain unfinished.

(Porter 1988)

In sum, for the lesbians involved in these organizations and groups, the necessary work of supporting gay men and other persons affected by AIDS goes on, but the mistrust and the struggling continue.

Finally, lesbians have become actively involved in the activist group ACT UP in many communities. While not without a struggle, they have grafted a feminist agenda onto a progressive AIDS platform and pushed through an understanding of the relationship between some women's issues and AIDS. The Women's Caucuses have led the struggle for recognition of women with AIDS against government bureaucracies such as the Centers for Disease Control and the Food and Drug Administration. In 1988, a prominent issue was the opening of drug trials to persons other than gay men; another was the structuring of CDC reporting categories that preclude the counting of lesbians.

The ACT UP actions, plus the expansion of women's AIDS programmes, the strong volunteer work in AIDS groups, and the leadership of gay and lesbian organizations, reflect the range of political activities lesbians have been doing as a result of AIDS.

CONCLUSION

Lesbians will continue to be affected in subtle and large ways by AIDS in the 1990s. Lesbians are now in the forefront of affirming homosexuality, sexual difference, and sexuality. Doing this has meant the willingness of more lesbians to be open about our sexual identity and much greater contact with gay men. It has meant increasing awareness of the link between AIDS and the possibilities of increased repression of sexual expression and the lesbian/gay communities. It has required more lesbians willing to take responsibility for a community it was often easy to let the men lead. To do this has resulted in considerably more inspection of the racism and sexism of the movement and the community overall.

This decade may see lesbians with feminist politics taking a second turn at shaping the agenda and contours of the lesbian/gay movement around political action and with regard to community services. It is already the case that lesbians have got more gay men to attend to issues of reproductive choice, domestic partnerships, and violence against women than was true in the past. A healthy tension will most likely continue between the need to coalesce and act like a community in the face of personal and political threats posed by AIDS and the insistence on a flexible, inclusive community subject to change. Not letting the community mean white gay men will remain an ongoing struggle in which lesbians will certainly play a very active part.

NOTES

1 This chapter is a revision of 'The Impact of AIDS on the Lesbian Community' given at the annual meeting of the Society for the Study of Social Problems, New York, August 1986. Special thanks to Dave Whittier and Nancy Stoller Shaw for helpful materials, to Anna DiStefano, Robin Lloyd, Stephen Murray for comments on an earlier draft, Rhonda J. Levine for many conversations, and Martin P. Levine for encouragement and inspiration.

2 This analysis relies on a number of different sources. For the earlier period, I interviewed nine lesbians in Central California, whose thinking about these particular issues at least partially reflects the demographic and structural features of AIDS in California. I reviewed brochures about AIDS expressly for women with AIDS from Atlanta, Los Angeles, Boston, and San Francisco, and my notes from AIDS conferences and programmes in which I participated. For the more recent period, I examined the media: issues of the 1988 and 1990 *Gay Community News* (Boston); issues of *The Lesbian News* (Los Angeles); all the issues of *Out/Look: National Lesbian and Gay Quarterly* published since 1988. Letters to the editor were particularly revealing. I talked with lesbian friends active in AIDS work in most of the largest cities in the US. Finally, I make use of my own experience and observations as a social scientist, an AIDS researcher, and as the chair of the major community-based organization serving people with AIDS and the gay and lesbian community in the US.

14

SEX AND CARING AMONG MEN
Impacts of AIDS on gay people[1]
Barry D. Adam

Though some anticipated that AIDS would affect gay people with a return to the closet and a retrenchment of civil rights, the actual effects of the last decade have been much more complex, with certain ironies and unexpected turns. Seen within the context of the larger historical evolution of homosexuality, the social response to AIDS has led to the growth of new social institutions and to variations in the identities of the gay worlds of Western Europe, North America, and Australia. AIDS has generated in the 1980s and 1990s an extensive range of new organizations whose purpose is to shift emphases in the sexual and social behaviour of gay men and whose financial resources (however inadequate when compared to the enormity of the problem) exceed those of the non-commercial social and political gay organizations of the past. The result has been a pattern of consolidation and transformation which defies simple assessments of gain or loss to gay people as a whole and which may have significant influence upon wider societal ideas about sex and caring among men.

BEFORE AIDS

At the risk of telescoping several important debates about its origins, suffice it to say that central to the emergence of the post-war gay and lesbian worlds have been the commercial venues which created public places for homosexually interested people. These commercial settings have not only facilitated the development of the modern gay world, but have influenced its content. Urban small businesses of the 1950s often opened the first publicly identifiable social spaces for gay life which otherwise existed more privately at home and in personal friendship networks or found an unsecured place in public streets and parks. Over time, this new public scene consolidated experience and identity, providing opportunities for gay men and lesbians to expand and develop social networks which became the nuclei of voluntary associations and interest groups. The historical outcome of network formation has been the generation of a 'gay community' with much of the institutional completeness characteristic of an ethnic group.

175

The ethnic model, which is deeply rooted in American legal and political traditions, offered a ready-at-hand organizing principle making homosexuality in the United States into a people with a territory (Adam 1987). While less salient in countries where ethnic pluralism plays a smaller role in the national imagination, in the United States homosexuality developed, through the decades of the twentieth century, as a gay and lesbian culture centred in urban enclaves, replete with their own residential areas, social services, press, recreational groups, churches, and political lobbies.

These historical changes contained implications for how people lived their personal relationships as well. The formation of a homosexual 'ethnos' in American society could be interpreted as part of a larger historical trend identified by Michel Foucault (1979), where sex has been made to speak as a final cause or 'essence' of personal identity. Yet at the same time as people were being differentiated by their sexuality into supposedly discrete categories of 'homosexuality' and 'heterosexuality', 'homosexuals' were adopting the terminology of being 'gay' or 'lesbian' to signify a protest that their interpersonal ties were always 'more' than the sexual script would allow. Lesbians and gay men were extricating themselves from conventional heterosexual family models of interpersonal bonding and shedding traditional role norms. This process involved both separation and participation in larger historical trends of the entire society.

From these foundations came the first tentative, low-profile homophile organizations of the 1950s and 1960s and then the intensive and more militant organizing of the 1970s, stimulated by the social challenges posed by the black, students', and women's movements of the day (Adam 1987).

An irony of the post-Stonewall period (given the often anti-business orientation of gay liberationists and lesbian feminists) was the impetus given to the commercial gay world as the gains won in the earlier 1970s created a climate of greater security for small business investment. In many ways, commercial venues remained predominant in the public sphere, directly involving a great many gay men and presenting the best-known face of gay life to those least engaged with it. While no doubt the majority of gay men, and even more lesbians, remained peripheral to the big-city 'core culture', the rise of the commercial world in the 1970s seemed to transform the 'mood' of the Stonewall generation, leading Dennis Altman (1982b: 52) to characterize its contemporary adherent as 'non-apologetic about his sexuality, self-assertive, highly consumerist and not at all revolutionary, though prepared to demonstrate for gay rights'. At its most extreme, these trends generated an image of gay men as superconsumers of both 'fast food' sex and a life-style built out of high disposable incomes. Though never true of a great many gay men, who could hardly afford this image or who found the rules of the sexual marketplace alienating, it did have an impact on both self and public perceptions of the gay world.

176

The role of the commercial bar scene and its impact upon personal relationships provided a ground for debates over identity and objectives for movement groups. Gay liberation movements of the early 1970s, partly through the adoption of New Left discourse, developed critiques of the commercial exploitation and shallowness of life in bars and baths. Many sought to create alternatives to amplify the possible locations and ways that lesbians and gay men could come together and interrelate.

The pervasive and efficient sex delivery systems developed by businessmen through the 1970s existed in tension with the ideal of a world of adhesive comrades and brothers envisioned by the critics of the 'gay ghetto'. For the critics, the unique potential inherent in homosexuality to rehumanize relationships among men became increasingly contained by a culture of orgasm without communication for participants in the commercial scene. Relationships among men, it seems, were participating in the growing sexual reductionism of the current century: male bonding in the commercial gay world tended to implode into its sexual aspect (though, of course, this apparent trend obscured a much more complex reality of variable engagement in 'ghetto' styles and opportunities by gay men as a whole). Another side of the debate, while celebrating an apparently emergent 'primary sexual communism' (Hocquengi.. m 1978: 97) shorn of traditional encumbrances and inhibitions, nevertheless confirmed the perception that the gay world was becoming increasingly sexualized through the 1970s.

The commitment to developing alternatives to the commercial scene led many of the movement groups of the early 1970s to evolve into community organizations which learned 'the ropes' of city politics and offered basic social services to a people traditionally ignored by established agencies (Adam 1987). By engaging in the unglamorous labour of political canvassing, fund raising, and coalition building, gay and lesbian groups made important inroads into electoral politics. They began to hear candidates willing to endorse equal rights ordinances and to address police relations. And, from time to time, an openly gay or lesbian candidate would win a seat on a city council or national parliament. Community organizations as well began to operate counselling, legal, and health services, ranging from peer-operated phone lines in small centres to professional centres in major cities where lesbians and gay men could expect compassionate and non-judgemental treatment along with respect for confidentiality.

These developments provided a framework which proved successful in mobilizing sizeable numbers of lesbians and gay men in the face of such crises as the moralist campaigns launched by the Christian right in the late 1970s or periodic police raids of bathhouses. On this foundation came the first responses to the personal distress and alarm created by AIDS at a time when governmental, public health, and social service agencies would take no notice of the impending epidemic.

For lesbians, the organizational demands posed by AIDS prompted debates concerning the setting of priorities around a disease with high social, but limited medical, consequence for them and which nevertheless threatened to overwhelm more pressing medical problems.[2]

For gay men, this social and political care system opened a potential for growth of a neglected model of male bonding. AIDS presented the possibility of a new shift for the end of this century not only of the social content of the 'gay' category but of general societal categories of male bonding. Though AIDS may possibly lead to the broadening of public understandings of the gay world and gay relationships, it may ultimately influence wider social conceptions of inter-male intimacy whether marked as 'gay' or not.

AIDS MOVEMENTS AND THE STATE

AIDS did not so much suppress the commercial 'sexualism' of the gay ghetto, despite the very real disarray pointed to in the work of Andrew Holleran (1988), as stimulate the growth of a less publicly visible aspect of gay community. As friends and lovers fell to the onslaught of the epidemic and many more showed signs of conscription to its front ranks, gay men organized from the beginning into groups devoted, of necessity, to an ethic of caring for one another. It is too stereotypical to think that AIDS 'taught' gay men 'a lesson', though there has been no lack of homophobes who sought to use AIDS for their own agenda. Commentators on the gay world have been frequently asked about how AIDS must have driven gay rights back ten years, but the reality is quite different. AIDS has been the impetus for a new wave of mobilization and a new set of organizations, some of which have developed unprecedented, routinized connections to state institutions, social welfare systems, and health bureaucracies (see Altman 1988). Indeed, in nations such as Hungary, Poland, and Costa Rica (Schifter 1989) where many of the structural preconditions for the development of a gay and lesbian movement had already emerged (see Adam 1987), the creation of AIDS organizations has, in a reversal of the previous pattern, created an opening for the mobilization of the first gay movement groups.

In North America, government responses have ranged from intransigent to tentative, and care for people with HIV infection has necessitated a reanimation of confrontational strategies. Among conservative governments with a political agenda of reducing social services, such as the Reagan-Bush administration in the United States and similar right-wing governments in the United Kingdom (Carter and Watney 1989), British Columbia, Queensland, and Bavaria, state agencies have resisted popular pressure to fund research into AIDS or to provide support services for people living with the syndrome (Adam 1989). AIDS has been an occasion for these governments to do as little as possible, thereby allowing, through acts of omission, the mass death of such traditionally stigmatized people as homosexuals, drug users, and impoverished blacks and hispanics, who, in any case, had little representation in the political constituency of conservative parties. At times, inaction has threatened to turn into overt hostility through reliance on police methods to control HIV transmission and the introduction of punitive laws designed to invade medical confidentiality or deny any sexuality at all to people with HIV antibodies. In the United States, where health care has never been guaranteed for all and where AIDS has struck hardest at groups traditionally poorly served by the medical system, government neglect has contributed to a rapid death rate and accelerating homelessness among people with AIDS.

Indeed, government neglect has provoked a new wave of militancy in the form of ACT UP groups across the continent. Having barely caught their breath from resisting the onslaught of the New Right in its effort to roll back civil rights gains in the late 1970s and early 1980s, gay men and lesbians have regrouped to counter the effects of bureaucratic inertia and political budgeting priorities which have sought to pit treatment funds against research funding, to encumber drug trials with a rigid and lengthy approval process while people die untreated at an exponential rate, and which have traditionally found the financing of military death machines more palatable than health research. In Canada, for example, the Conservative government announced cuts in health and education funding in late 1990 for the purpose of financing Canadian participation in the war on Iraq.

In more liberal administrations, however, state agencies which had traditionally feared political contamination from appearing to grant tax dollars to gay and lesbian projects have begun to turn to fledgling AIDS organizations for initiative and advice once the enormity of the health problem could no longer be ignored. In cities where community-based AIDS organizations won operating grants from various levels of government, relationships between AIDS activists and state bureauracies have become regularized and ongoing. By the late 1980s, as governments began to respond with budgetary allocations for AIDS services and research, existing charitable organizations and social welfare agencies, which had shown little previous interest in AIDS, began to find the subject attractive. While media and public hysteria about AIDS was peaking in 1983 to 1985, public institutions typically shunned the work (and outrage) of community-based AIDS groups. After the abatement of public hysteria and the initiation of state funding, AIDS groups in some places have found themselves embraced by the care-giving agencies around them and incorporated into a co-operative network of health and social service professionals, reaching in some places to the extent of benefiting from United Fund/United Way fund-raising efforts.

Yet even in jurisdictions where the state has taken a more co-operative approach to grass-roots AIDS organisations, the limitations imposed by state funding have prompted some activists to set up ACT UP groups to address drug testing problems, health delivery costs, and half-hearted public education programmes.

Even where the relationship between AIDS movements and the state is intentionally oppositional, the actions of both may ultimately have unintended consequences and unwittingly partake together in larger historical trends. This relationship is especially problematic in the generation of sexual advice. The articulation of 'safer sex' by community-based AIDS organizations has pressed forward the evolution of sexual speech which has served, as Foucault might have predicted, to create, organize, indeed produce a sexuality for the end of the twentieth century. State policies have shown considerable confusion and contradiction in this process. Safer sex promotion has typically endorsed a distinction between gay people and the 'general public' thereby failing to acknowledge the existence of gay men in its language and imagery while addressing itself to an audience the least at risk. Though the state has not shown reluctance to invade private sexual interaction in so far as half of the states of the United States continue to criminalize homosexual behaviour and the US Supreme Court confirmed that right of interference in 1986, it has entered gingerly upon the terrain of counselling people about how to avoid HIV while allowing that they can still have sex. Local, state, and federal authorities have been quick to try to censor erotic depictions used to convey safer sex messages and have been less ready to assume a responsibility to get the message out (Adam 1989). Often enough, the response to possible public infection thought 'safest' by local authorities has been to try to suppress sex between men altogether. The bathhouses were the first casualties of the zeal of public health authorities to 'do something' in a number of major cities.

Still, AIDS has provoked the state, for example, to introduce taboo topics such as anal intercourse and to acknowledge gay male relationships in the public school system. This step, which had been traditionally held back by conservatives fearful of giving youth 'ideas' about sex, has, of course, been taken with a heavy overlay of warnings. After lectures on celibacy and monogamy, condoms are presented as a poor 'third option' in the school system's moral hierarchy. In Ontario, for example, the first reference to a gay male couple ever prescribed for universal education takes the form of an apocryphal moral tale where one man abandons the other upon discovering the other's HIV infection. The man with HIV infection then flees to the embrace of his family of origin. If gay relationships are to appear for school students, curricular authorities will still rush to invalidate them.

But people never quite learn their school lessons as intended and young people continue to call gay phone counselling services to get a second opinion and look further for information about gay society. The predominant message may have forged AIDS into a sign for 'no sex' but it can never avoid simultaneously speaking of 'sex'. AIDS organizations and education workers find themselves not unwillingly being used as a source for finding out about sex by the young, the isolated, and the uninformed.

CULTURAL SHIFTS IN MALE INTIMACY

Gay men responded quickly to generate a 'care delivery' system which shows a different aspect of male bonding outside the homosexual modes encouraged by the commercial scene. This care, organized by community-based AIDS groups, includes a wide range of professional services, from counselling and legal assistance to food banks and therapeutic support, but it is also of the most mundane sort: running errands, house sitting, cat feeding, being there, nursing, and all the realm of domestic labour. Yet it is this most unglamorous and 'un-masculine' work which meets very real needs. Perhaps it is not surprising that, since its origins in the gay community, the care system has increasingly drawn in many women, who have already been well versed in the work of nurturance.

Care is nothing new in gay relationships, though its public recognition is. Even 'casual', short, and plural sexual relationships coded by the social script of the masculinist 'sex machine' had not infrequent moments of tenderness and care. The bedrock conventional oppositions between sex and love, casual and committed, promiscuity and fidelity never did fully capture people's experiences or do justice to the emotional epiphanies encountered along the way. These experiences were never fully contained by the ready-made discourses purveyed for making sense of them. Though 'everyone knew' that the baths were 'for' quick unencumbered sex – Hocquenghem's 'plugging in of organs' – less acknowledged were the possibilities opened by interactions with a range of people never met in the comparatively encapsulated everyday life of home and work. New buddies, friends, and lovers came out of the baths as they did in other sites of gay contact.

Friendship networks have always existed, but AIDS organizing drew upon and extended them, making visible the many gay men engaged in caring relationships who had been often overlooked both by young gay men new to the gay world and by the public images of what the gay world was about. AIDS has drawn upon and developed a cultural trend which has made visible the gay men engaged in caring relationships who had often been overlooked. AIDS has struck widely with devastating impact, bringing forth people once peripheral to community organizations and mobilizing many who had found politics irrelevant or insufferable. This development may, as well, have helped diversify visible modes of gay identity by making new opportunities for involvement for those uncomfortable with styles innovated by the Stonewall generation.

Just as caring had always remained inextricably involved in a sexualized culture, so too erotic values manifested their continuities in the 1980s as gay organizations were quick to invent 'safer sex' which enhanced some of the core virtues of sexual liberation: the affirmation and cultivation of eroticism beyond insertive or ejaculatory acts and the allowance for sexual multiplicity through the adoption of the simple technology of the condom to avoid HIV.

Today there is a possibility, still much denied and virtually tabooed in mass media presentation, that caring relationships, domestic partnerships, and love between men may be allowed to become visible as an ironic consequence of AIDS. Portraits of gay relationships have appeared in the 'gay literature' of the last decade, and in recent theatre and cinema such as the British historical romances, *Maurice* and *Another Country*, and more contemporary films such as *Making Love*, *My Beautiful Launderette*, *Torch Song Trilogy*, and *Law of Desire*. Still, this kind of innovation has yet to diffuse into mass communications systems beyond the tabloid exposé and its television talk show equivalent.

The care delivery systems, developed largely within the gay community and growing to encompass more than the gay community, suggest the possibility of a rehabilitation of invisible modes of inter-male bonding already well developed among gay men. This possibility is, however, undeniably limited by three very powerful alternative codes for making sense of male bonding. First, it has not taken long for profit-making enterprises to colonize the safe sex domain with 'fantasy phone lines' and video erotica designed to offer sex without bodies. With the putative waning of the sexual marketplace provided by the bars and baths, this solution to risky sex even more radically separates people from one another and, at the same time, markets (to both homosexuals and heterosexuals) their own orgasms for a fee.

Second, as AIDS awareness organizations become increasingly institutionalized, they are remade in the image of the professional and social service agencies the state conceives them to be. State funding agencies typically presume the model of the rational, bureaucratic delivery of services to a series of usually mutually isolated, passive clients and AIDS organizations feel a pull to compromise with, if not adopt, this model for financial security. ACT UP militants have attacked this approach for wanting to 'ease' people with AIDS into their graves without challenging the response of the established health research and delivery system in meeting the crisis.

The other hegemonic code easily mobilized in an era of AIDS is a symbolic 'final solution' which has governed mass depictions of homosexuals in this century (Adam 1978). Here male bonding is put forward only under the sign of death, allowing glimpses of the interior of a male love relationship only when one partner is fated to die. This paradigm is evident in television drama such as *An Early Frost* and in such US PBS presentations as *André's Mother* which portrayed the pathos of a widowed gay man and his dead lover's unaccepting mother.

182

Gay and AIDS activists have not been unaware of the power of symbolic representations of the syndrome and have often sought to address the connotative implications of media language which, for example, has referred to the 'AIDS virus' or 'AIDS victims'. Perhaps most notable has been the Names Project which has worked to commemorate those killed by AIDS and to rescue them from silence or invisibility (Ruskin 1988). It is no accident that the Names Project has periodically gathered together commemorative panels from across the continent to form a gigantic quilt which has been made to 'occupy' the heart of Washington thereby symbolically injecting those 'marginal' to the site/sight of the political system into the 'core' of state power.

Some European observers have found something very American about finding a silver lining in a disaster as profound as AIDS. Any depiction of ironically 'positive' consequences of the syndrome can never be allowed to overshadow the absurdity and suffering caused by a slow-acting but lethal virus discovered too late. People with AIDS, like residents who one day find they have been unwittingly living on top of a toxic dump, find that there is comparatively little to be done about a decade of damage unknowingly wreaked upon their bodies. Their pain is neither justification nor compensation for some surprising social effects of AIDS.

Yet, finally, AIDS does have the potential to rehabilitate some forms of male intimacy at the same time as it is destroying so many adherents of it. Out of AIDS militancy has come a rejuvenated gay militancy in the form of 'Queer Nation' in the United States and Canada and 'OutRage' in the United Kingdom, groups unafraid of direct confrontation and astute in getting past media gatekeepers to communicate their message. It is also forcing recognition of the need to support the relationships so often on the frontlines of the AIDS struggle, through the extension of the rights and benefits routinely accorded heterosexual relationships to same-sex partners.

NOTES

1 An earlier version of this chapter was presented to the Society for the Study of Social Problems, Berkeley/Oakland, California.
2 For the impact of AIDS upon women, see Beth Schneider, 'Lesbian politics and AIDS work' (this volume); Cindy Patton (1985); Diane Richardson (1987).

Part VI

SHIFTING SEXUALITIES
The lesbian case

Just as there is nothing fixed about 'the homosexual', so there is nothing fixed about 'the sexual'. All that is solid melts into air. The sexuality of modern gay men in the 1970s was often 'fast', but during the 1980s – with AIDS education playing a major role – it often shifted gears into a more affectionate, even romantic, mode. Certainly, 'non-penetrative' sex became a part of safer sex.

But for women the story shifts in a slightly different direction. Deprived of a sexual language by a predominantly male culture, lesbianism was largely constructed as either romantic or a male 'turn on'. The two articles presented here take us into the reformulation of lesbian desire. Diane Richardson argues for the inscription of a new lesbian language of sexuality, for new ways of talking about sexuality, enhancing and facilitating a lesbian sex. Anna Marie Smith argues for the need to place this language in a public and political context, to challenge and overthrow the hegemony of traditional politics and their discourses.

15

CONSTRUCTING LESBIAN SEXUALITIES

Diane Richardson

> I once perused a large and extensively illustrated book on sexual activity by and for homosexual men. It was astounding to me for one thing in particular, namely, that its pages constituted a huge lexicon of *words*: words for acts and activities, their sub-acts, preludes and denouements, their stylistic variation, their sequences.... Gay male sex, I realised then, is *articulate*. It is articulate to a degree that, in my world, lesbian 'sex' does not remotely approach.... I have, in effect, no linguistic community, no language, and therefore in one important sense, no knowledge.
>
> (Frye 1990: 310–11)

Why as lesbians do we rarely talk about sex?[1] One explanation is that this is an understandable reaction, given that it is the sexual aspects of being a lesbian that have tended to dominate how others see us. Another limit on how easy we find it to talk about sex, even among ourselves, is the knowledge that sex between women is often interpreted as a 'turn on' for men, as the pornography industry can easily testify. One other possible constraint is the history of anti-lesbianism within the feminist movement[2] which, especially in the early days, resulted in some lesbians experiencing a pressure to downplay their sexuality to avoid giving 'feminism a bad name' or scaring off heterosexual women (Schulman 1983). We can proclaim our identity and our politics, but to be publicly passionate is a different matter!

Some of the early feminist debates on sexuality also served to reduce the sexual for lesbians, particularly in the United States. For instance, although writers like Ti-Grace Atkinson (1974) and Catharine MacKinnon (1982) held a position similar to that of many lesbian feminists in rejecting sex with men, particularly vaginal intercourse, as oppressive to women, they did not necessarily advocate lesbianism. Atkinson believed, at least in her early writings, that any sexual expression perpetuated women's domination by men and emphasized celibacy. MacKinnon has similarly questioned the possibility of women being able to have non-oppressive sex in a male-dominated society, even when this is sex with another woman (1982, 1987).

One of the consequences of not discussing our sex lives is that we often have to struggle alone, or with lovers, in dealing with our sexual difficulties and worries. Breaking down the silence around lesbian sex is also important so that we can realistically assess what health risks, if any, we are taking sexually.

On a theoretical level, there are questions which need to be addressed about the relationship between sexual conduct and sexual identity: between being a lesbian and desiring and having sex with women. How vital is sex to lesbian identity and what kinds of sex at that? What do you have to do, sexually speaking, to be a 'real' lesbian? Do you have to *do* anything? Sexual activity *is* often seen as proof of our lesbianism; when we are first coming out being sexually involved may make us feel like we are 'one of the girls'. The relationship between sex and identity is also an important area of political debate within lesbian feminism, in particular discussions about political lesbianism. These are some of the issues which will be addressed in this chapter, but first I want to consider the question, What is lesbian sex?[3]

One way of answering this question is to ask it another way: What is a sexual partner? Or, how do you know you've had sex with a woman? Is it sex only if you have an orgasm? What if she comes and you don't? Is she a sexual partner or were you just giving a helping hand? What if you are both fully dressed and during a close embrace pressed up against her you 'accidentally' come without her realizing? What if what you did wasn't genital, say you stroked each other and kissed and caressed, would you later say you'd had sex with that woman? And would she say the same?

The answer, of course, is that it depends; it would depend on how you and she interpreted what happened. Sex cannot be defined simply in terms of what we do; it is the meaning we give to situations and behaviours which defines them as sexual – or not.[4] From this perspective, the important question is where do these meanings come from? What are the ideas and beliefs from which we construct our experience of lesbian sex?

Two interrelated sources can be identified: views of sexuality and views of female sexuality and lesbianism.

WHAT IS 'SEX'?

Prevalent ideologies concerning sexuality, such as those coming from religious, legal, medical, psychiatric, and psychological discourses, influence common-sense ideas about what is both 'normal' and 'appropriate' sexual behaviour. For example, it is commonly felt that it is 'normal' to be heterosexual but 'abnormal' to be lesbian or gay; or that it is 'normal' for men to be more interested in sex than are women. Similarly, some sexual practices are regarded as inherently better (normal, natural, more satisfying) than others, with vaginal intercourse privileged as the 'Real Thing'.

Such beliefs, influenced by views about sex as ultimately a reproductive function, continue to be perpetuated through discourses on sex despite a number of important contradictions. The existence of enormous sexual variation as documented by Kinsey (1948, 1953) and others, the fact that in the majority of cases the aim in heterosexual sex is not to reproduce, the evidence that it is a majority of women who say they do not have orgasms during vaginal penetration, all these challenge dominant definitions of sex as intercourse. For instance, *The Hite Report* found that two-thirds of the women who were interviewed did not have orgasm during vaginal intercourse although they came easily in other ways (Hite 1976). Other studies echo this finding that most women 'have a problem' having orgasms through vaginal intercourse (Hunt 1975). Sociologically speaking this tells us something about the power relations at play in defining good sex. If over 50 per cent of men didn't regularly achieve orgasm during intercourse would penetration be still seen as so important? Similarly would we still be talking about women 'having a problem'? (For whom exactly is not coming during intercourse a problem?) Is it a problem if you accept the many ways women have of reaching orgasm as part of what we call 'sex' and consider these to be as important and exciting as the activities which lead to male orgasms (Hite 1987)?

While sexual surveys may have raised some difficult questions for sexology, it was the 'discovery' of the clitoral rather than the vaginal orgasm by Masters and Johnson that appeared really to set the cat among the pigeons (Masters and Johnson 1966). Feminist writers on the whole greeted Masters and Johnson's work enthusiastically, interpreting their findings on female sexual response as challenging the idea that women must engage in vaginal intercourse (Jeffreys 1990). Some, like the American feminist Anne Koedt (1974), acknowledged the implications for lesbianism, in suggesting that sexual pleasure was just as obtainable from either men or women. With the advantage of hindsight however we might want to ask whether such enthusiasm was misguided (Coveney *et al.* 1984). Even if it is now acknowledged that the female orgasm always starts in the clitoris, vaginal intercourse is still seen as normal, necessary, and desirable within heterosexual relationships. After all, the necessity of penetration for male orgasm was not being questioned! It is clear from their writings that this is what Masters and Johnson themselves believed. Although the vagina may have been ascribed a subsidiary role in the experience of female orgasm, women were still told that the clitoris could be stimulated through vaginal thrusting.

The social construction of 'sex' as vaginal intercourse affects how other forms of sexual activity are evaluated as sexually satisfying or arousing; in some cases whether an activity is seen as a sexual act at all. For example, unless a woman has been penetrated by a man's penis she is still technically a virgin even if she has had lots of sexual experience. If you've not had intercourse, you've not really had sex. The perception of sex as vaginal intercourse is also enshrined in the law as well as in religious teachings. For example, the legal definition of rape in most countries is unlawful sexual intercourse which means the penis must penetrate the vagina. Other forms of sexual violence towards women such as forced oral sex or anal intercourse, or the insertion of other objects into the vagina, constitute the 'less serious' crime of sexual assault.

This view of sex as penis in vagina, as something done to a woman by a man, implies that lesbians don't really have sex they have 'foreplay'. (The fact that we don't talk about afterplay also says something about the dominance of a goal-orientated view of sex rather than sex as a process.) Lesbian sex has often been conceptualized as immature, not as satisfying as intercourse, second-best sex. Many psychoanalytic theorists, for example, would argue that mutual masturbation produces a less satisfying form of orgasm than vaginal penetration. Even if lesbian sex does involve penetration it is still not seen as an authentic and autonomous form of female sexuality; rather it is understood as an imitation of what all women are supposed to want, a man's penis inside them. This is exemplified by referring to objects which a woman may use to penetrate herself or another woman as 'phallic objects' or 'penis-substitutes'. From a different point of view we could define a penis as a finger/vibrator/dildo substitute.

Language is important in shaping sexual behaviour, not only in what it categorizes and labels as erotic but also through what it does not articulate. Do we, for instance, have a language which adequately expresses female sexual experience in general and lesbian sex in particular?

Sex is defined largely in terms of male experience. The vocabulary of sex is much more concerned with describing what happens to a man's body during sexual arousal than a woman's. Similarly, there are very few words for women's genitals, whereas there are a great many other terms for the penis. In many ways language is either silent about women's bodies and sexuality or, where it does exist, ridicules and insults them (Richardson 1990).

The language of sex also reflects and reinforces the idea that sex equals intercourse. There are a wide range of words for intercourse, but very few for other ways of making love such as body rubbing or cunnilingus. For instance, take the term 'mutual masturbation'. One of the problems with this phrase, in addition to the fact that it suggests that what you are doing is an imitation of masturbation with yourself, is its vagueness. It might include you and your partner taking it in turns to touch each other, touching your partner at the same time as she is touching you, touching her while touching yourself, touching yourself while she touches you or watching each other masturbate. One phrase to describe many different ways of having sex with another woman.

This is not however to suggest that just because some activities or parts of the body are not defined as specifically sexual they will not be part of a woman's sex life. On the contrary you might want to argue that opportunities for sex between women are restricted by labelling certain behaviours as sexual. Or, to put it another way, that defining some things and not others as sexual can serve to restrict opportunities for sexual pleasure, whereas the absence of labels can increase erotic potential.

For instance, Lillian Faderman, commenting on sexual relationships between women during the eighteenth century, claims that 'a narrower interpretation of what constitutes eroticism permitted a broader expression of erotic behaviour since it was not considered inconsistent with virtue' (Faderman 1981: 33).

In other words the phallocentric view of sex as penis in vagina meant sex between women was less easy to categorize as sexual and that therefore there was less pressure to restrict erotic interests in the same sex. It rendered sex between women as more invisible, but also more harmless.

Similarly, Foucault (1979) argued that language can shape behaviour through its absence and imprecise nature, as well as by what is defined as sexual. According to Foucault, sexuality has been regulated through talking about sex; control of female sexuality has not been through denial or silence but through discourses which categorize and define certain individuals, activities, situations, and parts of the body as potentially erotic.

WHAT'S A WOMAN SUPPOSED TO DO?

Fundamental to the social meaning of lesbian sexual practice are the views about female sexuality and lesbianism which emanate from the 'scientific' discourse about sex and sexuality. Two main stereotypes of lesbians emerge, apparently in contradiction with each other.

Sexualized

Despite conceptualizing male and female sexuality as different (but complementary), a comparison has been drawn between women's and men's same-sex relationships. The application of theories of homosexuality, which were primarily concerned with men, to lesbians contributed to sex and sexual desire being seen as central to definitions of lesbianism, despite prevailing views of female sexuality as sexually responsive rather than active.

This construction of lesbians (and, even more so, gay men) as essentially *sexual*, a social group defined by its sexuality, is made particularly apparent in the kind of concerns expressed about the relationships lesbians have with children, for instance, in the case of the employment of lesbians who work with children or, alternatively, of children living with lesbian mothers. In such cases the traditional perception of women as maternal is overshadowed by the notion of lesbians, either directly or indirectly, posing some sort of sexual threat to children.

As I have already suggested, the view of lesbians as highly sexed would seem to contradict dominant discourses of sex, in particular the view of female sexuality as 'passive', responsive, primarily concerned with meeting a man's needs and 'sex' as synonymous with intercourse. This might help to explain why some people apparently find it hard to imagine what lesbians can possibly do in bed (or wherever): hence that all too familiar question 'But what do you do?' which, translated, means without a penis what can you do! The allocation of sexual agency to lesbians is, however, congruent with the view of the lesbian as unlike real women in her interests and desires and, to varying extents, more like a man, where men's interest in sex largely goes unquestioned.

The portrayal of the lesbian as a pseudo-man has also been influential in the way sex between women, when it is acknowledged, has often been interpreted as a mimicry of vaginal intercourse. It is often assumed that sex between women usually involves dildos or 'penile substitutes' – the stereotype of the 'dildo-wielding dyke'. In addition, lesbians have been described as suffering from feelings of 'virile inferiority' and wanting a penis of their own. Some studies in the past have gone so far as to suggest that lesbians are not only psychologically 'masculine' but are biologically like men. For instance, earlier this century Lang put forward the hypothesis that female homosexuals were genetically male, albeit having 'lost all morphological sex characteristics except their chromosome formula' (Lang 1940). Others have suggested that lesbians are anatomically masculinized; for example, the notion of the lesbian who has an unusually long clitoris which can be inserted into the vagina of another woman. Again, this owes a great deal to the definition of lesbians as pseudo-men as well as to the idea that sex equals penetration of the vagina by a penis or 'penis-substitute', in this case the clitoris defined as a 'vestigial penis'.

The notion that lesbian sex necessarily involves 'role playing', that one woman plays the part of the 'man' and the other the part of the 'woman', is also widely believed by some people, including some lesbians (Kitzinger 1985). Thus, while the idea of a 'feminine' lesbian is potentially more challenging than that of the 'masculine' lesbian, it is contained by the assumption that such women are attracted to and form relationships with butch women and are not in any case 'real lesbians'. (The concept of two 'femmes' or two 'butches' having sex is much more challenging to these assumptions.)

At an individual level, such stereotyping can create anxieties in some lesbians about imitating heterosexuality. This may discourage them from engaging in certain kinds of sex: for example, lying on top of a woman and gaining sexual pleasure by rubbing against her body, or putting fingers or an object into the vagina of another woman, or having that done to themselves. As one woman said, 'If I want that I might as well go with a man'.

192

Others would argue that we need to construct alternative images which articulate the experience of certain kinds of sex between women as other than an imitation of heterosexuality. For instance, some women may very much enjoy the feeling of having their vaginas touched during sex precisely because they have rejected the way in which the potential pleasures of penetration have previously been defined, almost exclusively, in heterosexual terms and have reappropriated the vagina as part of lesbian love-making. However, there is still the question of language. Do we murmur to our partner that, as *The Joy of Lesbian Sex* (1977) puts it, we want to be finger-fucked? Or is this use of language one that harks back to the idea that what we are doing is heterosexual mimicry?

Desexualized

Other portrayals of lesbians have also been influential in the construction of lesbian sexuality, in particular the view, heavily influenced by psychoanalytic accounts, of the lesbian as 'mother-fixated', seeking, through her relationships with other women, to be mothered. Such a view within theoretical accounts of homosexuality in the past encouraged a tendency to see lesbian relationships as primarily emotional rather than sexual (e.g. Socarides 1979; Storr 1964). In part this can be understood in terms of the way women's sexuality has traditionally been seen as 'passive', needing to be brought to sexual fulfilment and orgasm by a man. But it can also be understood in terms of dominant definitions of sex. For if to the predominantly male 'experts' what lesbians do isn't real sex, then it's perhaps not altogether surprising that studies of lesbian relationships have often focused on emotional attachment rather than sexual behaviour.[5]

Some studies of lesbian history have also been seen as desexualizing lesbianism. For instance, Lillian Faderman's (1981) definition of lesbianism does not necessarily include genital contact. In rejecting what she sees as a male definition of lesbianism (and 'sex') as defined by genital contact, she describes women who had passionate friendships with other women as lesbians, where sexual contact may or may not have been part of their relationship. Critics of such a definition, such as Ruehl (1983), accuse Faderman of 'watering down lesbianism by playing down the sexual content' (Jeffreys 1984).

Others have appealed to social conditioning in describing lesbians as having a relatively low interest in sex. Lesbians, by virtue of their socialization as women, are likely to act 'just like other women' (Gagnon and Simon 1973). In keeping with the expectations of women generally, lesbians are described as sexually 'passive', for whom sex is primarily a way of expressing love. Some lesbian writers echo this view in claiming that lesbians, as women, are sexually inhibited and repressed. For example, Margaret Nichols states that: 'Two women together, each primed to respond sexually only to a request from another, may rarely even experience desire, much less engage in sexual activity' (Nichols 1987: 103).[6]

While Nichols is right to suggest that as lesbians we have to engage with the expectations of a heterosexual upbringing, her suggestion that we 'obediently comply' is highly questionable. As Annabel Faraday (1981) has pointed out, such a functionalist approach fails to take sufficient account of how we, as lesbians, question those definitions and negotiate new meanings. It is this process I want to consider next.

'WOMAN-IDENTIFIED WOMAN' TO LUSTFUL LESBIAN

Medicine and psychiatry may have played an important role in informing common-sense notions of both 'sex' and lesbianism. However, we are not simply passive recipients of that scientific legacy. Over the last twenty years lesbians have challenged what others have said about them, most obviously that lesbianism is a disease or mental illness. The question we next need to consider therefore is: how have lesbians defined lesbian sex for themselves? We might also ask how far the meanings derived from lesbian culture have challenged the heterosexual values incorporated in traditional medical and psychiatric definitions of sex.

For some lesbians, and indeed for some feminists, lesbianism is regarded as a sexual preference/practice; as being about who we desire and have sex with. However during the 1970s there was decreasing emphasis placed on lesbianism as a sexual and erotic experience, arguably partly as a reaction to the way psychiatry and medicine had previously defined lesbianism largely in terms of sexual orientation and sexual acts. Instead, there was greater emphasis on understanding lesbianism and indeed heterosexuality, in political terms. Lesbian feminists asserted that lesbianism is not simply a sexual practice but a way of life and political struggle – a challenge to the institution of heterosexuality. As Ti-Grace Atkinson put it, 'Feminism was the theory, lesbianism the practice.'

This analysis of lesbianism as more than a sexual preference, as a political choice, implied a critique of heterosexuality as an institution. It was a form of resistance to what Adrienne Rich (1984) later termed 'compulsory heterosexuality', the process whereby heterosexuality is instituted and maintained under conditions of male supremacy. In the United States the classic 'Woman-identified woman' paper by Radicalesbians, written in 1970, was one of the first attempts at defining lesbianism in political terms. It asserted that 'woman-identified lesbianism' was the political strategy necessary for women's liberation and the end to male supremacy. The implication for heterosexual feminists was that they should give up relationships with men and put their commitment, love, and emotional support into relationships with women. This included an acknowledgement of a sexual element in lesbianism:

> Until women see in each other the possibility of a primal commitment which includes sexual love, they will be denying themselves the love and value they readily accord men, thus affirming their second-class status.
>
> (Radicalesbians 1973: 243)

In Britain this idea that feminists should withdraw from sexual relationships with men and become political lesbians as a strategy to challenge women's oppression was put forward in a now famous paper, first published in 1979, by the Leeds Revolutionary Feminist Group, The paper, 'Political lesbianism: the case against heterosexuality' (1981) defined a political lesbian as a 'woman-identified woman who does not fuck men'. It was primarily concerned with not having sex with men rather than with lesbian sexual practice; the main issue was *identifying* as a political lesbian.

At the same time as many lesbian feminists, in the early 1970s, were defining lesbianism as political rather than sexual practice, lesbian and gay liberation movements were also engaged in redefining 'homosexuality'. In their emphasis on the importance of the development of a sense of lesbian/gay pride and the public affirmation of the validity of lesbianism/gay relationships through coming out, they too were primarily concerned with identity rather than sexual behaviour, with being rather than doing.

Some lesbians responded angrily to the arguments for political lesbianism on the grounds that it desexualized lesbianism (see Campbell 1980; Califia 1981; Onlywomen Press 1981).[7] Their concern was that lesbianism was becoming associated with a critique/rejection of heterosexuality and feelings of sisterhood for other women, rather than a positive and sexual attraction to women. Lesbianism stripped of its sexual element was better described as political celibacy.

Another common response to lesbian feminist critiques of heterosexuality is that they encouraged a view of lesbian sex as the only politically acceptable sexual practice; lesbianism was the model for describing good sex for women. This evoked a particular representation of lesbian sex. It was sex that was reciprocal, non-oppressive, equal, less goal-orientated, not penetrative or genitally focused. The term used by some writers (e.g. Nichols 1987) is 'politically correct lesbian sex', an expression that is generally used negatively to imply a curtailment of lesbian desires and sexual practices and provides a context for understanding critiques of 'vanilla sex'.

In recent years a concern with resexualizing lesbianism has become more evident. Never mind politicizing sex, let's put sex back into politics has been the rallying cry. In 1984 Susie Bright, editor of *On Our Backs*, the first American porn magazine for lesbians, declared that it was the Year of the Lustful Lesbian. Similarly, co-editor Debi Sundahl believes that a political and social revolution has begun as a result of lesbians producing erotica and pornography for other lesbians, not to mention live strip shows, sex toys, and so on (Sundahl 1985). The association of sexual liberation and the political liberation of women has been subject to serious criticism, particularly in recent analyses of the so-called sexual revolution of the 1960s (Ehrenreich, Hess and Jacobs 1987; Jeffreys 1990). Nevertheless, to disagree with the sentiments expressed by Sundahl and her contemporaries is to risk being characterized by some as a political dinosaur who is anti-sex or, even worse, anti-lesbian.

The libertarian stance urging us to celebrate sex can be seen not only as a reaction to the desexualization of lesbianism which many felt had occurred during the 1970s, but also partly as a response to the emphasis on the dangers of sexuality for women within feminist discourses, in particular debates around sexual violence and pornography. This is nothing new of course. Earlier this century feminists were divided over the emphasis placed on sex as danger/sex as pleasure, which inevitably led to differences in feminist campaigning around sexual and reproductive issues (Gordon and DuBois 1984).

Another factor in the emergence of discussions of lesbian sexual practice has been AIDS and the debates about safer sex it has generated (Richardson 1989). AIDS has created a context in which we are allowed to talk about sex. Indeed, telling each other what we do sexually has suddenly become not only permissible but a social requirement, a necessary and important part of lesbian health concerns. AIDS has, then, provided a 'legitimate' focus for lesbians to talk about sex generally, with safer sex as the starting point.

It is in this context of insisting that lesbianism *is* about sex that we have witnessed the emergence of lesbian sex-manuals such as *The Joy of Lesbian Sex* (1977), *Sapphistry* (Califia 1980, 1988), and *Lesbian Sex* (Loulan 1984), but more especially pornography and erotic fiction for lesbians by lesbians. This includes the production of magazines such as, in the United States, *On Our Backs* and *Bad Attitude*, in Britain, *Quim* and (with gay men) *Square Peg* and, in Australia, *Wicked Women*. There have also been a number of books of 'lesbian sexual fiction' recently published including *Serious Pleasure* (1989) and *More Serious Pleasure* (1990), *Lady Winston* (1987), *A Restricted Country* (1988), *Macho Sluts* (188), and, less controversially, *Lesbian Lovestories* (1989), not to mention the marketing of lesbian sex videos and films (see Smyth 1990) for a discussion of the latter. Lesbianism as sex has been politicized, and often in the name of feminism, but we need to ask, what as? What kind of lesbian sex is being represented? – especially as writers such as Bright (1988) and Califia (1988) are claiming the new sexual agenda to be revolutionary, a challenge to the heterosexual norms of the past.

A close examination of recent lesbian porn and erotica reveals that the dominant forms of sex represented are penetrative and/or sado-masochistic

(S/M) activities. Dildos or, as they are often referred to, 'cocks' appear with great regularity, as do chains, manacles, studs, leather straps, and whips. Stories about 'playing with power', of bondage and dominance, of S/M sex are what we have come to expect. Representations of lesbian desire as desire for a full vagina or, to a lesser extent, a full anus are the norm and include 'fist-fucking' as well as penetration with objects. Byron (1985) describes this as 'the renaissance of vaginal sex amongst lesbians', which she sees as borrowed from gay male porn and its emphasis on penetrative sex. There are some strange ironies here, not least that the celebration of the pleasures of penetration in lesbian porn has occurred at a time when, because of AIDS, penetrative sex has been challenged.

These developments have provoked discussion, debate, and, in some cases, outrage among many lesbians. The question I want to address here however is how far does this so-called resexualization of lesbianism reproduce, rather than challenge, traditional sexual values by placing a primacy on penetration and associating lesbian desire with eroticized power difference?

One answer to the question is that acts which may be regarded as oppressive/harmful/unsatisfying to women in heterosexual relationships will in a different context (i.e. between two women) have different meaning. At one level this is obviously true. The experience, both psychologically and physically, of a man's penis in your vagina is not the same as the experience of a woman's fingers inside you, not to mention bananas, vibrators, or dildos. It's also the case that a lot of lesbians enjoy touching themselves, being touched, and touching their lovers in their vaginas. Some lesbians also like to be touched in their anuses and rectums. Having said that, the concern is that in representing lesbian sex as primarily penetrative there becomes a pressure that lesbians should want to be touched or put objects in their vaginas – an expectation that passion means penetration.

Similarly, the focus in lesbian porn on sado-masochism challenges a sexual desire and practice which eroticizes mutuality and equality. Despite the appeals to sexual liberation, some lesbian porn writers clearly feel that sexual diversification has its limits: all things are not equal; it is not simply a case of whatever turns you on. It is implied that lesbians who don't like or desire a full vagina, who don't want to play with sex toys, who don't turn on to power are somehow conservative, prudish, immature, or boring sexually. They are 'bambis' or vanilla dykes, where vanilla is certainly not flavour of the month! Indeed, one might ask will it mean in future that you've not gone all the way with a woman, not really had sex, are not a 'real lesbian', unless you've, say, fist-fucked or tried bondage and dominance? Consider, for instance, Pat Califia's response to lesbians who don't like, for whatever reasons, what lesbian porn has to offer: 'If you don't like to read about pussy maybe you don't like pussy and you should be lickin' something else' (Califia 1988: x). This is doubly ironic when one considers another trend in lesbian porn, the portrayal of lesbians becoming aroused through heterosexual and gay male sex.

A central question has to be whether lesbian porn is liberating or constricting for lesbians. Quite clearly some believe it is the former and it is certainly the case that recent lesbian porn has challenged the soft-focus, romantic imagery of lesbianism which, from a feminist perspective, can be regarded as oppressive. It's also true that lesbian porn differs in certain respects from heterosexual porn, for instance while the penis is often the only focus of genital satisfaction in heterosexual porn the emphasis in lesbian porn is on the woman's desire and pleasure; it's she who comes, not the dildo, vibrator, or finger. Despite this, I want to argue that this so-called radical, liberatory discourse is in fact more of the same, colluding with rather than challenging dominant discourses of sex which are fundamentally oppressive to women. Thus we could see the recent emergence of lesbian porn and erotica, with its privileging of certain kinds of activities, as a pressure to accept as the norm for lesbian sex sexual values which have previously been associated with heterosexuality.[8] The experience of a full vagina is represented in ways that replicate the language, values, and imagery of heterosexual sex; even down to the 'female come shot' where 'fucking' ends in 'ejaculation' (Smyth 1990). In some cases the 'turn on' is that it actually is a penis in a vagina or anus.

Whatever we think about these developments what we are witnessing, in the absence of a diversity of cultural representations of lesbian sex, is a redefinition of what lesbian sex is. As I stated at the beginning of the chapter, the answer to the question 'What is lesbian sex?' will depend on the meanings available to us from social discourses about sex. As those meanings change then so may our desires and our practices. Different parts of the body may become more or less sexualized. I have already indicated how in recent lesbian porn the anus and the vagina have been more privileged than either the clitoris or breasts. Similarly, different activities may become eroticized as lesbian sex; 'fist-fucking' and bondage are part of lesbian consciousness in the 1990s in a way they never were in the 1950s and 1960s. We've come a long way since then, when lesbian sex was represented by one long smouldering kiss and then.... Or have we?

NOTES

1 The use of the word 'sex' to describe lesbian desire and sexual pleasure is not unproblematic (see Frye 1990; Hoagland 1988) and in choosing to use it I am conscious of the difficulties it presents.

2 This is not to imply that all feminists were anti-lesbian.

3 While it makes more sense in terms of transmission of HIV and sexually transmitted diseases to talk about sex between women, in terms of the social and political aspects of lesbianism it makes more sense to talk about lesbian

sex. As Campbell (1980) and others have pointed out, lesbianism is a specific sexual practice between women with its own history, it is not the same as sex between women.

4   What is highlighted here is the need to distinguish same-sex sexual attraction and relationships from the historically specific sexual categorizations and identities which provide the meanings and conditions in which individuals experience the former. It is these socially constructed meanings that are the basis for the experience of sexual desire: who does what to whom with what and in what order.

5   In both of these stereotypes of the lesbian – as sexualized and desexualized – an autonomous female sexuality is denied: in the former case by seeing a woman's interest in sex as 'pseudo-male' behaviour; in the latter by representing lesbianism as the mother–child dynamic.

6   Nichols goes on to argue that if sexual desire requires a 'barrier', some kind of tension, difference, power discrepancy, this is a problem for lesbian sexuality. She suggests that we need to find ways of introducing 'barriers' into our relationships to enhance sexuality and sexual desire. For instance, 'through the use of sex toys and props, through costume, through S/M (which maximizes differences between partners), by developing sexual rituals with our partners, and by introducing tricking into our relationships' (Nichols 1987: 108).

7   Heterosexual feminists also criticized the notion of political lesbianism, arguing for the 'right to choose' relationships with men (Jeffreys 1990).

8   Another concern expressed over the recent emergence of lesbian porn and erotica is what effect this will have on how lesbians are regarded and socially controlled.

16

RESISTING THE ERASURE OF LESBIAN SEXUALITY

A challenge for queer activism

Anna Marie Smith

[Lesbians are] not a problem. They do not molest little girls. They
do not indulge in disgusting and unnatural acts like buggery. They
are not wildly promiscuous and do not spread venereal disease.
  (Lord Halsbury, House of Lords, 18 December 1986, col. 310)

The emergence in recent years of several new activist projects has revitalized
the lesbian and gay communities. These projects include the Stop Clause
28 campaign, ACT UP and OutRage in Britain, and ACT UP and Queer
Nation in the United States and Canada. One of the many positive features
of this new wave of activism is the participation of lesbians. However, the
anti-lesbian and gay strategies which are being targeted by this wave of
activism are complex; they can work with and even amplify the differences
in our communities. In the context of this differentiation, we cannot assume
that the connecting work which is performed by the 'and' in the phrase
'lesbian and gay' is a straightforward matter.

The problem of representing a distinct lesbian presence was brought home
to me in a particularly effective manner in a lesbian and gay demonstration which was held in London on 16 February 1991. The march was
organized to protest three developments: Operation Spanner, the trial of
fifteen gay men and the conviction of eight of them for consensual s/m sex;
Paragraph 16, a section of the Department of Health's guidance notes on
fostering which implies that lesbians and gay men are unsuitable foster
parents; and Clause 25 of the Criminal Justice Bill which would allow the
courts to impose prison sentences for sexual offences relating to various
consensual sex practices between men. Over 7,000 lesbians and gay men
joined the march. I participated in the kiss-in at Piccadilly Circus which
was organized by OutRage as part of the demonstration. The gay men there
were eager to include lesbians in the kiss-in, and encouraged me and another
woman to climb to the top of the Eros statue, and to kiss and to pose for
the onlookers and cameras.

There was, however, something missing. The men on the statue reached
for a sign which included the word 'lesbian' to place behind us. Since

the s/m trial and Clause 25 were concerned solely with gay male sex acts, the only placards for the demonstration which referred exclusively to lesbians dealt with Paragraph 16: they declared that lesbians had the right to be mothers. There was, literally, no sign for the representation of a lesbian presence as a sexuality.

In this chapter, I want to discuss the representation of homosexuality in what can be called 'official discourse' in Britain: the legislation, court decisions, and statements by the political parties. I shall attempt to show that this discourse is organized in terms of a complex and yet consistent logic, a particular differentiation of homosexualities, and that one dimension of this logic is precisely the erasure of lesbian sexuality.[1] I shall then refer to the challenges that this erasure poses for resistance discourse[2], and the ways in which it is being countered in both Britain and the United States.

THE PROHIBITION OF THE PROMOTION OF HOMOSEXUALITY AND THATCHERISM

Section 28 is a fundamental part of official discourse on homosexuality. Although there have been no actual prosecutions of any local authorities under this legislation, it has had a tremendous informal effect on their policies: several existing and proposed programmes have been cancelled, grants to local groups have been cut, and visual arts exhibitions and theatrical productions have been censored and refused funding.

In Britain, official discourse on homosexuality has been previously organized around different agendas, such as changes to the definition of sexual offences and the 'age of consent' in the criminal code and the censorship of homosexual discourse through obscenity and blasphemy laws. Local government legislation became a site for this discourse in the mid- and late-1980s. Some local authorities became centres of resistance against Thatcherism through the construction of new political coalitions, giving feminists, black activists, and lesbians and gays an increased presence in local affairs.

The Thatcherite response to these initiatives took the form of both legislative and election campaign strategies. Unlike in the United States and Canada, the distribution of powers between central and local governments in the UK is not protected by a strong federal system. The abolition of the Greater London Council (GLC) was only one of the central government's many attacks on local government autonomy in the 1980s. Anti-lesbian and gay statements played a key role in the legitimation of this campaign. Lord Halsbury introduced a private member's Bill in the House of Lords in December 1986 which would have prohibited local authorities from giving 'financial or other assistance to any person for the purpose of publishing or promoting homosexuality' and from teaching the acceptability of homosexuality as a 'pretended family relationship'. Although this Bill was not passed, it brought attention to the position of the Conservative Party at a time of growing public concern around homosexuality and AIDS. In the 1987 election campaign, the Conservative Party used a billboard poster which depicted four books with the titles, *Young, Gay and Proud*, *Police Out of School*, *Black Lesbian in White America*, and *Playbook for Children About Sex*, and declared that these books represented 'Labour's idea of a good education for your children'. Section 28 therefore constituted one element in the Conservative Party's strategy to make Labour-controlled local governments appear naturally equivalent to permissiveness, moral degeneracy, the 'loony Left', the anti-democratic imposition of a foreign political agenda, and the promotion of anti-family feminism, anti-British black activism, and immoral homosexuality. Section 28 was not, then, the result of an irrational prejudice, or 'homophobia', but was actually central to one of the important strategies of Thatcherism.

The responsible homosexual versus dangerous gayness

Section 28 legitimates the abandonment of lesbian and gay issues by local authorities, the increased policing of gay male sex acts, the increased regulation of lesbian mothering, and even queer bashing. However, it also has a 'productive' role in that it promotes a differentiation of the lesbian and gay community. The parliamentary statements on this legislation, for example, are not solely limited to expressions of absolute intolerance for lesbians and gays; they also construct an opposition between what I shall call the responsible homosexual and dangerous gayness.

Most of the supporters of the Section claimed that it would not affect the delivery of services to lesbians and gays, that it would not be used to censor lesbian and gay materials, and that it would not locate lesbians and gays as second-class citizens[3] (Howard, HC 15/12/87, 1017, 9/3/88, 420; Wiltshire, HC 15/12/87, 1006, 9/3/88, 404–5; Earl of Caithness, HL 16/2/88, 596). The Earl of Caithness argued that the Section was 'not intended as part of some campaign against homosexuals' and that it is instead a 'modest and necessary measure to restrain the activities of some local authorities which have gone too far' (HL 1/2/88, 893). Lord Monson said that he supported the decriminalization of homosexuality legislation and that he recognized the 'genuine' rights of homosexuals, but added that these rights pertained to the 'bedrooms of consenting adults' and not to 'propagat[ion]' (HL 1/2/88, 928). The Lord Bishop of Manchester contrasted the 'bad gay' and 'bad straight' with responsible people, declaring that the conduct of the former was 'undisciplined, self-centred and out of control', while the latter group were 'not sleeping around, not molesting children and not breaking up other people's marriages and friendships' (HL 11/1/88, 965). Some of the supporters even argued that lesbians and gays should have supported the Section. They recognized and deplored the violence and discrimination against lesbians and gays, and claimed that the Section would counteract this backlash by curbing extremist activists and politicians (Howard HC 9/3/88, 421; Earl of Caithness, HL 16/2/88, 643).

Attempts were made by the supporters of Section 28 to speak on behalf of the responsible homosexual. The Earl of Halsbury stated that his favourite letter from his constituents about the Section was written by a male homosexual. He read the following passage to the House.

> I want to say how fed up I am with my fellow homosexuals. They have brought it upon themselves, their unpopularity. They are too promiscuous, too aggressive and exhibitionist. I cannot stand the sight of them. I wish they would keep themselves to themselves. . . . I cannot help what I am but I can help what I do.
>
> (HL 1/2/88, 874–5)

This distinction between the responsible homosexual subject and the activity of promoting homosexuality is also made in the context of the debates on Lord Halsbury's original Bill. Lord Campbell (HL 18/12/86, 312), the Earl of Longford (HL 18/12/86, 314–16), and Dame Jill Knight (HC 8/5/87, 998) express both their acceptance of law-abiding homosexuals and their alarm concerning the promotion of homosexuality. Homosexualities are similarly differentiated in the context of the decriminalization of certain male homosexual practices in 1967 and Clause 25 of the current Criminal Justice Bill. The Sexual Offences Act 1967 decriminalized only private sexual acts between adults over the age of 21. It was located in a series of law reforms on sexuality, obscenity, abortion, theatre censorship, and divorce. Based on the approach of the 1957 Wolfenden Home Office inquiry, these reforms had a dual purpose: to decriminalize private activities which do not harm other people and to intensify the regulation of public activities which were held to disrupt the social order. The 1967 Act introduced strengthened restrictions concerning offences involving 'minors', male soliciting ('cruising') and sexual practices in 'public' places. It defines the conception of 'public place' quite broadly as any place in which a third person is likely to be present. The reforms of the 1960s have had, therefore, a dual legacy, the decriminalization of private sexual acts and the dramatic escalation in the policing of 'public decency' offences (Weeks 1981b: 239–44, 274–5).

Clause 25 neither reverses the 1967 Act's decriminalization of private sexual acts between adults nor creates new sexual offences. It increases instead the severity of existing offences relating to 'public' sexual acts, including gross indecency (any sexual contact other than buggery between two men in a 'public' place), procuring an act of indecency, buggery (anal penetrative sex with a penis, 'however slight', in a 'public' place or involving a minor), and soliciting ('cruising' between two men or between a formerly male post-operative transsexual and a man; no sex act need actually occur, and no exchange of monies need be involved). In 1989, well over 2,000 men were convicted for soliciting, procuring, and indecency offences (Tatchell 1991).

Again, the emphasis is not on homsoexuality *per se*, but on those homosexual acts which are supposed to threaten the social order. Clause 25 defines the term 'sexual offence' which is used in Clause 2. Clause 2 states that the length of a custodial sentence is to be commensurate with the seriousness of the offence, except in the case of a violent or sexual offence, where the court may impose a longer sentence, 'if this is necessary to protect the public from serious harm from the offender'. In one of the debates on the Clause, the Home Office Secretary of State, John Patten, said, 'I fully understand the strong feelings evinced by Stonewall [a lesbian and gay legislative lobby group] and other organizations'. He nevertheless defended the Clause in that it only reflected the 'existing structure of sexual offences as they affect homosexual activity and heterosexual activity' (SCA 18/12/90, 314–15). Patten also referred indirectly to the criticism of the Bill by lesbians and gays in a letter to Robin Squire MP. He stated that he is 'of course, concerned that the Bill should be perceived as having an effect that was never intended', that he planned to amend the Bill so that the increased sentences would be used only 'in cases where there is a need to protect potential victims from serious harm from the offender concerned'. He added,

> I hope that, as a result, those who have been anxious about the possible effects of the Bill as it stands will be reassured that the only people who have anything to fear from the Bill are that small number of dangerous offenders from whose activities their intended victims need to be protected.

> (Patten 1991)

The Government has defined 'serious harm' in a subsequent amendment of the Bill as 'death or serious personal injury, whether physical or psychological', but has refused to remove the offences relating to consensual sex acts between men from Clause 25.

The reforms of the 1960s, Section 28, and Clause 25 all differentiate between a non-threatening homosexuality which has nothing to fear in terms of state intervention and a homosexuality which interrupts the social order and, as such, is subjected to social regulation. The former, the responsible homosexual, limits his or her expression of his or her homosexuality to a hidden and self-contained space which is defined in terms of fixed frontiers; he or she is, in other words, closeted in every sense. That he or she does not actually exist since no one can ever obtain a perfectly closeted status is beside the point; this is the ideal homosexual which the supporters of these laws accept as legitimate. The latter, the dangerous gayness, is a floating and excessive element, and includes the activities of flaunting,

204

exhibition, proselytising and promoting homosexuality, of invading the space of the normal and of seducing the otherwise normal. This gayness is dangerous not simply because it is different from heterosexuality. The politicians who support Section 28 and Clause 25 must include some type of homosexuality as legitimate and acceptable so as to locate themselves in the centre as the truly tolerant and moderate. Their discourse does not in fact work to eliminate homosexual difference; it does not promote a purely homogeneous heterosexual vision of British society. It attacks a difference of a particular type, a subversive difference which exceeds proper boundaries and which threatens to contaminate other space. It attacks dangerous gayness as a type of this difference, just as racist discourse singles out radical black activism and black criminality while claiming to accept the assimilated black entrepreneur as a legitimate citizen (Gilroy 1987: 57–8). The construction of the responsible homosexual subject/dangerous gayness difference and the acceptance of the former as legitimate therefore support the primary strategy, namely the attack on dangerous gayness.

Queer activism and the 'responsible homosexual'/ 'dangerous gayness' difference

The implications of this production of difference are complex, but two consequences stand out. First, this differentiation works with, rather than against, discourses in our own lesbian and gay communities. The figure of the self-disciplining responsible homosexual is not a figment of right-wing imagination; many letters to the editors of our community publications in Britain express a rejection of confrontational activist tactics in the same manner as the letter quoted by the Earl of Halsbury. In the US, an entire study has been written from the responsible homosexual point of view. *After the Ball* (Kirk and Madsen 1989) insists that the set-backs for lesbians and gays are due to the activities of our own enemies within: the excesses of effeminate gay men in drag, butch dykes, sado-masochists, pederasts, and gay men who promote and practise 'public sex'. These demonizations are organized around an extremely mysogynist, anti-'left', anti-working class, and pro-American nationalism agenda. The authors criticize Gran Fury's kiss-in advertisement, which features two fully uniformed sailors standing together and kissing, with the slogan, 'Read My Lips'; this representation of 'homosexual foreplay' is supposed to 'deliberately shock', 'antagonize', 'reinforce revulsions and inflame homohatred' (Kirk and Madsen 1989: 230). *After the Ball* actually includes a 'Self-Policing Social Code': the gay male reader is encouraged to agree not to have sex in public places, not to make sexual approaches to 'strangers who might not be gay', to come out only where it is 'possible and sensible' and only in a 'graceful manner', and to not 'talk gay sex and gay raunch in public' (p. 360). The lesbian reader is simply not addressed at all. The authors argue that we cannot win the recognition of our rights unless we exclude the marginal elements from our communities and promote a 'sanitized' image of ourselves. Similar arguments have been made in both the US and Britain against the usage of the term 'queer'; many have argued that by calling ourselves 'queer', we are only reproducing anti-lesbian and gay insults, rather than empowering ourselves. It is also often claimed that the extremism of activists will jeopardize our attempts to secure legislative reform. These arguments, however, confuse strategies with identities. Groups such as ACT UP, OutRage, and Queer Nation are not attempting to invalidate formal strategies, such as lobbying for legislative reform through their informal activism. There is often a great deal of overlap between these two types of strategies, in terms both of membership and of joint planning. Queer activism is not exclusive, then, in terms of strategy, but positions itself as one strategy among many.

However, queer activism *is* exclusive in terms of identity. The new activist groups do not, and should not, represent the responsible homosexual position. The confrontational queer identity is a critique and a displacement of the homosexuality which wants to occupy a legitimate space within an unchanged social order. Again, the impossibility of total acceptance, in that it depends on perfect closetedness, is irrelevant: many lesbians and gays dream of the type of acceptance which is promised (and infinitely postponed) by right-wing politicians.

This is not to say that being 'out' is inherently 'progressive', or that being closeted in itself constitutes a treasonous 'selling out'; we are all constantly crossing and re-crossing the closet/queer nation frontier, and some of us cannot visit our 'homeland' as often as we would like to. This is also not to say that we should ignore the extent to which we all internalize anti-lesbian and gay hatred, and sometimes get caught up in damaging games of blaming ourselves and our 'representatives' for our oppression. The responsible homosexual is more than just closeted and does not just seek acceptance. He or she attempts to achieve acceptance in the terms promised by official discourse and by furthering the demonization and exclusion of dangerous gayness. The responsible homosexual therefore functions as the 'contra' force within the community; his or her presence allows right-wing politicians to speak in our name as the representatives of the true homosexuals. He or she allows them to say: 'We are not really against homosexuals *per se*, we are simply against the criminals, the perverts, the extremists, and so on, who happen to be homosexual'. Queer activism rightly stands against this incitement of self-surveillance, self-discipline, and assimilation. It attempts to speak to all lesbians and gays, but it does not, and should not, speak for all of us. Queer activism therefore subverts the differentiating logic of official discourse by inviting all lesbians and gays to identify with the dangerous gayness position.

206

CONTESTING THE REPRESENTATION OF LESBIAN-NESS

The queer identity should not, however, be exclusive in terms of gender. The problem here is that where lesbian-ness appears in official discourse on homosexuality, it is usually located within the responsible homosexual category. Lord Halsbury, for example, argues that in contrast to the excesses of some male homosexual practices, lesbians are 'not a problem'.

> They do not molest little girls. They do not indulge in disgusting and unnatural acts like buggery. They are not wildly promiscuous and do not spread venereal disease.
>
> (HL 18/12/86, 310)

He claims that gay men attempt to conceal their dangerous practices by placing the term 'lesbian' before the term 'gay' in the names of community groups, such that the relatively harmless lesbian leads on to the vicious gay' (HL 18/12/86, 310). This distinction is consistent with legislation on sexual offences. Lesbian practices were not referred to in the 1533 Act of Henry VIII on sodomy, the 1861 and 1885 laws on sodomy and gross indecency, the 1898 Vagrancy Act, the 1967 Sexual Offences Act, or Clause 25 of the 1991 Criminal Justice Bill. When attempts were made in 1921 to include lesbian practices in the category of gross indecency, Lord Desart argued that this inclusion would be inappropriate in that it would only bring lesbian sex 'to the notice of women who [had] never heard of it, never thought of it, never dreamed of it' (Weeks 1977: 106–7).

This representation of lesbian-ness constitutes the erasure of the very possibility of lesbian sexuality. It is structured in terms of a sexist conception of women's subjectivity: that women are, by nature, passive, moderate, non-assertive, and so on. Roger Scruton, a British right-wing philosopher, claims that because the 'moderating effect' of female presence is lacking in male homosexuality, the latter takes the form of an 'imperative force' which promiscuously seeks immediate gratification in a socially destructive manner. Female homosexuality, as the mere addition of two moderating forces, is supposed to be centred on lasting partnership and not on sexual excitement. Scruton concludes that a lesbian cannot possess the same sexual drive as a gay man because if she did 'act like a man' in this way, she would no longer attract other women (Scruton 1986: 307–8). A similar erasure of lesbian sexuality has taken place in the United States in the context of AIDS research. When asked why the Center for Disease Control has not carried out any research on woman-to-woman transmission of the virus, an official replied, 'Lesbians don't have much sex'. Official discourse on AIDS has 'over-sexualized' the activities of gay men and 'desexualized' lesbian sexuality (Maggenti 1990:243).

The dangerous lesbian figures:
black lesbian groups and lesbian mothers

In Britain, lesbian-ness is nevertheless identified in official discourse as a dangerous element in two ways. First, the figure of the lesbian or, more precisely, the black lesbian is used to invalidate the Labour Party's support for a whole range of feminist, black, disabled, and lesbian and gay projects. This tactic was used, for example, in leaflets distributed by the Conservative Party local constituency association in Surbiton before the May 1991 elections. They claimed that the London Boroughs Grant Scheme should be eliminated so that 'public money' would no longer be spent on '"loony left" projects such as black lesbian groups'. References to the illegitimacy of funding for black lesbian projects were also made by both left- and right-wing politicians throughout the debates on the abolition of the GLC (Tobin 1990).

Second, lesbian-ness in the position of the parent is represented as a dangerous element in official discourse. In the Section 28 debates, both gay male parents and lesbian parents were named as pseudo-parents who led pretend families. The second part of the Section, the prohibition of the teaching of the 'acceptability of homosexuality as a pretended family relationship' was designed to block the displacement of the traditional patriarchal family by these dangerous simulacra. In terms of fostering, Paragraph 16 of the recently issued guidelines to the 1989 Children Act instructed social services departments that

> It would be wrong arbitrarily to exclude any groups of people from consideration. But the chosen way of life of some adults may mean that they would not be able to provide a suitable environment for the care and nurture of a child. No one has the 'right' to be a foster parent. 'Equal rights' and 'gay rights' policies have no place in fostering services.

Paragraph 16 was withdrawn after intesive lobbying by lesbian and gay groups.

Lesbian parenting was targeted again in the Human Fertilisation and Embryology Act 1990. Following a right-wing campaign against the provision of artificial insemination services by government-licensed clinics to single heterosexual women and lesbians, the Conservative Party successfully added to this Bill Section 13(5) which states:

> A woman shall not be provided with [artificial insemination] treatment services unless account has been taken of the welfare of any child who may be born as a result of the treatment (including the need of that child for a father).

Clinics must follow government guidelines to retain their licences. The April 1991 draft of these guideline states that the doctors and counsellors of each clinic have to decide whether or not prospective mothers who do not have male partners would be able to meet the child's needs fully. In 1991, claims were made in both the popular and the 'quality' press that women who had not had sex with men should not be allowed to bear children. It is important to note that, in this so-called 'virgin birth' scandal, the rights of both lesbians and single heterosexual women were attacked on an equal basis. This representation of lesbian reproduction as dangerous is another form of the attack on women's right to control our own bodies and women's right to act as the head of a 'family' and to have our 'families' recognized as legally equivalent to the traditional patriarchal family. The defence of lesbian mothering should therefore be regarded as a logical extension of demands for access to abortion, and for the reform of marriage, divorce, and family laws.

However, the construction of a link between the defence of lesbian parenting and the defence of gay male sexuality from the oversexualization, demonization, and criminalization in official discourse may be more difficult. The London-based Lesbian Action for Parenting and Reproductive Rights rejected the strategy of connecting the campaign against Clause 25 and the Operation Spanner trial[4] with the campaign against Paragraph 16. In a letter to a community paper, they stated that the former are 'issues about gay male practice (which many of us would not condone anyway) and are of a very different order from the attacks on lesbians bringing up children' (Lesbian Action 1991). Instead of joining a broad-based coalition to resist all of these attacks on lesbian and gay rights, they declared that they would form a lesbian-only group against Paragraph 16. This statement is a typical example of the responsible homosexual argument from the lesbian separatist point of view: 'public' sex acts between men are excluded as illegitimate such that the lesbian separatist campaign gains the appearance of acceptability. Keith Alcorn, an OutRage activist and community paper columnist, attempted to counter their argument from what I have called the queer activist position. He stated that 'lesbian parenting is an issue of sexual practice just as much as Clause 25 and Operation Spanner' (Alcorn 1991), thereby attempting to identify lesbian parenting as equivalent to the sexual forms of dangerous gayness.

Although I support Alcorn's attempt to include both lesbians and gay men in resistance campaigns, the attack on lesbian parenting *is* of a different order than criminalization of 'public' gay male sexuality. The lesbian mother is a dangerous figure in official discourse because she displaces the male head of the family. Lesbian mothering, however, does not constitute a sexuality. The defence of lesbian parenting, albeit an important struggle for lesbian and gay movements, does nothing to address the problem of the erasure of lesbian sexuality in official discourse.

Queer activism and the representation of lesbian sexuality as a visible presence

How should queer activism deal with this problem? First, it should be recognized that the exclusion of lesbian sexuality from official discourse on homosexuality constitutes a thoroughly anti-lesbian strategy. The effects of inclusion in official discourse are highly ambiguous. As Lord Desart noted in 1921, criminalization can promote deviant identifications. This is not to say that we want our sex practices equally criminalized and demonized like gay men's sex practices, but that the reduction in lesbian-ness to harmlessness is a subtle and extremely effective attack on our hard-won presence. Lesbians should continue to work with gay men to change the official agenda on sexuality as it affects them, but they should also continue to work with us in our efforts to get on the agenda. Resistances around criminalization and demonization offer important opportunities for gaining visibility and empowerment. It is crucial that lesbian participation in these resistances not be reduced to the status of a supplementary support for gay men, but that the erasure of lesbian sexuality be addressed. For example, in response to the Center for Disease Control's failure to recognize that lesbians *do* have sex, the Women's Caucus of ACT UP San Francisco demanded that research on woman-to-woman transmission of the HIV virus and the seroprevalence of HIV in lesbians and bisexual women be conducted. The Women's Caucus led an act of civil disobedience outside the VIth International Conference on AIDS in June 1990; one of their signs read 'CDC – Dykes Fuck Too!' Referring to the 16 February demonstration in London against Operation Spanner, Clause 25, and Paragraph 16, Cherry Smyth argued that lesbians should work to ensure that:

> we are not simply tagged on to equality campaigns in connection with procreation and the family . . . we have never had the safety to take the same public space for sexual adventures as gay men, yet we solicit, procure, indecently assault and fuck each other in SM scenarios and want the right to be acknowledged for our sex and sexuality, just as gay men rightly demand.
>
> (Smyth 1991)

She suggested that lesbians should carry banners declaring (In)visible Lesbians', 'Lesbians Solicit and Fuck Too', and 'Grossly Indecent Lesbian'. These strategies may appear paradoxical in that through our struggle for visibility as sexual women, we are risking the extension of criminalization and demonization to lesbian-ness in addition to male gayness. However, the cost of invisibility is so great that this risk is more than worth taking. In any event, the representation of lesbian-ness as desexualized innocence is nothing but a retreat to the responsible homosexual position and a betrayal of the risk-takers.

Second, it should be recognized that some of the most serious threats to the establishment of a visible lesbian presence as a sexual presence come not from the 'state' but from 'our own' community.[5] In Britain, many 'women's' bookstores and even 'lesbian and gay' bookstores still refuse to stock our lesbian erotica, calendars, videos, and 'zines.[6] Women in 'safe spaces for "women"', nightclubs and community centres, are verbally and physically attacked for wearing fetish gear. The 'lesbian' archives in London reject material relating to the lesbian s/m subculture, the support phoneline on policing for 'lesbians' refuses to deal with calls from s/m dykes, transsexual lesbians were banned from a 'lesbian' sexuality conference, and the organizing committee for the 1989 'lesbian' pride march attempted (unsuccessfully) to ban leather from the march. In London, several lesbians who were associated with the fetish club, Chain Reaction,[7] have been fired from their jobs and denied housing by 'women's' centres and housing associations. The Sheba collective, which published Joan Nestle's book, *A Restricted Country* (1988), and the collections of lesbian erotica, *Serious Pleasure* (1989) and *More Serious Pleasure* (1990), have been called 'pornographers' and have been charged with promoting violence against women. These authoritarian campaigns are waged within the lesbian communities in the name of 'anti-sexism' and 'anti-racism'. They not only threaten the survival of a wide range of low-budget sexual projects by lesbians, but also dilute the meaning of the terms 'sexism' and 'racism' such that they are equated with just about anything which challenges the lesbian separatist view of the world. This abuse of these terms hardly contributes to the actual struggles against sexism and racism which are of crucial importance, both to the 'Left' in general and to queer activism. The policing of lesbian sexuality from within the lesbian 'community' may be somewhat less intense in some parts of the US and Canada, but these 'sex wars' are far from over. Queer activism should address the policing of lesbian and gay sexuality in all its forms, both from the outside and from within 'our' nation.

Finally, it should be recognized that the erasure of lesbian sexuality in official discourse is not a random strategy but the product of sexism. Queer activists may have a sophisticated grasp of the operation of power relations around sexuality, but this certainly does not guarantee that we are adequately aware of the complexities of sexism. Commenting on the dynamics within Queer Nation New York, Maria Maggenti notes that the group had not dispelled her 'lesbian existential dread' that:

> the map of the new queer nation would have a male face and that mine and those of my many colored sisters would simply be background material. We would be the demographic cosmetics, as it were, to assuage and complement the deeply imbedded prejudices and unselfconscious omissions of so many urgent and angry young men.
> (Maggenti 1991)

When the problem of sexism disrupted Queer Nation San Francisco in February 1991, the women's caucus, LABIA (Lebians and Bisexuals in Action), chose not to walk out of the group but to organize a forum on sexism. Their forum included a session on lesbian sex practices; true to the Queer Nation style, this presentation was designed to put lesbian sexuality 'in the face' of the gay men in the group. This kind of consciousness-raising around sexism and the desexualization of lesbian-ness is central to the success of queer activism.

NOTES

I would like to thank Ken Plummer for his suggestions and encouragement, Queer Nation LABIA (Lesbians and Bisexuals in Action) for allowing me to attend one of their meetings, and OutRage for being fabulous.

1 For the purposes of this essay, I am analysing only the right-wing variant of official discourse; this is not to suggest that other variants do not exist.
2 My research is theoretically framed within the 'discourse analysis' approach and draws on the 'post-Marxist' texts of Ernesto Laclau and Chantal Mouffe (1985) and Stuart Hall (1988). In terms of the conception of 'resistance', and the relation between 'official discourse' and 'resistance discourse', I am borrowing from Foucault's analysis of power relations.
3 References to the *Official Report*, the Hansard record of parliamentary debates, will be noted as either HC (House of Commons), HL (House of Lords) or SCA (Standing Commitee 'A'), date, and column number.
4 Fifteen men were tried for consenting sado-masochistic sex in private at the Old Bailey in December 1990. The eight sadists in the group were found guilty of keeping a disorderly house, causing or aiding and abetting actual bodily harm, assault, and other offences relating to the possession of drugs and the publication of photographs, and were given prison sentences ranging from twelve months to four and a half years. Six others were given suspended sentences, conditional discharge, or were fined for causing and aiding and abetting bodily harm, assault, aiding and abetting a disorderly house, and charges relating to the possession and sending through the post of photographs. One man was given two years' probation for aiding and abetting others to cause injury to himself. In passing sentence, Judge Rant accepted that all of the participants had consented, but declared that the courts had to 'draw the line between what is acceptable in civilized society and what is not'. The appeal, in February 1992, was rejected, and the House of Lords will now be making a decisive ruling on whether sado-masochistic sex should be illegal or not. It should be noted that there is a precedent to this case which involved two women. Brenda Morris was found guilty and sentenced to six months' imprisonment for assault, running a disorderly house and possession of pornographic material in Birmingham in July 1982. Morris worked as an s/m prostitute for both men and women, and had videotaped an s/m session between herself and a non-paying female partner. The charges were brought against the wishes of her partner, who testified in court that she had given her consent to Morris. (I would like to thank the English Collective of Prostitutes for providing me with the research materials relating to this case; the ECP is the only group which protested against this court ruling.) There is no statutory right to privacy in the UK, and the European

Convention of Human Rights, which includes this right, has not yet been incorporated into British law.

5 Lesbians' sexual spaces are also subjected to actual police harassment. Joan Nestle (1988) documents the police raids on lesbian bars in New York in the 1950s. A lesbian sex party in Los Angeles was raided by plain clothes and uniformed police in February 1991. *Screambox*, a lesbian 'zine in Los Angeles, had organized this 'Jill-Off' party as a benefit, borrowing the concept from Queer Nation and ACT UP jack-off party benefits. The organizers were charged with liquor law offences. It became evident that the plain clothes police had been at the party for several hours before the raid.

6 *On Our Backs*, a magazine devoted to 'Entertainment for the Adventurous Lesbian' and Fatale Videos are available from Blush Entertainment, 526 Castro, SF, CA 94114. Tigress Videos are available from Tiger Rose Distributing, PO Box 609, Cotati, CA 94928. The queer 'zines which include lesbian sexual content are: *On Our Rag*, Box 21, 3542 18th St., SF, CA 94110; *Taste of Latex: Entertainment for the Sexually Disenfranchised*, PO Box 460122, SF, CA 94146–0122; *Scream Box*, 7985 Santa Monica Blvd., Suite 109–51, Los Angeles, CA 90046; *JD's*, PO Box 1110, Adelaide St. Stn., Toronto, Canada M5C 2K5; and *Quim*, BM Box 2182, London WC1N 3XX, UK.

7 Chain Reaction was a fetish club in London for women which was organized by a collective. It ran bi-weekly at the Market Tavern, a gay men's bar, from 1987 to 1990. Several new clubs and projects, including the 'zine *Quim*, and a London version of the Clit Club, have emerged since its closure.

Part VII

MAKING THE FUTURE
Radicalism, rights, and citizenship in the UK

All the articles in this book have signposted changes in lesbian and gay experiences: they all move us beyond traditional notions of homosexuality. As such they are not only sociological descriptions but essays on political possibilities, fragments of futures.

These last essays turn more explicitly to aspects of campaigning. The history of the 'homophile movement' might stretch back a hundred years, but the gay and lesbian movement really comes into its own from the early 1970s onwards as one of the new social movements shaping new communities, identities, and politics. From its inception, and like other movements, it has been riddled with internal schisms and conflicts as to appropriate strategies of change. The three articles presented here are concerned with the UK situation, but they have wider implications for the continuing issue of how to move ahead.

17

ABSEIL MAKES THE HEART GROW FONDER

Lesbian and gay campaigning tactics and Section 28

Vicki Carter

> In the struggle of any oppressed group, the process is as important as the goals, for it is through that process that a new sense of community and acceptance is forged.
>
> (Altman 1982a: 125)

Lesbian and gay political action around legislative attacks is the subject of this chapter. The struggle around Clause 28,[1] which took place in Britain in 1988, is the central example, but I also look to North America for an international perspective. Highlighting different tactics used in these campaigns, I suggest that those encompassing an element of revolt and outrage convey a message which questions more than the law, using symbolic politics. This symbolic element is vital for it is this that can resonate through the culture for longer than it takes to win or lose a specific campaign.

Lesbians have played a crucial role in these campaigns, many coming to gay politics via feminism and passing through a period of radical feminism. Never having relied heavily on traditional campaigning methods of lobbying and exerting institutional pressure, radical feminism developed symbolic strategies on the streets with spray paint and at actions like the women's peace camps. The necessity for combined lesbian and gay involvement that legislative attacks engender encourages different groups to work together. Lesbian experience with its symbolic angle can then pervade the whole campaign.

A STORY FROM NORTH AMERICA

In California, roughly ten years before Clause 28 raised its ugly head in Britain, an anti-gay initiative was launched by Senator Briggs. It became known as Proposition 6,[2] and was similar in wording and intention to Clause 28. It states:

1. A District School Board would be *required* to dismiss or refuse to hire, any person who has engaged in homosexual *activity* or *conduct*

if the Board believes such activity renders the person unfit for service.

The proposition defines homosexual *activity* as the public or indiscreet commission of an act of sodomy or perversion.

Homosexual *conduct* is defined as the 'advocating, soliciting, imposing, encouraging or promoting private or public homosexual activity directed at or likely to come to the attention of school children and/or other employees.'

David Goodstein owner of the national gay magazine *The Advocate* proposed that 'All gay people could help best by maintaining low profiles ... and keeping out of sight of non-gay voters' (Freeman and Ward 1978: 16). Although this approach was used at one end of the political spectrum, the majority of groups that organized to fight the proposition paid little heed to his advice. 'A quarter of a million people poured into the streets here [in San Francisco] on June 25th chanting their message over and over again. "No on the Briggs Initiative, gay rights now." It was the largest gay rights march in the city's history' reported the *Militant* newspaper (Back page 42#26 77/78). The protest was mirrored in Los Angeles. The arguments were carried across California, reaching out to small isolated communities as well as the bleak ghettos of the cities. The campaign was co-ordinated from women's centres and gay centres. Unions were mobilized, as were the Afro-American community and the Chicano community. A broad-based 'No on Prop 6' Campaign was built which had strength and breadth.

The proposition voted on by the Californians was not passed despite a field poll which anticipated that it would be voted in by a two to one margin. This was a resounding victory. Many campaigners realized that only by embracing their lesbian and gay sexuality as an identity could they openly organize themselves and win the battle. Many 'came out' to their communities, unlike previous campaigns which were 'nearly all attempts to fend for themselves individually, by running for cover, adopting the duplicity of closetry and playing the heterosexist game through marriage and conformity' (Adam 1987: 107).

THE BRITISH STORY: SECTION 28

Bearing in mind the struggle that had already taken place in California I shall now look at the central example in this chapter, the campaign to get Clause 28 deleted from the Local Government Bill[3] of 1988 before it was passed into law by the British Government.

On 15 December 1987 it was first debated in Parliament, at the Bill's second reading. Despite the Labour Party's apathy many lesbians and gays immediately grasped the implications of this clause. The *Sun*'s headline on 16 December read 'SCREAMING GAYS BRING COMMONS TO A HALT!'; *The Independent* on the same day commented that 140 people in the public gallery followed the debate, cheering and hissing the speakers. Thus began the campaign which from the outset aroused enormous interest from the press, lesbians and gays, and finally from a broad Left/Liberal following.

The clause was not a government initiative but a Private Amendment put forward by the Conservative Member of Parliament David Wiltshire. The previous year Lord Halsbury had put forward a Bill with similar intent, which had fallen, due partly to the impending General Election, but due also to the government minister responsible for the Bill recognizing that there was danger that it was open to misinterpretation. A year later, however, with further success in the General Election, the Government decided to back the Clause.

In the meantime there had been various right-wing uproars regarding, among other things 'loony left' local authorities. The charge was that they did not cater for 'ordinary people' as they laid too much stress on providing services for minority groups. One such uproar concerned the Positive Images Campaign implemented by London's Haringey Borough Council which aimed to redress the balance of negative images of minority groups. A group known as the Parents Rights Group lobbied for the reversal of this policy. These right-wing actions gave the Government renewed vigour and confidence to press ahead with anti-lesbian and gay legislation.

Strategies of struggle

Under the broad coalition of *Stop the Clause*, a strategy developed to co-ordinate the campaign which fought the legislation. London and Manchester served as nerve centres, but most cities and many towns throughout Britain had independent groups. Developed from small nuclei of politically active lesbians and gays formed during previous lesbian and gay campaigns, many had been working towards eradicating discriminatory practices. As the campaign gained momentum it attracted a much larger and diverse following from lesbians and gays in general and also from heterosexuals.

Three broad strategies of struggle can be identified as having been utilized during the campaign. An examination of the tactics employed by each group and the impact that they can be seen to have had on its overall success will help to clarify the impact of these actions and of the whole campaign.

The lobbyists

This strategy followed the traditional middle-class formula of letter writing, influencing the influentials, nurturing institutional pressure, and lobbying. Perhaps the best known group was the *Arts Lobby*, patronized by well-known actors such as Ian McKellen (who subsequently accepted a knighthood) and Michael Cashman who had played a gay character in the TV soap opera *EastEnders*. Stage-managed from the Drill Hall Arts Centre in London, this campaign emphasized the number of playwrights, musicians, and artists whose work might be censored under the clause. They argued that homosexuality was respectable and produced a long list of famous lesbians and gay men, as well as raising large sums of money at benefit performances.

The group had a high profile in the media, photographs of members often getting into the papers, being portrayed as the 'respectable' faces at the forefront of the campaign. They had a very white, male, middle-class image, partly at the insistence of the press, thus misrepresenting the whole campaign. The first mass demonstration on 9 January 1988 was reported in the *Guardian* as 'The protest – led by Mr. Cashman'; above this there was a photograph which exclusively depicts Cashman holding part of a banner which actually was held predominantly by lesbians. Like it or not, the only positive comment in the mainstream press was going to depict a white male middle-class version of the events which disregarded the considerable input of the lesbians and did nothing to break down any prejudices held about other less 'respectable' lesbians and gays. However, their impact on the white middle classes was considerable, winning over a section of public opinion that might otherwise have remained stoically uninterested.

The mass movement

The second broad category of struggle aimed for mass mobilization of the general public to protest against the clause. *Haringey Stop the Clause* nicely represents this type of organization. The tactics implemented by them were used by other local groups and indeed the national groups. Made up of Haringey Council workers, trade unionists, students, activist groups (such as the Socialist Workers Party and the Revolutionary Communist Party), and non-aligned lesbians and gays, the group had about forty members. The format was weekly meetings held at Haringey Civic Centre where policy was discussed and actions planned. Public meetings with speakers were organized and small groups lobbied workers, especially those working for Haringey Council who would be implementing the legislation locally. People were asked to sign petitions, buy badges, and take stickers and leaflets about the clause. Underground stations were a favourite site for this task, to enable contact with a cross-section of people. Small demonstrations were organized in strategic places where the message was put across with placards, loud hailers, and banners as well as much stamping of feet, it being winter. Leaflets and posters about both local and national actions were widely distributed. Fairly close contact was kept with the main London *Stop the Clause* office, at the University of London Student Union, money raised being split between the national and local campaigns. This strategy proved to be the most popular, with national demonstrations rallying thousands of supporters.

Local groups were well positioned to identify where local action was needed, but co-ordination with the national group could highlight those actions that were perceived to be efficacious at a national level. *Haringey Stop the Clause*'s largest event was the lobby of the council meeting on 25 April 1988 where Conservative Councillor Peter Murphy attempted to implement the clause even before it was law. For this event publicity was distributed by both local and national groups. The local group did much of the groundwork for the lobby, but relied on the national group for funds, expertise, and national press mobilization.

Lesbians played a crucial role, both in Haringey and nationally. Many had been involved earlier in the year in the campaign against the Alton Bill, concerning abortion rights. Their extant networks and experience were fully utilized. Many had women's rights, class, and race issues high on their agendas and highlighted them in this campaign. It was not only lesbians who argued for their inclusion, but it was they as a group who most consistently argued for taking on board these issues. Thus the campaign not only demanded Clause 28 be deleted from the bill but that this was a bigoted attack on lesbians and gays of all classes and colours. We insisted that we should have the right to promote our life-styles in the same way that straight people continually promote theirs.

Guerrilla tactics

The third strategy for struggle could be described as an anonymous underground one. The major proponents became known as *Abseilers against the Clause*, a title arising from their first major action, of abseiling into the House of Lords during the debate about the clause on 1 February 1988. Between this event and its passing into law they got onto the BBC's *Six O'Clock News* on national television, confounding the news reporters and causing total chaos. They also chained themselves to the railings outside Buckingham Palace to draw attention to the clause campaign. Reminiscent of Greenham Common peace camp campaigns and women's liberation tactics, their actions had style, lesbian style. With a complete disregard for authority and total autonomy from the mainstream campaign they were prepared peacefully to break the law and assert the right to promote their life-styles. Within this strategy can also be included those small groups and individuals who made sure that toilet doors, underground trains, nice bits of clean wall, and bridges were artfully decorated with graffiti and stickers.

There was an element of revolt inherent in this strategy, which differentiates it from the other strategies. Using tactics of non-violence and theatricality their actions captured people's imaginations. The inevitable smile provoked on the face of the activist helped fuel the campaigners.

My own personal glee, when I first heard of the abseiling mission, filled me with a sense of pride in our whole campaign. At these moments there was a feeling that the campaign was a success and that our message was being put across in a way that truly reflected the style of our community.

The symbolic impact of Clause 28

These groups were not exclusive, involvement in one did not preclude involvement in others, and contact between groups was good. There was in-fighting and disagreement but the overall impression remained one of unity. The links between lesbians and gay men, unfamiliar as they were with working together, may have been fragile but there was strength in the unity which was refreshing. Many lesbians and gay men did not become involved in the campaign or, at most, put money in a collecting tin at their local bar. However, for many others it was the first taste of political action and the moment when their sexuality became more than simply a social facet.

The clause became law, as part of the Local Government Bill, when it received Royal Assent from the Queen on 24 May 1988. Since then it has been implemented only five times by local authorities although thirty-seven have sought a legal opinion on it (Thomas and Costigan 1990). This is a remarkably small take-up rate and might suggest that councillors[4] have been influenced by the arguments used in the campaign and are actually unwilling to use it. This could be seen as a victory, for if those who have the power are unwilling to use it then the clause is useless. However, despite its low level of implementation, one could suppose that its presence is actually acting as a deterrent. Groups may well not even try to get funding, or may be quietly discouraged from applying, because of confusion and anxiety regarding what is permissible under the law. This is an effective means of silencing us: there is no need for visibly oppressive actions but we are prevented from benefiting from local government support.

From the outset the chances of getting the clause deleted and thus gaining a legal victory were minimal, as the government had a good majority. The objective of this struggle then was not solely concerned with this law, but provided an opportunity for defiance and promoting our life-styles as valid alternatives to heterosexuality. This is ironic indeed: legislation aimed at stopping promotion of lesbianism and homosexuality unwittingly provoked this very phenomenon. Whenever the law regarding sexuality is changed it signals a redrawing of parameters. The irony is that the aim of brushing issues under the carpet with legislation actually causes them to explode into public debates which can paradoxically strengthen the community. The important question hence becomes whether that strength lasts longer than the campaign.

WHY ABSEILING IS EFFECTIVE

In any campaign or political action it is crucial that we know who and what we are in struggle against. Josh Gamson, in a discussion of AIDS activism, questions how domination is maintained, proposing that it is through a process of the 'delineation of "normal" and the exclusion of the "abnormal"', rather than via any direct force or institutionalized oppression (Gamson 1989: 352). Through this process 'the dominator becomes increasingly abstracted and invisible, while the dominated, embodied and visible . . . becomes the focus of attention' (Gamson 1989: 357). People actually dominate and silence themselves to avoid the stigma of abnormality. ACT UP in the USA has utilized this stigmatization of their identity to flaunt their difference and thereby disrupt the categorization process, by actively being themselves. Symbols are seized that uphold the domination of lesbians and gays; in reclaiming them the workings of the system that oppresses are exposed.

In this way, the abseilers can be seen to have utilized their stigmatization in their actions by aiming for institutions that wield enormous symbolic and traditional power: the House of Lords, the BBC, and Buckingham Palace. This juxtaposing of lesbians with the power of the nation subverts that power by flaunting the 'abnormal' (that is, being themselves) where the 'normal' (the institutions) are housed. It is this same juxtaposing that brings on that wicked smile when we hear about the action. These are symbolic actions but they form an essential part of a strategy which aims to confront a less tangible form of oppression.

The campaigns that I have described illustrate the importance of the method of struggle, not only for the actual legal outcome, but more importantly for the overall symbolic impact. Loss of rights is of course the prevalent issue at the moment of confrontation, but if the campaign goes further than this so that lesbians and gays can assert the vibrancy of their life-styles, then it also swells their collective strength.

QUEER FUTURES

Inspired largely by AIDS activists and specifically by the group ACT UP new groups both sides of the Atlantic have evolved, with bright ideas and the energy to implement them. In the States they are known collectively as Queer Nation, in Britain as OutRage. Both groups use guerilla tactics, based largely on confrontational methods, aiming to draw attention to themselves and the issues in their own self-styled manner. Made up of lesbians and gay men, some have formed separate lesbian and black communities, to address issues of gender and colour which many view as a priority.

OutRage in London held their first demonstration in June 1990, highlighting police activity regarding cottaging. Feelings were running high after the murder of three gay men in Ealing in London and the apparent lack of police activity. OutRage have subsequently organized various demonstrations, the most notable being the kiss-in at the Eros statue in Piccadilly, London, where hundreds of lesbians and gays armed with lip gloss descended to test the law. Under an 'indecency between men' clause in the Sexual Offences Act 1967 it is ruled that, among other things, for homosexuals, kissing outside the home is an offence. No one was arrested and the demonstration was both fun to participate in and successfully proved the point that to arrest people for such acts is ridiculous.

The American group Queer Nation, as the name suggests, is built on contradictions. 'Queer' lays down a challenge to lesbians and gays who aim for assimilation (as well as to heterosexuals): it asserts that we are different and proud of it. 'Nation' in contradiction affirms the sameness of those already marginalized and aims to draw together diverse strands. These contradictions, inherent in the movement, keep the activists in a constant state of confrontation both within the groups and out on the streets where their actions take place. Organizing marches, kiss-ins, and be-ins, 'fighting to keep queer turf safe from bashings' (Bérubé and Escoffier 1991: 16), they are certainly challenging many American lesbians and gays and prompting 'gays bash back' stories in the press. This movement, love it or hate it, seems to be generating considerable excitement in the States. The refusal to be silenced represents an emergent intolerance to oppression and a proactive stance to replace the reactive one that has been so prevalent recently among lesbians and gays.

Back in Britain, simultaneously with OutRage a lobbying group has been formed called Stonewall. They also aim to be proactive rather than reactive. With lobbying as their mainstay, their tactics are significantly different from those of the other two groups. Well-known people are associated with the campaign, such as Ian McKellen, Michael Cashman, and one of Britain's best-known lesbians, Pam St Clement. Assimilation could be said to be their aim, which gives their campaign a respectability scorned by the other two groups. Their campaign has only a limited brief which is to change the legal system which they see as underpinning the oppression of lesbians and gays. Such an élite group may change the statute book but will this change the reality of being a Queer Nation?

There are, however, some problems with OutRage: a few of their demonstrations have seemed to be too press orientated, leaving the dyke or faggot at the gay bar feeling a little left out. This is clearly a dangerous situation. While press coverage is obviously important, so too is building a sense of community and joint identity which will not be achieved by élite groups of activists looking for the limelight. Despite this worry, their tactics, which aim for a symbolic message are effective and exciting, and certainly have more style than lobbying.

The outlook

There is still an enormous amount of change needed before lesbians and gay men are free of oppression. The way in which we go about working for this will inform the success that we achieve. Lobbying may eventually change laws, but is it not far better to change people's opinions so that the law must follow suit? The more people that are involved in the struggle for change, the more valid, pervasive, and representative that change will be. For example, most of the overtly sexist laws are gone but women are still earning substantially lower wages, often subjected to male violence, and more often than not bearing the brunt of housework and child care in the family. Legal parity has not changed the reality of many women's lives.

Clause 28 enabled many of us to cut our political teeth and was an important moment for the lesbian and gay community here, as was the battle over the Briggs initiative in California. Lesbians were at the forefront of the campaign and in California the Afro-American and Chicano communities were fully involved. This perspective can only broaden our horizons, and enrich our campaign. These campaigns must be remembered as successes. Abseiling is still a word that means something different to lesbians than to the general public.

It is important that we keep going, keeping the pressure up and staying stroppy. We should never accept that another gay bashing has occurred, let alone gone unsolved by the police; never quietly accept that a lesbian has lost her children because of her sexuality; never accept harassment on the streets or in our workplaces. We must also continue to challenge ourselves, not allowing issues of gender, race, and class to be pushed aside during the struggle, but not allowing ourselves to become fragmented either. We all need a voice if we are going to evolve a community that is capable of including us all. If a white, middle-class male movement has success, whose success will it be?

It is time now that we draw up our own agenda, so that we do not waste our energy on these nasty, punitive, indeed bigoted pieces of legislation. What excites me about Queer Nation and OutRage is their uncompromising attitude. I too want to be fired up about my politics, feel that rush of anger keep me yelling at the top of my voice out there on the streets. I think I *am* different. I'm not looking for approval and I certainly don't need anyone's permission to be myself. I *like* being a lesbian and *like* too to be in the thick of a demonstration to prove it. Not everyone feels the same way; some people may like writing letters and peaceably arguing for legal change, but it doesn't turn me on. It simply isn't publicly challenging enough; it feels too much like another private action. Too much of my life has been closeted. I don't want to keep my politics closeted; I want people to know that I am a lesbian and proud of it: I want to demonstrate that on the streets with lesbian style. The defiant image of the abseilers in the House of Lords still fills me with pride and a desire to be equally wicked. That feeling is our political hope.

NOTES

1 Clause 28 was also known by other names. It began as Clause 27 of the Local Government Act then, as further clauses were added, it became Clause 28. When it passed into law it became known as a section and the act also became known as a bill, as happens to all legislation.
2 A Proposition is state legislation which is voted on by the electorate, similar to referendums in Britian. It is an often-used mechanism in California usually with a number of propositions to vote on at any one time.
3 Local government in Britain is administered by local authorities, which are independently elected bodies with specific local responsibilities. Many have a majority of Labour councillors, which often brings them into conflict with the Conservatives at a national level.
4 Councillors are the elected local government officials who make the decisions on policy and spending for their area.

18

DANGEROUS ACTIVISM?

Jason Annetts and Bill Thompson

The price we have paid for the creation of a gay community may be a culture that is too inward-looking, too ready to accept unnecessarily limited ambition.

(Altman 1987)

While gay activists have correctly prioritized AIDS as a social issue, there is a danger in making AIDS *the* battle front for every debate, from medicalization to discrimination, that affects lesbians and gays. For some, the AIDS experience encouraged the option of a single-issue strategy – a 'symbolic politics' (Watney in Watney and Carter 1989) – whereby the previous rationales for gay rights were almost replaced by righteous indignation demanding redress against a New Right backlash.

This new strategy was justified by erroneous lessons drawn from the American AIDS experience and a misperception of British homophobia. Yet proponents appeared oblivious to the potential trap faced by all minority social movements promoting a single issue: creating a mentality of 'victimization', rather than taking advantage of wider possibilities.

Given the vast amount of energy available, the interests of lesbians and gays are best served by avoiding gay 'victimology'. Surviving the AIDS 'backlash' means reassessing the lessons of the AIDS decade and adopting a pragmatic rather than idealistic strategy.

THE AMERICAN MODEL

The British AIDS experience has often been evaluated in a pessimistic and alarmist fashion – escalating infection, deliberate government inaction, and violent homophobia following a media-induced public panic – proven by constant references to a political and/or religious New Right backlash. This replicated early American commentary which argued that:

The virulence of the far right, with its growing structural power, makes it a considerable political and ideological force in AIDS

227

organizing ... manipulating fear by using AIDS to defeat lesbian
and gay rights bills and attempting to limit the community's freedom
of expression and right to congregate.

(Patton 1985: 13)

The dominant imagery that crossed the Atlantic was that of another Nazi-
style holocaust:

The elective tyranny of parliamentarianism depends these days, like
the National Socialism, 'on citizens who are willing to give up personal
identity and individualized ways of life and let themselves be managed',
as one survivor of Dachau and Buchenwald has noted.

(Watney, *Gay Times* February 1988: 39)

As we have demonstrated elsewhere, this simple comparison exaggerated
the strength of conservative familial values on both sides of the Atlantic
and ignored the possibility that recent attacks upon the lesbian and gay
communities reflected the conservative's fear that society was becoming
more pluralistic (Thompson 1992). Contrary to some British activists'
impressions the power of the fundamentalist Christian–free market–
Republican alliance was always grossly exaggerated (Hemmelstein 1983;
Liebman in Liebman and Wuthnow 1983). The American New Moral
Right's successes really amounted to defeating the odd liberal all-affirmative
action proposition and blocking the Equal Rights Amendment for women.
They failed to secure any social legislation like the Family Act, and the
Meese Commission was a poor return for their eight-year support of the
Reagan administration (Hunter 1983; Bruce 1988; Thompson 1992). Proof
of the Moral Majority's failure can be seen in their desperate return to
symbolic crusades against 2 Live Crew, Mapplethorpe exhibitions, and anti-
satanism. Moral panics like these occur when there is no consensus of values
in society and fears are deliberately provoked in an attempt to reimpose
a consensus (see Ben-Yehuda 1990).

In any event, Britain is not America and there are three reasons why
the USA could not set a global trend. Gay sex acts are still illegal in many
American states, unlike European countries where even Ireland is having
to toe the EEC line. Despite Thatcherism, Europe is still essentially welfare
orientated, and health care is not seen as the responsibility of the individual,
which accounted for many early USA problems (Altman 1986). Being more
centralized than the federalist United States, European bureaucracies will
have a long-term interventionist interest. It is, therefore, impossible and
unhelpful to generalize AIDS experiences. It could even be argued that,
given the relatively small HIV figures in Europe, governments have been
fairly swift in response and resource provision.

The only real similarity between the British and American AIDS
experience is the analysis offered concerning a 'backlash'; an attempt by

some gay activists to utilize AIDS to re-mobilize the lesbian and gay subculture as a politicized community promoting an agenda which includes:

> restructuring the delivery of healthcare, more community involve-
> ment in the development of research priorities, re-framing social
> concepts of sexuality.
>
> (Patton 1985: 158)

Transferred to Britain, this programme has been enlarged to include: countering family ideology, direct government funding for gay community projects, a Bill of Rights, and even proportional representation (Watney in Watney and Carter 1989). In order to achieve this, gays and lesbians are supposed to engage in 'critiques' of parliamentarianism, of civil-rights organizations, and of the institutions of medicine, the police, and health education among others.

However desirable, and necessary, many of these demands may be, this programme is not an exclusively gay one, and hardly follows specifically from the AIDS experience. Exploiting AIDS in this way could backfire: first, by selling the soul of the community to one political programme, thereby alienating large sections of that community; second, by insisting AIDS is the root of the problem, thereby creating a greater threat than a backlash – a victim mentality.

FOREVER VICTIMS?

During the 1980s, many disadvantaged groups in the USA attempted to redress their grievances through the language of victimology. Beginning as a demand by crime victims for redress within the criminal justice system (Karmen 1990), this quickly became the adopted strategy of all structur-ally disadvantaged groups, whose leaders argued that the concept of group 'rights' replaced the liberal concept of individual rights and justified positive discrimination. Ironically, the end result has often been the disabling perpetuation of a 'victimization' mentality and strategies which play into the hands of persecutors. Sometimes overt, sometimes not, AIDS activists' discourses began to reflect a similar tendency.

At its high point, this gay victimology argued that the liberation of the 1970s gave way to a potential holocaust in the post-AIDS 1980s:

> On top of the death of our friends, and our own fears for ourselves
> and those closest to us, gay men currently face a massive resurgence
> of militant aggressive homophobia.
>
> (Watney 1987: 4)

At this stage, this 'victimization' was complemented by a concept of gay heroism, whereby:

AIDS affects a generation of gay men which has already long ago refused to accept second class citizenship ... and if in these terrible times we should wish to alleviate the pains of our losses – of freedom and friends – then we might think of AIDS as a monstrously ironic means to this end, and of our loved ones who have died as martyrs to that great cause.

(Watney 1987: 148)

This early dramatic contrast between a simplified good and evil, the beleaguered gay volunteers battling to save hetero-humanity from its moralistic-induced ignorance, sounded uncomfortably like the simplistic dualities promoted by the religious campaigns in the same period.

In truth, proof of the threat to the gay community rested not upon a public reaction, but substitutes culled together to create a gay victimology. The most frequently told horror stories merely referenced tabloid newspaper bigotry, especially Murdoch's notorious paper, the *Sun*. Yet this was highly selective reading, given this newspaper's 'equal opportunity policy' of tirade targets covering football hooligans, lager louts, punks, blacks, Asians, women, non-Thatcherite Tories, the 'loony left', pop stars, movie stars, other newspapers, and even the Royal Family. While quoting such bigotry could easily give the impression that the gay community was beleaguered, *Sun* columnists do not necessarily reflect or even promote public attitudes.

The second backlash indicator we were referred to was the opinion polls. It was alleged that:

recent evidence has shown, there has been a shuddering setback in public attitudes to homosexuality – a very significant drop, for instance, of about 20 per cent polled, who are in favour of continuing liberalisation of the law. This is very significant, and is obviously very closely related to the AIDS crisis.

(Weeks 1989b: 128)

On the contrary, the British Social Attitudes survey, taken at that time, was clearly encouraging. While AIDS may have produced a percentage increase in those who believed gay orientation was 'wrong', the figure was still less than for those who thought divorce was 'wrong'; and respondents had actually become more intolerant of discrimination against gays in 'key' areas, such as teaching and government – the accepted means to test prejudice (5th Report 1988). Our own survey, conducted at the very height of the media AIDS 'panic', just before the 1987 election, clearly demonstrated a similar tendency. Students, communists, petty criminals, gypsies, the mentally ill, and fascist National Front members were all regarded as far more threatening to public order than lesbians and gays, despite the belief that PWAs had brought it upon themselves (Pritchard and Thompson 1987). Similar trends were seen in the United States. Despite alleged public panics, a Gallup Poll recorded that 59 per cent of the population had *not* changed their views, one way or the other, concerning homosexuality. Likewise, New York City finally secured an anti-discrimination statute in 1986, after almost two decades of fruitless attempts (Greenberg 1988: 478).

The third dubious indicator was the assertion that all gay fatalities and street attacks followed directly from the AIDS-induced homophobia, as if nothing of this kind had occurred before 1981. It did, in large numbers, as many lesbians and gays can testify. Consequently, the assertions concerning police duplicity sounded like a moral panic, emulating 'Sunsational' reportage:

> Ongoing research . . . has now identified 48 murders of gay men which have happened in the period of almost four years from December 1986.
>
> (*Gay Times* October 1990)

A homophobic conspiracy? Only if one was to discount all other possibilities, including violent robbery and so on. Given an average of 600 murders per year in Britain, murders of twelve unknown gays a year would be an under-representation of that social group. If homophobia was rife, surely we would have witnessed over-representation. Gay men can, like anyone else, be mugged, robbed, or killed for the simple reason that they were in the wrong place at the wrong time; it may have nothing to do with their sexuality. To claim all murders are homophobic, desensitizes us to those cases which really are.

This holocaustic impression was further reinforced by scouring the global gay experience for cases of oppression which were not occurring here, and to imply Britain was not alone: 800 yearly imprisonments in Russia, a Buenos Aires clampdown on gay street life, increasing murder of gays in Sao Paulo, and so on. While each case was a cause for concern, the addition of the ultimate urban legend concerning the systematic extermination of several million gays in Iranian death camps (*Action* February 1990) hinted at the purpose of this reporting: to convince British lesbians and gays that the holocaust is coming, and that all backlash horror stories should be taken seriously.

The fourth bogus backlash indicator was stereotyping the evangelical Christian response to AIDS, by constantly repeating the 'Wrath of God' statements made by a few figures on the fundamentalist fringe. This was disingenuous; vast numbers in the far from homogeneous evangelical camp thought otherwise. Even a cursory reading of their proliferating AIDS texts revealed an emphasis upon 'caring', not retribution (see Dixon 1987; Collier 1987; White 1987). Their leading medical doctor demanded:

Where are your tears? Go and find your tears of grief for those who
are suffering, dying and (you say) who are in line for judgement. When
you have found your tears, then talk to me of judgement – but start
with yourself.

(Dixon 1987: 151)

Not only did many evangelicals reject the anti-gay sentiments of their
American cousins, the major fundamentalist pressure group, the CARE
Trust, established Mildmay as *the first* AIDS hospice in Europe.

The most melodramatic backlash proof offered was a charge of deliberate,
callous inaction by the Government towards gay deaths and the alleged
recriminalization of gay sexuality. The gay victimology asserted that
because gays were considered non-persons, AIDS became a government
issue – i.e. funding appeared – only when heterosexuals began to die (Watney
1987)!

Yet, if all these indicators did reflect a backlash, we were faced with two
bizarre anomalies. First, why did government make no attempt to legislate
against specific sexual acts, let alone lesbians and gays *per se*? It is unlikely
they would do so. Even in America, where various churches had rallied
against 'deviant' sexual behaviors, Altman tells us AIDS was not used to
foster political advantage. Incredibly:

the President did not respond to the AIDS epidemic, neither did he
use it in his appeals during the 1984 campaign to conservative morality,
and even in local races AIDS seemed to be rarely mentioned.

(Altman 1986: 184)

In Britain, apart from a half-dozen public figures, the reaction was similar.
The initial AIDS fear, as even the maligned evangelicals noted at the time,
was due to ignorance and a lack of public information. Second, as the concept of AIDS as a purely homosexual disease receded in line with clinical
findings (attention moving to intravenous drug users and the Third World),
what reason did some gay activists have for keeping the old associations
alive?

'Holocaust' promoters have deliberately invoked, first, Clause 28 of the
Local Government Act 1988 and, second, Section 25 of the Criminal Justice
Bill 1990, as proof of government *re*criminalization of gay sex in the wake
of AIDS. Such connections were questionable. The former emerged out
of CARE Trust's mobilization against gay sex education, and had nothing
to do with the AIDS backlash, as Graham Webster-Gardiner recently
admitted.[1] The more recent Clause 25 was a bumbling move in a
bureaucratic attempt to bring all penalties 'up to date'. It created no new
category of crime. While we may object to the use of indecency, solicitation,
and procuration laws to harass, heterosexuals are subject to similar restrictions, reflecting a thirty-year-old policy to curb public manifestations of

victimless crimes (see National Deviance Conference 1980). The real complaint is, as it has always been, that lesbians and gays are subject to arrest as well as disapproval for showing any form of public affection, and that 'offences' such as kissing in public should be *de*criminalized. Whatever was happening, Clause 25 is not a *re*criminalization.

In short, proof of a virulent backlash rested upon erroneous generalizations about public attitudes and the misrepresentation of other events. And this brings us closer to the single-issue trap.

THE SINGLE-ISSUE TRAP

Homophobia horror stories and victimology follow inevitably from symbolizing political issues. This form of crusading has been seen before, and the end results are frequently disastrous for those involved, as the separatist feminists' anti-pornography crusade demonstrates. Following the collapse of the welfare-orientated demand of the early women's movement, an obsession with the threat of pornography, based ultimately on the belief that all penetrative sex amounts to an act of violence against women akin to rape (see Dworkin 1989: 55–6), led to demands to prioritize pornography as *the* issue. (Bouchier 1983; Banks 1981; Snitow 1985; Duggan *et al*. 1985; Duggan 1984). As many feminist activists adopted this strategy, other women fighting structural and organizational inequality through precedent-setting court cases often found they were alone; many young women shied off joining the movement; and little attempt was made to discover the real pattern of pornography's links to sexual violence. As more and more images were labelled pornographic, the demand to censor all sexually orientated images emerged. Attempts were also made to ban sexually orientated women's organizations from the London Lesbian and Gay Centre, and any woman who did not accept the anti-pornography analysis was denied 'feminist' identification and sometimes physically attacked (see Chester and Dickey 1988). Ultimately, the 'prioritize pornography' faction abandoned economic and social liberation completely in favour of this symbolic gesture, and has now even openly joined forces with pro-life/anti-permissive moral lobbies. Since 1989, for example, their leading MP Clare Short shared platforms with speakers from the fundamentalist CARE Trust, which also supplied many activists for the 'feminist' anti-soft core pornography Off the Shelf campaign (see Thompson and Annetts 1990 for details). As a result of this 'feminist' duplicity, the Obscene Publications Squad and Customs Service have felt confident enough to increase their harassment of all sexual minority literature. Recent court cases have even included an attempt to outlaw *Modern Primitives* special issue on body art!

The lesbian and gay community can learn from this disastrous phase in the history of the feminist movement, which promotes a tokenistic measure rather than real equal rights issues. Being a parallel social movement demanding equality, it is a near-perfect comparison. Both groups have campaigned around one issue for many years: AIDS for gay activists; pornography for women activists. These strategies were promoted as a means of uniting the group's total perceived membership in one cause, designated as being typical and symbolic of the oppression faced in everyday life. The single-issue pornography strategy has inevitably backfired. It not only invited ridicule from the public, and contempt from many sexually active women now alienated from the feminist movement; but all women are now paying the price. Feminist bookstores are raided, art shows closed, and films censored all in the name of eliminating pornogrpahy. Worse, at least one woman has been incarcerated for alleged 'Satanic' child sex abuse on the basis that she once had a lesbian affair, and that such sexual proclivities were proof of a desire to abuse children (see Rabinowitz 1990).

Now that feminist activists are beginning to learn from their mistakes, will gay activists have to learn the same hard way? This almost seems the case. Not content with victimology, some gay activists appeared to desire approbation. Christians, for example, are constantly vilified in the gay media, by being denounced as the 'Jesus-in-jack-boot fraternity' whether or not they support the homophobic Rev. T. Higton (*Gay Times* April 1988: 21). Is the cause of gay and lesbian rights really advanced by lamenting the *Sun's* sensational and derogatory phrases in one breath, and emulating, even surpassing, them in another?

These personal attacks are no substitute for a detailed analysis of the situation. We need a clear and detailed appraisal of advances and setbacks for lesbian and gay rights, not the creation of further rifts between gays and wider publics.

BACKLASH POLITICS

In both Britain and America, AIDS hit the gay community long after liberation politics had been displaced by the self-contained subculture of bars, clubs and bathhouses. As there were no gay 'rules', the vast subculture did not automatically lead to a unified or politically orientated community (Altman 1986: 108–9). But whereas sex and sensualism had been more fun than 'boring' politics, for others non-political hedonism now appeared deadly. According to some activists, the apparently self-sufficient gay community would have to mobilize; one way or another AIDS was going to be a political watershed and the subculture was to become a community of common interest (Patton 1985; Weeks 1989a). These activists then offered themselves as the leadership needed to carry this process out. But their single-issue AIDS strategy had its downside.

Since they were committed to taking full advantage of this new community of interest, pluralism was not to be tolerated. Promoting the politics of (sexual) diversity threatened to give way to telling gays and lesbians what to think and which papers *not* to read, insisting they must mobilize over AIDS issues on pain of ostracism, and urging the vote for one political party. Ironically, AIDS had brought the potential of oppression within the gay community, as much as outside it. Like conservative Colonel Blimps we must – given AIDS – all pull together and not question our leaders. Like separatist feminists, we must subscribe to the leaders' interpretation, or we have no right to be part of the movement. As for fundamentalist Christians, salvation is by only one path.

The 1990s will present the gay community with many opportunities to extend equality and representation, but these could be easily lost in the single-issue trap. Like Altman we can:

> understand the fears of those who see AIDS as opening the way for
> new pogroms and who compare current right-wing rhetoric with the
> early stages of the Nazi persecution of the Jews, but I think their fears
> are somewhat exaggerated.
>
> (Altman 1986: 183–4)

This is definitely the case in Britain, where activists fail to see that their lamentations regarding the community's 'complacency' over AIDS may be the result of overkill,

Readers of the gay press cannot fail to have noticed that at the very time we are being sold a holocaust scenario, the news is not all bad: Australia has seen the repeal of the repressive anti-homosexual laws in Queensland, banning discrimination against PWAs and giving legal recognition to gay relationships in immigration law; despite reports of gay fatalities in Bahia province, Brazil, Salvador city has now banned discrimination against gays; Denmark has introduced marital rights for gays; homosexual activity has been decriminalized in Hong Kong; the gay age of consent was reduced from 18 to 14 in Iceland; and the Irish government included gays in its Incitement to Hatred Bill.

Of course, all is not well, but placing events in context and avoiding panic will help us to plan more effective action in future. The last thing we need is single-issue, symbolic politics which keeps us in a self-imposed ghetto:

> leading us to accept too easily that what we are and do is of relevance
> only to ourselves, rather than being part of the broad panorama of
> human behaviour.
>
> (Altman 1987: 18)

Rather than see ourselves as victims, perhaps it is time we took a further step from the closet, transcended the limits of separation and segregation in the ghetto, and returned to the question of free and open identity in society at large.

Two recent events point the way out of the trap towards this end. The founding of OutRage to address all forms of continual discrimination emphasizes that there is more to gay activism than AIDS. AIDS is one issue among many. Second, through their alliance with heterosexual civil libertarians, OutRage members helped ensure that Liberty, the British Civil Liberties Union, reaffirmed its commitment to combating discrimination, and will again actively work for its elimination. Avoiding the single-issue trap and a victim mentality by actively working together to change attitudes, rather than sniping at any 'enemy' from the safety of the ghetto to secure what will inevitably become tokenistic redress from 'right-on' politicians, will help ensure that the next decade sees real advances in gay politics.

NOTE

1   On 4 March 1991, Gardiner told a meeting of the Conservative Graduates Association exactly how and why his Conservative Family Campaign pushed through Clause 28. The CFC's motive was to restrict gay sex education material, following in the footsteps of CARE Trust and other fundamentalist crusades in the previous decade. It, therefore, did not reflect an AIDS backlash. Both Peter Tatchell and Bill Thompson were present at that meeting.

EQUAL RIGHTS FOR

Strategies for lesbian and gay eq
in Britain

Peter Tatchell

By comparison with most other European countries – and with much of
Australia, Canada, and the United States – Britain has more homophobic
laws and less legal protection for lesbian and gay people. Thousands of
homosexuals suffer criminalization and discrimination in Britain every year.
In 1989 around 3,000 men were convicted or cautioned, and 40–50
imprisoned, for consenting homosexual relations, contrary to laws which
criminalize victimless gay behaviour, but rarely its heterosexual
equivalents.[1] Many other lesbians and gay men are subjected each year
to discrimination – often officially sanctioned – in employment, housing,
child custody and adoption, health care, immigration, local council grants,
customs' censorship, youth care orders, membership of the armed forces,
and so on. In total, about twenty different points of law, either explicitly
or by omission, discriminate against the lesbian and gay community.[2] The
end result is that homosexuals are officially relegated to a second-class citizenship: denied equality in law and subject to institutionalized discrimination
in virtually every aspect of our lives.

Unlike lesbians and gay men in many other democratic countries, British
homosexuals have no legal recourse to a Constitution or a Bill of Rights
which guarantees fundamental freedoms and which can be used to redress
government homophobia and claim equality of treatment in law. Instead,
as with everyone else in Britain, we are consigned to the legal status of
subjects of the Crown, rather than free citizens with inalienable rights. This
is reinforced by the dominant political discourse, where the notion of full
and equal citizenship for all people is notoriously weak. The absence of
equality for lesbians and gay men is thus both symptomatic and reflective
of a broader legal and political culture which is traditionally hostile and
suspicious of egalitarianism and citizens' rights. Campaigning for lesbian
and gay equality therefore also involves challenging a much deeper and
more general ingrained resistance to the principles of citizenship and
equality.

THE LIMITATIONS OF REACTIVE
POLITICS AND SEPARATISM

The historic restrictions on our rights as lesbian and gay people have fostered an overwhelmingly defensive and oppositionist agenda within the homosexual rights movement. Faced with so many state-sponsored denigrations of our dignity, invasions of our private lives, and assaults on our civil liberties, much of our political campaigning is reactive. We rush from pillar to post fighting each new outrage that is launched against us: Section 28, Paragraph 16, Clause 25, and Operation Spanner. The list goes on and on.

The end result of this 'fire brigade activism' is not merely a defensive politics, but an absence of any thought-out, coherent political strategy for lesbian and gay equality. Looking back over innumerable recent campaigns, in each case it has seemed obvious what we are up against. We want the government, the church, the police, the media, and the judges to get off our backs. But what are we ultimately aiming to achieve? Faced with homophobic attacks, of course we have to respond. However, we also need to find a way to set our own agenda and make our own demands. If we want to win support and maximize the effectiveness of our campaigning, we need to demonstrate clearly what we stand for, as well as what we are against. This requires us to formulate alternative policies, and strategies for their achievement, which are principled, plausible, and persuasive.

Not that the struggle for lesbian and gay equality can be reduced to a simple battle for legislative change. There are many diverse fronts on which we need to fight. However, the successes of other endeavours will always come up against the barrier of legal inequality, and be limited in their achievements, until we enshrine in law the principle and practice of equal rights for lesbians and gay men. Though law reform is neither a panacea for social prejudice nor a short-cut to social acceptance, it is a fundamental precondition for the realization of full equality for homosexual men and women. It can help create a legal framework and a social atmosphere which actively de-legitimizes discrimination and positively encourages equality. Indeed, a campaign for radical legislative changes is potentially a highly effective way of exposing injustice, provoking debate, raising public awareness, and challenging bigotry. It can also be a stepping-stone towards shifting the debate around sexuality onto the even more far-sighted and liberating agenda of the cultural construction of sexual desire and the inherent bisexual potential of all human beings. For all these reasons, there is much to be recommended in a legislative agenda for homosexual rights.

Considerable work along these lines has already been done by the lesbian and gay rights lobbying organization, the Stonewall Group. Its proposed Homosexual Equality Bill attempts, in a single piece of legislation, to abolish the inequalities in sexual offences law concerning same-sex behaviour, to outlaw discrimination on the grounds of sexual orientation, and to grant legal recognition to relationships involving lesbian and gay couples.[3] This is a very concrete and valuable legislative agenda. It establishes a useful benchmark, setting out in clear terms much of what we are fighting for. But it has its weaknesses. First, instead of questioning the existing framework of law and proposing a radical overhaul, which would be to the benefit of gay and non-gay people alike, this Bill has the more limited aim of merely ensuring that homosexuals are treated equally with heterosexuals. In other words, it seeks equality on heterosexual terms, largely accepting the current parameters of legislative principles and practice. Second, the Stonewall legislation does not cover all aspects of law. It gives no explicit recognition to issues such as child custody, political asylum, obscenity regulations, and donor insemination.

In its defence, the Homosexual Equality Bill deliberately sets out to cover only the keys aspects of lesbian and gay inequality. Its stated aim is to secure the legislation of the 'minimum necessary' rights to ensure 'basic' equality, rather than to provide an exhaustive programme for 'full legal equality'. The rationale for this approach is to maximise public and parliamentary support and to thereby hasten its successful enactment at the earliest possible opportunity. Whatever its current limitations, the implementation of this Bill would, as its explanatory notes rightly suggest, provide a positive framework 'for further changes in the law'. This approach is quite understandable. The scale of legal discrimination against lesbians and gay men is so great and so severe that our number one priority must be to get rid of the worst excesses of inequality as fast as we can, even if that means postponing some of our longer-term objectives to a later date.

However, there is a third and much more persuasive criticism of the Stonewall strategy. It is the view that seeking to legislate for lesbian and gay rights by means of an exclusive and separate Homosexual Equality Bill is the least likely way to win law reform. Indeed, it is bound to draw flak from every homophobe in the country, providing a 'sitting target' for tabloid newspapers and right-wing MPs to wage a ferocious anti-gay campaign. It would encourage our opponents to use all their traditional manipulations and misrepresentations, including the false, but often in the past successful, claim that such legislation is an attempt to give special privileges to lesbians and gay men over and against heterosexuals. Pursuit of a 'go-it-alone' lesbian and gay strategy would therefore tend to render our legislative agenda more vulnerable and marginal, and therefore make it much more difficult for us to win broad public support.

AN 'ALL-IN' STRATEGY FOR EQUALITY

To deflate and undermine our opponents' arguments we need a more subtle and sophisticated strategy for homosexual equality which can positively encourage alliances and build support for our cause from beyond the lesbian and gay community. After all, since we don't comprise a majority of the population, we are not in a position to legislate homosexual equality solely by our own efforts. We are invariably dependent on the solidarity and support of others, some of whom may also be dependent on us to get their equality agendas through parliament.

This realization points to a possible alternative strategy for lesbian and gay rights: the integration of legislative initiatives for homosexual equality within a broader agenda of 'equal rights for all'. Our embrace of this comprehensive equality strategy would explicitly refute the claim that our demands are concerned with divisive and sectional interests. Instead, it would make it abundantly apparent that we are fighting for *everyone*'s right to enjoy equality and to be spared discrimination. In this sense, we would be seizing the moral high ground and putting forward a universalist equality agenda. It's a strategy with a general and wide appeal, which makes it much harder for our opponents to default and defeat. As such, it stands a far greater chance of success. What would it entail?

A broad-based legislative strategy for equal rights would involve the formulation of a comprehensive equality agenda which integrates diverse equal opportunities commitments within a unified policy framework, based on the concept of full and universal citizenship and geared to the realization of equal rights for all people. The basic principles underlying this all-encompassing equality agenda would be the same for everyone, including lesbians and gay men and other discriminated groups in society such as women, black people, and the disabled. These principles are:

- Full equality in law
- Legal protection against discrimination
- Equality of access and opportunity
- Positive action to monitor, promote, and enforce equality.

Such principles state both the goals of equality and the mechanisms for their achievement. They are universal and comprehensive, addressing the concerns of all individuals and communities, particularly those suffering disadvantage and marginalization, as lesbians and gay men do.

What, then, are the specific policies which would give these four principles practical effect? There are many to choose from. However, to ensure a sharp political focus and maximize our chances of success, it might be advisable to concentrate on a small number of the most important and effective policies instead of a diffuse and endless shopping list of demands. The three policies which, more than any others, would ensure equality across-the-board for everyone are:

- A Bill of Rights
- An Anti-Discrimination Act
- A Department for Equal Opportunities

Between them, they offer both the ends and the means to equality in general, and to lesbian and gay equality in particular. Though these policies wouldn't sweep away all aspects of discrimination overnight, their comprehensive character would swiftly demolish the central pillars of lesbian and gay inequality, creating a new legal framework of rights and redress which could be used to tackle any remaining, or future, discrimination.

These 'all-in' policies for equality, which are inclusive of equal rights for lesbians and gay men, have a number of advantages over the 'go-it-alone' strategy of separate and exclusive legislation. To enact individual laws to combat each distinct type of discrimination would be unwieldy and immensely time-consuming. It would result in a parliamentary log-jam of legislation and take years to get through. It might also risk creating divisions and rivalries between different discriminated sectors of the population as each sought legislative priority for the remedy of their particular grievances. In contrast, these three comprehensive policies for equality would remove the need for a mass of different laws to deal with each specific type of discrimination. They would enable most forms of inequality to be remedied promptly and concurrently through one or two all-encompassing Bills.

This integrated and broad-based strategy for equality may also help avoid marginalizing policies, such as lesbian and gay rights, which are frequently deemed to be controversial and are often relegated to the political sidelines. By not legislating these policies in isolation, but incorporating them into a generalized equality agenda, they would remain in the forefront of parliamentary priorities for equal rights. At the same time, they would be less vulnerable to media vilification, electoral backlash, and parliamentary opposition.

All-embracing policies for equality have the added advantage of tending to unite the many different discriminated groups in society, giving them a common interest in pooling their resources and working together around a common agenda for equality. This alliance-building strategy brings people together, fostering cohesion and strength, to the mutual benefit and empowerment of everyone suffering inequality. In contrast, an exclusivist and separatist legislative agenda is more prone to pull them apart. There is, of course, no automatic community of interest or bond of solidarity between different disadvantaged and discriminated peoples. That cannot be assumed, as the examples of misogynistic gay men and homophobic black women testify. However, with commitment and endeavour, it can be achieved, as shown by the examples of 'Lesbians and Gays Support the Miners' during the 1984–5 strike and the diverse heterosexual backing given to the lesbian and gay campaign against Section 28 in 1988.

A Bill of Rights, an Anti-Discrimination Act, and a Department for Equal Opportunities are not a panacea. Collectively, however, they can help to create a new democratic and egalitarian culture which enshrines positive and inviolable rights for everyone, without distinction, and which constrains the hitherto largely untrammelled power of the state over the individual. While these legal protections don't guarantee that the state would never be able to violate individual rights, they do make it much more difficult.

A Bill of Rights

The existence of a Bill of Rights would discourage the enactment of discriminatory government legislation and the handing down of prejudiced court judgements. Failing that, it would provide a mechanism for them to be challenged and overturned. What might a Bill of Rights consist of? Most importantly, it should embody the principles of equal rights, equality of opportunity, and non-discrimination for all people – including lesbians and gay men:

> Everyone shall be entitled to full and equal rights under the law, equality of opportunity, and to legal protection against discrimination on any grounds whatsoever, including sex, race, national or social origin, religion, language, political opinion or belief, age, sexual orientation, disability or medical condition.

These Bill of Rights proposals are universal and all-inclusive. They guarantee that all those who suffer disadvantage and discrimination will have their inequalities recognized and remedied on an equal basis. Such proposals develop and expand the anti-discrimination principles set out in the Dutch constitution and in the European Convention on Human Rights (ECHR).[4]

There is, already, growing pressure from within the Labour and the Liberal Democrat parties and from the constitutional reform pressure group, Charter 88, for the incorporation of the ECHR into British law. Though this would be an important advance for individual liberties, the ECHR has a number of flaws and inadequacies. It offers, for example, no explicit protection against discrimination to the disabled, people with HIV, the elderly, or lesbians and gay men. All these people are omitted from Article 14 of the ECHR. To be acceptable as the basis for a Bill of Rights, the ECHR would therefore have to be amended to guarantee that its 'rights and freedoms' apply 'without discrimination' on the grounds of 'age, sexual orientation, disability, or medical condition'.

Critics argue that a Bill of Rights would undermine the elected parliament and give more power to the unelected judges. However, all our existing parliament-made laws are already open to interpretation and enforcement by the judges, and very often they exercise their judgement in a discriminatory manner. A Bill of Rights would, if it was well drafted, actually restrict the judiciary's interpretative leeway and opportunity for bias. It would also strengthen the individual's ability to get effective redress against the abuse of state power. Indeed, if Britain had a Bill of Rights, the discriminatory age of consent laws, which specify that gay men have to be 21 before they can lawfully have sex, would have been struck down a long time ago; and legislation like Section 28, which makes it illegal for local authorities to 'promote homosexuality', would never have got onto the statute books.

Looking at the experience of other European countries, those which have a Bill of Rights or equivalent constitutional guarantees of human rights – such as the Netherlands, Denmark, Sweden, and Norway – tend to have significantly greater social equality and far fewer violations of personal liberties. While they may not be perfect societies, their lesbian and gay citizens live in a much more accepting social atmosphere, with far less victimization. That, surely, is preferable to the present abysmal treatment of lesbian and gay people in Britain?

An Anti-Discrimination Act

A Bill of Rights would enable discriminatory legislation and court rulings to be contested and annulled. However, it could not be easily used to remedy instances of day-to-day discrimination against indivduals by other people and institutions (such as a hotel manager, employment agency, hospital nurse, or local authority). To enable individuals to remedy these forms of prejudice effectively and swiftly requires an Anti-Discrimination Act which is directly enforceable against all forms of unequal treatment, both *de jure* and *de facto*:

> It shall be unlawful to discriminate against a person, or group of persons,
> (a) in any circumstances whatsoever – including employment, partnership, housing, sexual offences, education, health care, censorship, political asylum, child custody, immigration, fostering and adoption, military service, donor insemination, government and judicial administration, and the provision of goods and services; and
> (b) on any grounds whatsoever – including sex, race, national or social origin, religion, language, political opinion or belief, age, sexual orientation, disability, HIV status, or other medical condition.

This Anti-Discrimination Act could usefully include a specific prohibition of incitement to hatred to give all peoples the same protection which is now, rather divisively, restricted to racial minorities.

> It shall be unlawful for any individual, organization or media to publicly and intentionally threaten or incite hatred against a person, or group of persons, on the grounds of their sex, race, national or social origin, religion, language, political opinion or belief, age, sexual orientation, disability, HIV status, or other medical condition.

These laws against discrimination and incitment to hatred are important not only because of the concrete and proactive legal powers they confer to fight unequal treatment, but also because of the egalitarian culture they help to legitimate and nurture. It is this indirect, diffuse cultural effect which is just as crucial for lesbians and gay men, since this ultimately helps to create a safe social space where homosexual people feel secure and free from the dread of victimization.

Legislation outlawing discrimination, including on the grounds of sexual orientation, already exists in Norway, France, Denmark, and Sweden, plus some of the states in Australia, the USA, and Canada. Similar all-inclusive statutes against incitement to hatred are currently enforced in Ireland, Norway, and Denmark. These initiatives don't, of course, guarantee absolute equality; but they do provide powerful mechanisms to tackle discrimination. These countries' achievements for their lesbian and gay citizens, partly due to anti-discrimination and anti-incitement to hatred laws, are infinitely preferable to the virtual 'homosexual rights-free zone' which exists in Britain.

The enactment of an Anti-Discrimination Act would have major implications for existing British legislation, particularly concerning key issues such as partnership and sexual offences. These would therefore need to be reformed simultaneously through a secondary Bill attached to the main anti-discrimination statute.

Danish-style civil marriage legislation for same-sex partners, which is discussed by Henning Bech in this book, may not be the best model to follow. Apart from the difficulty of getting exclusively lesbian and gay legislation through parliament, judging from the limited take-up rate of same-sex civil marriages in Denmark, this form of partnership recognition leaves unregistered lesbian and gay couples without any legal protection. It might therefore be more effective to aim for a comprehensive, sexuality-blind Co-Habitation Act which would ensure legal rights for all unmarried partners living togeher, regardless of their sex or sexuality. This legislative formula would cover both homosexual and heterosexual couples alike, and, therefore, be in everyone's interest:

> Any two people living together, tied by bonds of affection in a relationship resembling marriage, shall, irrespective of their gender or sexual orientation, be automatically entitled to legal recognition as partners and next-of-kin for the purposes of visiting rights to hospitals, schools, prisons, and similar institutions; taxation regulations and social security benefits; inheritance of wealth and property or tenancy in the event of a partner's death; the fostering or adoption of children; residence rights for a foreign partner of a British citizen; and access to all the benefits which are granted to married persons

244

and their spouses by employers, including maternity/paternity and compassionate leave and corporate perks and concessions.

Sexual offences laws would also require concomitant reform through a secondary bill linked to the primary anti-discrimination legislation. The best way to handle this would probably be through a complete overhaul of sexual offences laws. As well as introducing new statutes to cover the rape of a male and rape within marriage, this revision could include the repeal of all consensual offences and the removal of all references to gender and sexual orientation. Sexual offences law would thus make no mention of, or distinction between, male and female persons or between heterosexual and homosexual behaviour. The result would be to abolish discriminatory offences like 'indecency between men' and 'the procuration of homosexual acts'.

This overhaul of sexual offences law could also be an opportunity to equalize the age of consent at 16, and to introduce a policy of not prosecuting people aged 14 to 18 for sexual relations with 14- to 16-year-olds, unless there is a complaint from the persons involved. This would end the way the present law criminalizes tens of thousands of teenagers and it would bring our laws into line with progressive policies elsewhere in Europe.[5] The offence of sexual acts in non-private places could be revised so that a person would be liable to prosecution only if an identified member of the public witnessed explicit acts and was offended by them, thereby stopping the practice of bringing indecency charges against gay and bisexual men solely on the evidence of police officers, usually as a result of surveillance and entrapment operations. The soliciting and procuring laws – which criminalize men for 'cruising' and 'chatting up' other men in the street, and for aiding and abetting the commission of homosexual acts (even lawful ones) – ought to be repealed. Sexual relations involving members of the armed forces and the merchant navy could be decriminalized, providing they take place during off-duty hours in a person's private quarters or off-base/vessel. Such reforms might usefully go hand-in-hand with a sexual offences clause that specifically legalizes all sexual behaviour which is not explicitly declared unlawful. This would help restrict the opportunities for judges to interpret legislation and establish case law precedents in ways not intended by parliament. These radical reforms – focused on the principles that the law should not discriminate between heterosexual and homosexual acts and that consensual behaviour should not be a crime – are clearly in the interests of both gay and non-gay people. They therefore have the potential to mobilize support from a large and diverse cross-section of society in the name of non-discriminatory and non-judgemental sexual offences legislation.

A Department for Equal Opportunities

In addition to a Bill of Rights and an Anti-Discrimination Act, the third vital policy in a comprehensive equality agenda is a Department of Equal Opportunities. It's no good having the right policies unless there is also a mechanism for putting them into effect. That requires a powerful government department headed by a minister with cabinet rank and executive authority to monitor, promote, and enforce equality of access and opportunity for everyone. This must include the power to intervene proactively in all government departments, local authorities, and public and private sector enterprises. The Department's remit could include the setting of equality targets and equality codes of practice, and the requirement that all institutions compile annual equality audits and undertake equality impact assessments before new policies are finalized.

This 'all-in' approach of a Department for Equal Opportunities – which tackles every form of discrimination and implements equality initiatives for everyone – has the potential to unify diverse communities, encourage solidarity and evoke a sense of fairness and justice for all. In contrast, there is currently a great deal of pressure for an exclusive Department for Women, particularly from the Labour Party. Though well intentioned, this is an inherently discriminatory policy which prioritizes women's rights over the rights of other discriminated sectors of society such as black people and homosexual men and women. Indeed, it is a policy which is likely to breed resentment and tension from those it excludes. Equality is indivisible. Citizenship should be universal. Everyone suffering inequality has a right to expect that their inequalities will be tackled on an equal basis with the inequalities suffered by others. The idea that there are hierarchies of oppression – that some people's rights are more important than others and more worthy of redress – must be rejected. That is the kind of thinking that has led to the constant marginalization of lesbian and gay rights and the persistent de-prioritization of action against homophobia. It is an attitude steeped in the Orwellian nightmare of *Animal Farm*, where some are more equal than others. Women's rights are, of course, immensely important. However, they are no more, or no less, important than the rights of others. As lesbians and gay men, for example, we have a right to expect that the inequalities we experience are tackled on an equal basis with the inequalities experienced by others. The same applies to other highly discriminated sections of society such as ethnic minorities, young and elderly persons, the disabled, those with HIV, members of travelling communities, ex-offenders, and working-class people. All equally deserve respect, recognition and remedy.

By campaigning for lesbian and gay equality around a broad-based agenda of 'equal rights for all', we fight on the strongest possible ground with the best chance of success. Not only do we make it more difficult for our opponents to accuse us of special pleading, but we also raise consciousness, encourage solidarity, and mutually empower all disadvantaged and discriminated peoples. By so doing, we campaign for an equality agenda which benefits *everyone* suffering oppression and injustice.

NOTES

1 For details of how sexual offences law discriminates against gay and bisexual men, see my original research (Tatchell 1991, 1992). British law has never explicitly penalized lesbian behaviour, though lesbian women have occasionally been arrested under public order and morality laws.

2 The main discriminatory points of law concern sexual offences, employment, housing, immigration, military service, child adoption, and partnership (for an exposition of these, see Tatchell 1992). During the 1980s, there were five attempts, through Private Members' Bills and amendments to government legislation, to remedy inequalities faced by lesbians and gay men. All were overwhelmingly defeated.

3 The draft Homosexual Equality Bill is jointly sponsored by the Stonewall Group, Liberty, the Campaign for Homosexual Equality, and the Association of London Authorities. Copies are available from: Stonewall Group, 2 Greycoat Place, London SW1P 1SB (071-222 9007).

4 Article 1 of the Dutch constitution states: 'Discrimination on the grounds of religion, belief, political opinion, race or sex, or on any grounds whatsoever, shall not be permitted.' The words 'or on any grounds whatsoever' have been interpreted and accepted by parliament and the courts as prohibiting discrimination on the basis of sexual orientation. The European Convention on Human Rights (ECHR) was signed by the member states of the Council of Europe in 1950. The Council of Europe is separate from, and much larger than, the European Community. It brings together twenty-six European nations committed to strengthening parliamentary democracy and human rights. The principles of the ECHR are enforced by the Court of Human Rights in Strasbourg, which is empowered to order signatory states to remedy violations of the Convention. Council of Europe policy and ECHR rulings with respect to lesbian and gay rights are discussed in Tatchell (1992).

5 The age of consent for both heterosexuals and homosexuals is 14 in Italy and Albania; 15 in Sweden, Poland, France, Greece, Czechoslovakia, and Denmark; and 16 in the Netherlands, Spain, Belgium, Switzerland, Portugal, and Norway. In the Netherlands and Spain, sex involving 12- to 16-year olds is not prosecuted unless there is a complaint. The average age of consent in Europe is 16. For further details see Tatchell (1992).

A BRIEF GUIDE TO
FURTHER READING

The past twenty years has not only witnessed an enormous proliferation in the diversity of lesbian and gay experiences, it has also witnessed a substantial increase in writings which describe, analyse, theorize, and fictionalize these experiences. A rich, complex, and thoughtful literature has emerged as many fragments for a lesbian and gay studies. It would now be impossible to provide a truly comprehensive listing of these writings – even in the pages of a book-length bibliography (though there have been attempts). What follows therefore is a short selection of references with the limited goal of enabling the reader new to lesbian and gay studies to pursue general key sources, especially the social topics discussed in this volume.

INTRODUCING LESBIAN AND GAY STUDIES

In building a lesbian and gay studies there are a number of valuable bibliographic resources. See: Cal Gough and Ellen Greenblatt *Gay and Lesbian Library Service* (1990) McFarland & Co.; Wayne R. Dynes *Encyclopaedia of Homosexuality* (1990) Garland Press; Wayne R. Dynes *Homosexuality: A Research Guide* (1987) Garland; Robert Ridinger *The Homosexual and Society: An Annotated Bibliography* (1990) Greenwood; Dolores J. Maggiore *Lesbianism: An Annotated Bibliography and Guide to the Literature 1976–86* (1988) Scarecrow.

There are a number of earlier bibliographies. William Parker's *Homosexuality: A Selective Bibliography*, originally published in 1971, has gone through revisions (1985) Scarecrow Press; but Martin Weinberg and Alan Bell's *Homosexuality: An Annotated Bibliography* (1972) Harper & Row has not. There is a short 'Select Guide to Research' as Appendix Two of Ken Plummer's earlier edited collection *The Making of the Modern Homosexual* (1981) Hutchinson: all references here were published before 1980.

Two useful earlier edited collections of articles for a lesbian and gay studies are: Margaret Cruishank (ed.) *Lesbian Studies* (1982) The Feminist Press; Louie Crew (ed.) *The Gay Academic* (1978) ETC publication. A highly readable and well-referenced introduction to many issues is: Warren J. Blumenfeld and Diane Raymond *Looking at Gay and Lesbian Life* (1988) Beacon Press.

Two valuable articles which review the state of the field at the end of the 1980s (though overwhelmingly North American-based) are: Jeffrey Escoffier 'Inside the ivory closet' *Out/Look* (1990) no 10; Will Roscoe 'Making homosexuality: the challenge of a lesbian and gay studies' *Journal of Homosexuality* (1988) 15 (3): 1–40. See also the critical analysis in Diane Fuss's *Essentially Speaking* (1990) Routledge. For an introduction to some of the theoretical debates, see Edward Stein (ed.) *Forms of Desire* (1990) Garland; Lawrence Maas (ed.) *Dialogues of the Sexual Revolution* 2 volumes (1990) Haworth Press. Some of the papers of the major Amsterdam Conference on *Lesbian and Gay Studies*, held in 1987, are gathered in D. Altman *et al.* *Homosexuality, Which Homosexuality?* (1990) Gay Men's Press.

The crucial issue of homophobia and heterosexism is discussed in these classic sources: John DeCecco (ed.) *Bashers, Baiters and Bigots: Homophobia in American Society* (1985) Harrington Park Press; Suzanne Pharr *Homophobia: A Weapon of Sexism* (1988) Chardon Press; Adrienne Rich 'Compulsory heterosexuality and lesbian existence' in *Signs* (1980) 5 (4); George Weinberg *Society and the Healthy Homosexual* (1971/83) St Martin's Press.

On the new cultural studies, which emerged during the latter part of the 1980s, the key starting point is Michel Foucault's *The History of Sexuality* (1979) Penguin. See also Teressa de Lauretis 'Queer theory' (1991) *Differences* 3 (Summer); Jonathan Dollimore *Sexual Dissidence* (1991) Oxford; Diana Fuss (ed.) *Inside/Out: Lesbian Theories/Gay Theories* (1991) Routledge; Eve Kasofsky Sedgwick *Epistemology of the Closet* (1991) Harvester.

COMPARATIVE HOMOSEXUALITIES

The section in this book which examines Turkey and Mesoamerica signposts the increasing concern for homosexualities to be studied in a global and comparative perspective – anthropologically, historically, cross-culturally. The following are a few valuble starting points in comparative analysis: David Greenberg's *The Construction of Homosexuality* (1989) Chicago is the most comprehensive sociological introduction to this field, with a bibliographic source of 100 pages. Historically, the collection of readings contained in Martin Duberman, Martha Vicinus and George Chauncey Jr (eds) *Hidden from History* (1989) New American Library is most valuable for insights into a range of historical contrasts, and Evelyn Blackwood's *The Many Faces of Homosexuality: Anthropological Approaches to Homosexual Behaviour* (1986) Haworth Press does the same for anthropology. The 2nd *ILGA Pink Book* (Utrecht 1988) surveys law, life, and politics country by country round the world.

Specific studies that examine particular cultures and male homosexualities include: Stephen Murray *Oceanic Homosexualities* (1992) Haworth; Stephen Murray *Male Homosexuality in Central and Southern America* (1987) Gay Academic Union; Bret Hinsch *Passion of the Cut Sleeve: The Male Homosexual Tradition in China* (1990) University of California; Eric Allyn and John P. Collins *The Men of Thailand* (1991) Bua Lung; Joseph Carrier *Urban Mexican Male Homosexual Encounters* (1975) PhD Dissertation University of California Irvine; Fred Whitam *Male Homosexuality in Four Societies: Brazil, Guatemala, the Philippines and the US* (1986) Praeger; Richard Parker *Bodies, Pleasure and Passion: Sexual Culture in Contemporary Brazil* (1991) Beacon Press; Gary Kinsman *The Regulation of Desire: Sexuality in Canada* (1987) Black Rose Books.

On the Danish experience, see the theoretical work by Henning Bech *Nar maend modes: homoseksualiteten og de homoseksuelle* (translated as *When Men Meet: Homosexuality and the Homosexuals*) (1987) Gyldendal. See also the two volumes of life stories: Henning Bech *Mellem Maend (Among Men)* (1989) Tiderne Skifter; Karen Lutzen *At Prove Lykken* (*Try Your Luck*) (1988) Tideren Skifter.

Comparative study is also important within cultures. The North American situation provides a series of studies to suggest the dangers of incorporating contrasting cultures within a 'WASP' model. See:

Joseph Beam (ed.) *In the Life: A Black Gay Anthology* (1986) Alyson; Evelyn Beck *Nice Jewish Girls: A Lesbian Anthology* (1989) Beacon Press; Cherie Moraga and Gloria Anzaldua (eds) *This Bridge Called My Back* 2nd ed. (1984) Women of Color Press; Juanita Ramos (ed.) *Companeras, Latina Lesbians: An Anthology* (1988) Latina Lesbian Herstory Project; Will Roscoe (ed.) *Living the Spirit: A Gay American Indian Anthology* (1989) St Martin's Press; James T. Sears *Growing Up Gay in the South: Race, Gender and Journeys of the Spirit* (1990) Haworth Press; Ron Schow, Wayne Schow, and Marybeth Raynes *Peculiar People: Mormons and Same Sex Orientation* (1991) Signature Books; Carla Trujillo (ed.) *Chicana Lesbians: the Girls our Mothers Warned Us About* (1991) Third Woman Press; Mark Thompson *Gay Spirit: Myth and Meaning* (1987) St Martin's Press; Walter Williams *The Spirit and the Flesh* (1986) Beacon.

COMMUNITIES AND IDENTITIES

This has been the classic area of modern lesbian and gay studies, and it has produced a substantial literature. For some general reviews of the whole field, see: John De Cecco (ed.) *Bisexual and Homosexual Identities* (1984) Haworth Press; William DuBay *Gay Identity* (1987) McFarland & Co; John C. Gonsiorek and James Rudolph 'Homosexual identity: coming out and other developmental events', in J. Gonsiorek and J. Weinrich (eds) *Homosexuality* (1991) Sage pp.161–76; Richard Troiden *Gay and Lesbian Identity* (1988) General Hall.

On **gay identity and community**, see in particular Dennis Altman *The Americanization of the Homosexual, The Homosexualization of America* (1982) St Martin's Press; Joseph Harry and William DeVall *The Social Organization of Gay Males* (1978) Praeger; Gilbert Herdt (ed.) *Gay Culture in America* (1992) Basic; Martine Levine (ed.) *Gay Men* (1979) Harper & Row; Lon Nungesser *Homosexual Acts, Actors and Identities* (1983) Praeger; Kenneth Plummer

Sexual Stigma (1975) Routledge; Carol Warren *Identity and Community in the Gay World* (1974) Wiley; T.S. Weinberg *Gay Men, Gay Selves* (1983) Irvington.

On **lesbian identity and community**, see in particular Trudy Darter and Sandee Potter (eds) *Women-Identified Women* (1984) Mayfield; Betsy Ettore *Lesbians, Women and Society* (1980) Routledge; Barbara Gelpi (ed.) 'The lesbian issue' *Signs* (1984) 9: 553–791; Karla Jay and Joanne Glasgow (eds) *Lesbian Texts and Contexts: Radical Revisions* (1990) New York University Press; Celia Kitzinger *The Social Construction of Lesbianism* (1987) Sage; Susan Krieger *The Mirror Dance: Identity in a Women's Community* (1983) Temple University Press; Barbara Ponse *Identities in the Lesbian Community* (1978) Greenwood; Deborah Wolf *The Lesbian Community* (1980) University of California; Bonnie Zimmerman *The Safe Sea of Women* (1990) Beacon Press.

For key debates on the nature of identity, see: Steven Epstein 'Gay politics, ethnic identity: the limits of social constructionism' *Socialist Review* (1987) 17: 9–54; Ann Ferguson 'Is there a lesbian culture?', Ch. 7 of her *Sexual Democracy* (1991) Westview (and originally in Allen Jeffner (ed.) *Lesbian Philosophies and Cultures* (1990) State University of New York Press).

NEW RELATIONSHIPS AND THE FAMILY DEBATE

This is the area most likely, in this author's view, to become the 'hot research topic' of the 1990s. Already there are some important contributions. See: Kath Weston *Families We Choose: Lesbians, Gays, Kinship* (1991) Columbia University Press; Fredrick W. Bozett and Marvin B. Sussman (eds) *Homosexuality and Family Relations* (1990) Haworth Press; Frederick W. Bozett (ed.) *Homosexuality and the Family* (1989) Haworth Press; John de Cecco (ed.) *Gay Relationships* (1988) Haworth Press.

On more specific areas see:

Married homosexualities Jean Gochros *When Husbands Come Out of the Closet* (1989) Haworth Press; Michael Ross *The Married Homosexual Man* (1983) Routledge; Fred Klein and T.J. Wolf (eds) *Bisexualities* (1985) Haworth Press.

Lesbian mothering/gay parenting Bernice Goodman *The Lesbian: A Celebration of Difference* (1977) Out and Out Books; Gillian Hanscombe and Jackie Forster *Rocking the Cradle* (1981) Sheba; R. Barrett and R. Robinson *Gay Fathers* (1990) Lexington; Frederick Bozett *Gay and Lesbian Parents* (1987) Praeger; Joy Schulenburg *Gay Parenting: A Complete Guide for Lesbians and Gay Men with Children* (1985) Doubleday; Cheri Pies *Considering Parenthood* 2nd ed. (1988) Spinsters/Aunt Lute; Sandra Pollack and Jeanne Vaughn (eds) *Politics of the Heart: A Lesbian Parenting Anthology* (1987) Firebrand.

Couples Betty Berzon *Permanent Partners: Building Gay and Lesbian Relationships that Last* (1990) Dutton; J. Harry *Gay Couples* (1984) Praeger; D.P. McWhirter and A.M. Mattison *The Male Couple* (1984) Prentice-Hall; Donna M. Tanner *The Lesbian Couple* (1978) Lexington.

Young people, coming out and families Mary V. Borhek *Coming Out to Parents: A Two Way Survival Guide for Lesbians and Gay Men and their Parents* (1983) Pilgrim Press; Ann Muller *Parents Matter: Parents' Relationships with Lesbian Daughters and Gay Sons* (1987) Naiad; Carolyn Welch Griffin *et al. Beyond Acceptance: Parents of Lesbians and Gays Talk about their Experience* (1986) Prentice-Hall; Loralee MacPike's *There's Something I've Been Meaning to Tell You: An Anthology about Lesbians and Gay Men Coming Out to their Children* (1985) Naiad; Gilbert Herdt (ed.) *Gay and Lesbian Youth* (1989) Haworth Press; Ritch C. Savin Williams *Gay and Lesbian Youth: Expression of Identity* (1990) Hemisphere.

Friendships Janice Raymond *A Passion for Friends: Towards a Philosophy of Female Affection* (1986) Beacon Press. For two non-gay perspectives, see: Graham Allan *Friendship: Developing a Sociological Perspective* (1989) Westview; Lillian Rubin *Just Friends: The Role of Friendship in Our Lives* (1985) Harper & Row.

ON AIDS

The literature here is vast, as are the bibliographical resources available. Only a few sources will hence be listed – primarily of sociological interest. For a helpful guide to resources, which includes a 'bibliography of bibliographies' see: Ellen Greenblatt's 'AIDS information in libraries', Ch. 14 of Cal Gough and Ellen Greenblatt *Gay and Lesbian Library Service* (1990) McFarland, along with Appendices XIII and XIV. See also: Virginia A. Lingle and M. Sandra Wood *How to Find Information about AIDS* (1988) Haworth Press.

Some of the many social discussions include:
Erica Carter and Simon Watney (eds) *Taking Liberties: AIDS and Cultural Politics* (1989) Serpent's Tail; Douglas Crimp (ed.) *AIDS: Cultural Analysis, Cultural Activism* (1988) MIT Press; Peter Aggleton, Graham Hart and Peter Davies (eds) *AIDS, Social Representations, Social Practices* (1989) Falmer; Cindy Patton *Inventing AIDS* (1990) Routledge; Joan Huber and Beth Schneider (eds) *Social Contexts of AIDS* (1992) Sage.

ON SEXUALITIES

For the debate on lesbian sexuality, see: Sheila Jeffreys *Anticlimax* (1990) Virago; Feminist Review *Perverse Politics: Lesbian Issues* (1990) 34; Pat Califia *Sapphistry: the Book of Lesbian Sexuality* 3rd ed. (1988) Naiad; JoAnn Loulan *Lesbian Passion: Loving Ourselves and Each Other* (1987) Spinsters/Aunt Lute; Judith Roof *A Lure of Knowledge: Lesbian Sexuality and Theory* (1991) Columbia University Press; Joan Nestle *A Restricted Country* (1987) Firebrand Books.

On gay male sex, see: Charles Silverstein and Edmund White *The Joy of Gay Sex* 2nd ed. (1986) Pocket Books; Mark Thompson (ed.) *Leatherfolk: Radical Sex, People, Politics and Practice* (1991) Alyson.

THE POLITICS OF HOMOSEXUALITY

The clearest and briefest introductions to the politics of the gay and lesbian movements are: Barry Adam *The Rise of a Lesbian and Gay Movement* (1987) Twayne; John D'Emilio *Sexual Politics, Sexual Communities* (1983) University of Chicago Press; Toby Marotta *The Politics of Homosexuality* (1981) Houghton Mifflin; Jeffrey Weeks *Coming Out* 2nd ed. (1990) Quartet.

Among the classic early statements are: Dennis Altman *Homosexual Oppression and Liberation* (1971) Outerbridge & Dienstfrey; Sidney Abbott and Barbara Love *Sappho was a Right-On Woman* (1972) Stein & Day. See also: Simon Shepherd and Mick Wallis (eds) *Coming On Strong* (1989) Hyman; Jeffrey Weeks *Sexuality and its Discontents* (1985) Routledge; Jeffrey Weeks *Against Nature; Essays on History, Sexuality and Identity* (1991) Rivers Oram Press; Shane Phelan *Identity Politics: Lesbian Feminism and the Limits of Community* (1989) Temple; Mariana Valverde *Sex, Power and Pleasure* (1985) The Women's Press; Alan Berube and Jeff Escoffier *et al.* 'Queer/Nation' *Out/Look* (1991) 11 (Winter); Joshua Gamson 'Silence, death and the invisible enemy: AIDS activism and social movement "Newness"' in M. Buraway *et al.* (eds) *Ethnography Unbound: Power and Resistance in the Modern Metropolis* (1991) University of California Press; Carole Vance (ed.) *Pleasure and Danger* (1984) Routledge; Carol Anne Douglas *Love and Politics: Radical Feminist and Lesbian Theories* (1990) Ism Press.

On the European and UK background, see: Peter Tatchell *Europe in the Pink: Lesbian and Gay Equality in the New Europe* (1991) Gay Men's Press; M. Colvin and J. Hawksley *Section 28: A Practical Guide to the Law and its Implications* (1989) National Council for Civil Liberties, London.

BIBLIOGRAPHY

Abercrombie, N. *et al.* (1980) *The Dominant Ideology Thesis*, London: Allen & Unwin.

Adair, N. (1978) *Word is Out*, San Francisco: New Glide Publications.

Adam, B. (1978) *The Survival of Domination*, New York: Elsevier/Greenwood.

Adam, B. (1987) *The Rise of a Gay and Lesbian Movement*, Boston, MA: G.K. Hall.

Adam, B. (1989) 'The state, public policy, and AIDS discourse', *Contemporary Crisis* 13: 1–14.

Aggleton, P. and Homans, H. (eds) (1988) *Social Aspects of AIDS*, London: Falmer.

Aggleton, P., Hart, G., and Davies, P. (eds) (1989) *AIDS, Social Representations, Social Practices*, London: Falmer.

Alcorn, K. (1991) 'Mediactive', *The Pink Paper* 4: 23 February.

Allan, G. (1989) *Friendship: Developing a Sociological Perspective*, Boulder, CO: Westview.

Allen, J. (ed.) (1990) *Lesbian Philosophies and Cultures*, Albany, NY: State University of New York Press.

Allyn, E. (1990) *An Interview with 'Uncle' Goh Bhaknam*, Bangkok: Bua Luang.

Allyn, E. and Collins, J.P. (1988, 1991) *The Men of Thailand: Noom Thai*, Bangkok: Bua Luang.

Altman, D. (1971) *Homosexual: Liberation & Oppression*, New York: Outerbridge & Dienstfrey (1974: Allen Lane).

Altman, D. (1982a) *The Homosexualization of America*, New York: St Martin's Press.

Altman, D. (1982b) 'What changed in the seventies?', in Gay Left Collective (eds) *Homosexuality: Power & Politics*, London: Allison & Busby.

Altman, D. (1986) *Aids and the New Puritanism*, London: Pluto.

Altman, D. (1987) 'What price gay nationalism?, in M. Thompson (ed.) *Gay Spirit: Myth and Meaning*, New York: St Martin's Press.

Altman, D. (1988) 'Legitimation through disaster', in E. Fee and D. Fox (eds) *AIDS: The Burdens of History*, Berkeley, CA: University of California Press.

Altman, D. *et al.* (eds) (1989) *Which Homosexuality?*, London: Gay Men's Press.

Andrews, G. (ed.) (1991) *Citizenship*, London: Lawrence & Wishart.

Annetts, J. (1990) 'The politics of AIDS: the Moral Right in perspective' (unpublished undergraduate dissertation, Reading University).

Arterburn, J. (1988) *How Will I Tell My Mother?*, New York: Oliver Nelson.

Atkinson, T. G. (1974) *Amazon Odyssey*, New York: Links Books.

Axgil, A. and Fogedgaard, H. (1985) *Homofile kampr: Bÿsseliv gennem tiderne (Years of Homophile Struggle: Gay Life Through the Ages)* Rudkobing (Denmark): Grafolio.

Baetz, J. (1980) *Lesbian Crossroads: Personal Stories of Lesbian Struggles & Triumphs*, New York: William Morrow.

Banks, O. (1981) *Faces of Feminism*, Oxford: Martin Robertson.

Barnhart, E. (1975) 'Friends and lovers in a lesbian counterculture community', in N. Glazer Malbin (ed.) *Old Family/New Family*, New York: Van Nostrand.

Bech, H. (1987) *Nr mnd mÿdes: Homoseksualiteten og de homoseksuelle (When Men Meet: Homosexuality and the Homosexuals)* Copenhagen: Gyldendal.

Bech, H. (1989a) '"Homoseksualitetet". En presentation og diskussion af postionerne i den aktuelle videnskabelige strid: "essentialisme" versus "konstruktionisme"', ('"Homosexuality". A presentation and discussion of the positions in the ongoing scholarly debate: "essentialism" versus "constructionism"'), *Nordisk Sexologi* 7 (2–3): 129–42.

Bech, H. (1989b) *Mellem mnd: 20 livshistorier (Among Men: 20 Life Stories)* Copenhagen: Tiderne Skifter.

Bech, H. (1989c) 'Vetenskabsteoretiska och metodiska problem i homosexualitetsforskningen samt framtida forskning om homosexualitet – teman og metoder' ('Epistemological and methodological problems in research on homosexuality and future research on homosexuality – themes and methods'), in *Homosexuell forskning: Seminarium arrangerat av socialstyrelsen*, Stockholm: Socialstyrelsen.

Bech, H. (1991) 'Recht fertigen: über die Einfhrung homosexueller Ehen in Denmark' (working title), *Zeitschrift für Sexualforschung* (FRG) 4 (3) forthcoming.

Bech, H. and Lützen, K. (1986) *Lyst eller nÿd? Kvinders og mnds homoseksualitet. Redegorelse fra kommissionen til belysning af homoseksuelles situation in samfundet* (Pleasure or Compulsion? Women's and Men's Homosexuality. Report from the Minister of Justice's Committee for the Elucidation of the Situation of Homosexuals in Society), Copenhagen: Justitsministeriet.

Becker, H. (1963) *Outsiders*, New York: Free Press.

Bell, A.P. and Weinberg, M.S. (1978) *Homosexualities: A Study of Diversity among Men and Women*, London: Mitchell Beazley.

Benjamin, W. (1973) 'The work of art in the age of mechanical reproduction', in *Illuminations*, London: Fontana. (German original published in 1937.)

Benjamin, W. (1982) *Das passagen-Werk* Vols I–II, Frankfurt am Main: Suhrkamp. (Originally written c. 1927–40.)

Ben-Yehuda, N. (1985) *Deviance and Moral Boundaries*, Chicago: University of Chicago Press.

Ben-Yehuda, N. (1985) 'The sociology of moral panics: towards a new synthesis', *Sociological Quarterly* 27 (4).

Ben-Yehuda, N. (1990) *The Politics and Morality of Deviance*, Albany, NY: SUNY.

Berman, M. (1982) *All that is Solid Melts into Air: The Experience of Modernity*, New York: Simon & Schuster.

Bérubé, A. and Escoffier, J., *et al.* (1991) 'Queer/Nation', *Out/Look* 11 Winter.

Beshtain, J.B. (1982/3) 'Homosexual politics: the paradox of gay liberation', *Salmagundi* 58–9: 252–87.

Bittner, E. (1963) 'Radicalism and the organization of radical movements', *American Sociological Review* 28: 928–40.

Blackwood, E. (ed.) (1986) *The Many Faces of Homosexuality: Anthropological Approaches to Homosexual Behaviour*, New York: Harrington Park Press.

Blumstein, P. and Schwartz, P. (1983) *American Couples*, New York: William Morrow.

Boffin, T. and Gupta, S. (eds) (1990) *Ecstatic Antibodies: Resisting the AIDS Mythology*, London: Rivers Oram Press.

Bolak, H. (1990) 'Aile ici kadin erkek ilisklerinin cok boyutlu kavramlastirilmasina yonelik oneriler', in S. Tekeli (ed.) *Kadin Bakis Acisindan 1980' ler Turkiye' sinde Kadin*, Istanbul: Iletisim Yayincilik.

Boone, J. and Cadden, M. (eds) (1991) *Engendering Men: the Question of Male Feminist Criticism*, London: Routledge.

Boston Lesbian Psychologies Collective (ed.) (1987) *Lesbian Psychologies*, Chicago: University of Illinois Press.

Bouchier, D. (1983) *The Feminist Challenge*, London: Macmillan.

Bouhdiba, A. (1985) *Sexuality in Islam*, London: Routledge.

Bowles, G. and Klein, R.D. (1983) *Theories of Women's Studies*, London: Routledge & Kegan Paul

Bozett, F.W. (ed.) (1987) *Gay and Lesbian Parents*, New York: Praeger.

Bozett, F.W. (ed.) (1989) *Homosexuality and the Family*, New York; Haworth Press (and the *Journal of Homosexuality* 18 (1/2)).

Bradbury, M. (1988) *The Modern World*, London: Secker & Warburg.

Bray, A. (1982) *Homosexuality in Renaissance England*, London: Gay Men's Press.

Bright, S. (1988) (ed.) *Herotica*, California: Down There Press.

Brittan, A. (1989) *Masculinity and Power*, Oxford: Basil Blackwell.

Bronski, M. (1984) *Culture Clash*, Boston, MA: South End Press.

Bruce, S. (1988) *The Rise and Fall of the New Christian Right*, Oxford: Oxford University Press.

Butler, J. (1990) *Gender Trouble: Feminism and the Subversion of Identity*, London: Routledge.

Butters, R., Clum, J.M., and Moon, M. (eds) (1990) *Displacing Homophobia: Gay Male Perspectives in Literature and Culture*, Durham: Duke University Press.

Byron, P. (1985) 'What we talk about when we talk about dildos', *The Voice* 5 March.

Califia, P. (1979) 'A secret side of lesbian sexuality', *The Advocate* 27 December.

Califia, P. (1980) *Sapphistry: The Book of Lesbian Sexuality* (3rd edition 1988), Florida: Naiad.

Califia, P. (1981) 'Feminism and sadomasochism', *Heresies* 3, 4 (12): 30–4.

Califia, P. (1988) *Macho Sluts*, Boston MA: Alyson.

Campbell, B. (1980) 'A feminist sexual politics: now you see it, now you don't', *Feminist Review* 5: 1–18.

Carr, A. (1989) 'Gay men's relationships and unsafe sex', *National AIDS Bulletin*, 3 (5), June 27–31, and 56, AFAO, Canberra.

Carrier, J.M. (1975) *Urban Mexican Male Homosexual Encounters*, PhD dissertation, University of California, Irvine.

Carrier, J.M. (1976) 'Family attitudes and Mexican male homosexuality', in C. Warren (ed.) (1976) *Sexuality*, London: Sage.

Carrier, J.M. (1989a) 'Sexual behaviour and the spread of AIDS in Mexico', *Medical Anthropology* 10: 129–42.

Carrier, J.M. (1989b) 'Gay liberation and coming out in Mexico', *Journal of Homosexuality* 17 (3/4).

Carro, J.L. (1989) 'From constitutional psychopathic inferiority to AIDS: what is the future for homosexual aliens? Overview: domestic implications of immigration policy', *Yale Law and Policy Review* 7 Fall–Winter (end): 201–28.

Carter, E. and Watney, S. (eds) (1989) *Taking Liberties*, London: Serpent's Tail.

Cass, V.C. (1979) 'Homosexual identity formation: a theoretical model', *Journal of Homosexuality* 4 (3): 219–35.

Cass, V. C. (1984) 'Homosexual identity formation: testing a theoretical model', *Journal of Sexual Research* 20: 143–67.

Castells, M. (1983) 'Cultural identity, sexual liberation and urban structure', in *The City*, London: Edward Arnold, Ch. 14.

Chester, G. and Dickey, J. (1988) *Feminism and Censorship*, Dorset: Prism.

Chirimuuta, R. and Chirimuuta, R. (1989) *AIDS, Africa and Racism*, London: Free Association Books.

Cohen, J.L. (1985) 'Strategy or identity: new theoretical paradigms and contemporary social movements', *Social Research* 52 (4): 663–716.

Cohen, S. (1973) *Folk Devils and Moral Panics*, London: Paladin.

Coleman, E. (1982) 'Developmental stages of the coming out process', in W. Paul *et al.* (eds) *Homosexuality: Psychological, Sociological and Biological Issues*, London: Sage; also *Journal of Homosexuality* 7 (2/3): 31–43.

Collier, C. (1987) *The Twentieth Century Plague*, Tring, Herts: Lion.

Colvin, M. and Hawksley, J. (1989) *Section 28: A Practical Guide to the Law and its Implications*, London: National Council for Civil Liberties.

(Comm. Rep) (1988) *Homoseksuelles vilkr: Betnkning fra kommissionen til belynsing af homseksuelles situation i samfundset (The Situation of Homosexuals: Report by the Committee for the Elucidation of the Situation of Homosexuals in Society)* Copenhagen: Justitsministeriet.

Connolly, W. (1991) *Identity/Difference*, New York: Cornell University Press.

Cook, B.W. (1979) 'Women alone stiff my imagination: lesbianism and the cultural tradition', *Signs: Journal of Women in Culture and Society* 5: 718–39.

Cory, D.W. (1965) *Lesbianism in America*, New York: MacFadden.

Coveney, L., Jackson, M., Jeffreys, S., Kaye, L., and Mayony, P. (1984) *The Sexuality Papers*, London: Hutchinson.

Covina, G. and Galana, L. (eds) (1975) *The Lesbian Reader*, Oakland, CA: Amazon Press.

Coyle, A.C. (1991) *The Construction of Gay Identity*, (unpublished) PhD thesis, University of Surrey.

Crimp, D. (ed.) (1988) *AIDS, Cultural Analysis, Cultural Activism*, Cambridge, MA: MIT Press.

Cruikshank, M. (1980) *The Lesbian Path*, Tallahassee, FL: Naiad.

Daly, M. (1978) *Gyn/Ecology: The Metaethics of Radical Feminism*, Boston, MA: Beacon.

Dank, B. (1971) 'Coming out in the gay world', *Psychiatry* 34: 180–97.

Darty, T. and Potter, S. (eds) (1984) *Women-Identified Women*, Palo Alto, CA: Mayfield.

Davies, P.M. (1984) *The Control of Disclosure: A Sociological Study of Networks and Gay Identity*, (unpublished) PhD thesis, University of Wales.

Davis, M. and Kennedy, E.L. (1986) 'Oral history and the study of lesbian sexuality in the lesbian community: Buffalo, New York, 1940–1960', *Feminist Studies* 12 (1): 7–26.

Davis, M. and Kennedy, E.L. (1987) 'The reproduction of butch-fem roles: a social constructionist approach', in *Conference Papers: Homosexuality, Which Homosexuality?* Amsterdam: Vrije Universiteit, pp. 187–201.

De Cecco, J. (ed.) (1988) *Gay Relationships*, New York: Harrington Park Press.

De Lauretis, T. (ed.) (1991) 'Queer theory: lesbian and gay sexualities', *Differences* 3 (2).

D'Emilio, J. (1983) *Sexual Politics, Sexual Communities: The Making of a Homosexual Minority in the United States*, Chicago: University of Chicago Press.

D'Emilio, J. and Freedman, E. (1988) *Intimate Matters: A History of Sexuality in America*, New York: Harper & Row.

Department of Immigration and Ethnic Affairs (now and Local Government) (1983) Internal Submission to the Minister 1983, Immigration Policy and Secretariat Division, Canberra.

Department of Immigration and Ethnic Affairs (1984) *Australian Population and Immigration Research Program, Family Reunion Study*, AGPS Canberra.

DiLapi, E. (1989) 'Lesbian mothers and the motherhood hierarchy', *Journal of Homosexuality* 18 (1/2): 101–21.

Dixon, P. (1987) *The Truth About AIDS*, Eastbourne, Sussex: Kingsway.

Dollimore, J. (1991) *Sexual Dissidence: Augustine to Wilde, Freud to Foucault*, Oxford: Oxford University Press.

Douglas, C.A. (1990) *Love and Politics: Radical Feminist and Lesbian Theories*, San Francisco: ISM Press.

Duberman, M., Vicinus, M., and Chauncey Jr., G. (eds) (1989) *Hidden From History: Reclaiming their Gay and Lesbian Past*, New York: Penguin.

Duffy, S.M. and Rusbult, C.E. (1986) 'Satisfaction and commitment in homosexual and heterosexual relationships', *Journal of Homosexuality* 12 (2): 1–23.

Duggan, L. (1984) 'Censorship in the name of feminism', *The Village Voice* October.

Duggan, L. *et al.* (1985) 'False promises: feminist anti-pornography legislation in the US', in V. Burstyn (ed.) *Feminists against Censorship*, Toronto: Douglas & McIntyre.

Dundes, A., Leach, J.W., and Özkök, B. (1970) 'The strategy of Turkish boys' verbal duelling rhymes', *Journal of American Folklore* 83: 329.

Dworkin, A. (1989) (ed.) *Pornography: Men Possessing Women*, New York: Dutton.

Dyer, R. (1991) *Now You See It*, London: Routledge.

Echols, A. (1989) *Daring to be Bad: Radical Feminism in America 1967–1975*, Minneapolis: Minnesota Press.

Edwards, T. (1991) *The AIDS Dialectics*, PhD thesis, Department of Sociology: University of Essex.

Ehrenreich, B., Hess, E., and Jacobs, G. (1987) *Re-making Love: The Feminization of Sex*, London: Fontana.

Emerson, J.P. (1970) 'Nothing unusual is happening', in T. Shibutani (ed.) *Human Nature and Collective Behaviour*, Englewood Cliffs, NJ: Prentice-Hall.

Epstein, S. (1987) 'Gay politics, ethnic identity: the limits of social constructionism', *Socialist Review* 17: 9–54.

Epstein, S. (1988) 'Nature vs. nurture and the politics of AIDS organizing', *Out/Look* 1 (3): 46–50.

Escoffier, J. (1989) 'Can gay men and lesbians work together', *Out/Look* 2 (2) (Fall).

Escoffier, J. (1990) 'Inside the ivory closet', *Out/Look*, Fall.

Ettore, E.M. (1980) *Lesbians, Women & Society*, London: Routledge & Kegan Paul.

Faderman, L. (1981) *Surpassing the Love of Men: Romantic Friendships Between Women from the Renaissance to the Present*, London: Junction Books.

Faderman, L. (1986) 'Love between women in 1928: why progressivism is not always progress', *Journal of Homosexuality* 12 (3/4): 23–42.

Faderman, L. (1991) *Odd Girls and Twilight Lovers: A History of Lesbian Life in Twentieth-century America*, New York: University of Columbia Press.

Faraday, A. (1981) 'Liberating lesbian research', in K. Plummer (ed.) *The Making of the Modern Homosexual*, London: Hutchinson.

Featherstone, M. (1991) *Consumer Culture and Postmodernism*, London: Sage.

Feminist Review (1990) 'Perverse politics', Lesbian Issue 34.

Ferguson, A. (1989) *Blood at the Root: Motherhood, Sexuality and Male Dominance*, London: Pandora.

Ferguson, A. (1990) 'Is there a lesbian culture?', in J. Allen (ed.) *Lesbian Philosophies and Cultures*, New York: State University of New York Press.

Ferguson, A. (1991) *Sexual Democracy*, Oxford: Westview.

Ferguson, R., Gever, M., Minh-ha, T., and West, C. (1990) *Out There: Marginalization and Contemporary Cultures*, London: MIT Press.

Fernbach, D. (1981) *The Spiral Path: A Gay Contribution to Human Survival*, London: Gay Men's Press.

Fiske, J. (1987) *Television Culture*, London: Routledge.

Foucault, M. (1977) *Discipline and Punish: The Birth of the Prison*, Harmondsworth, Middx: Penguin. (French original published in 1975.)

Foucault, M. (1979) *The History of Sexuality*, Vol. 1, London: Allen Lane.

Fraser, N. (1990) 'Talking about needs: interpretive contests as political conflicts in welfare state societies', in C. Sunstein (ed.) (1990) *Feminism and Political Theory*, Chicago: University of Chicago Press, pp. 159–84.

Freedman, M. (1975) 'Homosexuals may be healthier than straights', *Psychology Today* March: 28–32.

French, M. (1990) *Changing Partners: Gays, Lesbians and Heterosexual Marriages*, (unpublished) MPhil. thesis, University of Essex.

Frye, M. (1983) *The Politics of Reality*, New York: The Crossing Press.

Frye, M. (1990) 'Lesbian "sex"', in J. Allen (ed.) *Lesbian Philosophies and Cultures*, New York: State University of New York Press.

Fuss, D. (1990) *Essentially Speaking*, London: Routledge.

Fuss, D. (ed.) (1991) *Inside/Out: Lesbian Theories/Gay Theories*, London: Routledge.

Gage, S. (1986) 'Lesbians, AIDS and safe sex', *Lesbian News* May: 50–1.

Gagnon, J.H. and Simon, W.S. (1973) *Sexual Conduct: The Social Sources of Human Sexuality*, Chicago: Aldine.

Gamson, J. (1989) 'Silence, death and the invisible enemy: AIDS activism and social movement "Newness"', *Social Problems* 36 (4) October.

Gay Community News (1989) 'Literary activist Joseph Beam dies at 33', 8–12 January: 1.

Gay Left Collective (1980) *Homosexuality: Power and Politics*, London: Allison & Busby.

Gergen, K.J. (1991) *The Saturated Self: Dilemmas of Identity in Contemporary Life*, New York: Basic Books.

Giddens, A. (1990) *The Consequences of Modernity*, Oxford: Polity Press.

Giddens, A. (1991) *Modernity and Self-Identity*, Oxford: Polity Press.

Gilroy, P. (1987) *There Ain't No Black in the Union Jack*, London: Hutchinson.

Gochros, J.S. (1989) *When Husbands Come Out of the Closet*, New York: Haworth Press.

Goffman, E. (1970) *Stigma: Notes on the Management of Spoiled Identity*, Harmondsworth, Middx: Penguin.

Gonsiorek, J.C. and Weinrich, J.D. (eds) (1991) *Homosexuality: Research Implications for Public Policy*, London: Sage.

Goodman, B. (1977) *The Lesbian: A Celebration of Difference*, New York: Out & Out Books.

Goodman, N. (1978) *Ways of World Making*, Indianapolis: Hacket Publishing.

Gordon, L. and Dubois, E. (1984) 'Seeking ecstasy on the battlefield: danger and pleasure in nineteenth-century feminist thought', in C.S. Vance (ed.) *Pleasure and Danger*, London: Routledge & Kegan Paul.

Gough, C. and Greenblatt, E. (1990) *Gay and Lesbian Library Service*, Jefferson, NC: McFarland.

Grahn, J. (1984) *Another Mother Tongue: Gay Words, Gay Worlds*, Boston, MA: Beacon.

Grammick, J. (1984) 'Developing a lesbian identity', in T. Darty and S. Potter (eds) *Women-Identified Women*, Palo Alto, CA: Mayfield.

Greenberg, D.F. (1988) *The Construction of Homosexuality*, Chicago: University of Chicago Press.

Habermas, J. (1984/1989) *The Theory of Communicative Action* Vols. I (1984) and II (1989), London: Heinemann. (German original published in 1981.)

Habermas, J. (1989) *The Structural Transformation of the Public Sphere: An Inquiry into a Category of Bourgeois Society*, Oxford: Polity Press. (German original published in 1962.)

BIBLIOGRAPHY

Hacettepe Institute of Population Studies (1989) *1988 Turkish Population and Health Survey*, Ankara: Hacettepe University Publication

Hall Carpenter Archives (1989a) *Inventing Ourselves: Lesbian Life Stories*, London: Routledge.

Hall Carpenter Archives (1989b) *Walking After Midnight: Gay Men's Life Stories*, London: Routledge.

Hall, S. (1988) *The Hard Road to Renewal*, London: Verso.

Hall, S. (1991) 'Ethnicity: identity and difference', *Radical America* 23 (4): 9–22.

Hall, S. *et al.* (1978) *Policing the Crisis: Mugging, the State, and Law and Order*, London: Macmillan.

Halperin, D. (1990) *One Hundred Years of Homosexuality*, London: Routledge.

Hammond, D. and Jablow, A. (1987) 'Gilgamesh and the Sundance Kid: the myth of male friendship', in H. Brod (ed.) *The Making of Masculinities: The New Men's Studies*, Boston, MA: Allen & Unwin, pp. 241–58.

Hanley-Hackenbruck, P. (1989) 'Psychotherapy and the "coming out" process', *Journal of Gay and Lesbian Psychotherapy* 1 (1): 21–40.

Hanmer, J. (1990) 'Men, power and the exploitation of women', in J. Hearn and D. Morgan (eds) (1990) *Men, Masculinities and Social Theory*, London: Unwin Hyman.

Hanscombe, G. and Forster, J. (1981) *Lesbian Mothers: A Challenge in Family Living*, London: Sheba.

Harding, S. (1986) *The Science Question in Feminism*, Milton Keynes: Open University Press.

Hart, J. and Richardson, D. (eds) (1981) *The Theory and Practice of Homosexuality*, London: Routledge & Kegan Paul.

Havelin, A. (1968) 'Almenhetens holdninger til homofile og homoseksualitet' ('Public attitudes to homophiles and homosexuality') *Tidsskrift for samfunnsforskning* (Norway) 9 (1): 42–74.

Hearn, J. (1987) *The Gender of Oppression: Men, Masculinity and the Critique of Marxism*, Brighton, Sussex: Wheatsheaf.

Hemmelstein, J. (1983) 'The New Right', in R. Liebman and R. Wutnow (eds) *The New Christian Right*, New York: Aldine.

Hemmings, S. (1980) 'Horrific practices: how lesbians are presented in the newspapers of 1978', in Gay Left Collective (eds) *Homosexuality: Power and Politics*, London: Allison & Busby, pp. 157–71.

Hencken, J.D. (1984) 'Conceptualisations of homosexual behavior which preclude homosexual self-labelling', in J. De Cecco (ed.) *Bisexual and Homosexual Identities*, New York: Howarth Press.

Henriksson, B. (1991) 'Sexual identity, Aids and the Moral Left', paper given at international conference on 'Social Aspects of Aids', London, May (Stockholm Institute of Social Studies).

Herdt, G.H. (1981) *Guardians of the Flute*, New York: McGraw Hill.

Herdt, G.H. (1984) *Ritualized Homosexuality in Melanesia*, Berkeley, CA: University of California Press.

Herdt, G. (ed.) (1989) *Gay and Lesbian Youth*, New York: Haworth Press.

Herdt, G. *et al.* (eds) (1992) *Gay Culture in America*, New York: Basic.

Hertoft, P. (1985) 'Homoseksualitet er ingen sygdom' ('Homosexuality is not an illness') *Politiken* (Denmark) 27 October.

Hess, B. (1972) 'Friendship', in M. Riley, M. Johnson, and A. Foner (eds) *Ageing and Society*, Vol. 3: *A Sociology of Age Stratification*, New York: Russell Sage, pp. 357–93.

Hinsch, B. (1990) *Passions of the Cut Sleeve: The Male Homosexual Tradition in China*,

261

Berkeley, CA: University of California Press.
Hirdman, Y. (1990) *'Att lgga livet til rtta': Studier i svensk folkhemspolitik ('To Put Life in Order': Studies in Swedish 'Folkhem' Politics*), Stockholm: Carlson.
Hite, S. (1976) *The Hite Report*, New York: Macmillan.
Hite, S. (1987) *Women and Love*, New York: Alfred A. Knopf.
Hoagland, S.L. (1988) *Lesbian Ethics: Towards New Values*, Palo Alto, CA: Institute of Lesbian Studies.
Hocquenghem, G. (1978) *Homosexual Desire*, London: Allison & Busby.
Holleran, A. (1988) *Ground Zero*, New York: Morrow.
Hooker, E. (1961) 'The homosexual community', *Proceedings of the XLVth International Congress of Applied Psychology*, Copenhagen.
Hughes, R. (1988) *The Fatal Shore*, London: Pan.
Humphreys, L. (1971) *Tea Room Trade*, London: Duckworth (2nd edition 1975).
Hunt, M. (1975) *Sexual Behaviour in the 1970s*, New York: Dell.
Hunter, J.D. (1983) 'The Liberal reaction', in R. Liebman and R. Wuthnow (eds) *The New Christian Right*, New York: Aldine.
Irving, J. (1990) *Disorders of Desire*, Philadelphia: Temple University Press.
Jackson, P.A. (1989) *Male Homosexuality in Thailand*, Amsterdam: Global Academic Publishers.
Japenga, A. (1986) 'Gay women and the risk of AIDS', *Los Angeles Times* 2 April.
Jay, K. and Glasgow, J. (eds) (1990) *Lesbian Texts and Contexts: Radical Revisions*, New York: New York University Press.
Jeffreys, S. (1984) 'Does it matter if they did it?', *Trouble and Strife* 3: 25–9.
Jeffreys, S. (1989) 'Does it matter if they did it?', in *Not a Passing Phase: Reclaiming Lesbians in History 1840–1985*, Lesbian History Group, London: The Women's Press, pp. 19–28.
Jeffreys, S. (1990) *Anticlimax*, London: The Women's Press.
Jenness, V. (1987) *It's all a State of Mind: Social Categories, Constructed Conceptions, and Lesbian Identities*, (unpublished) Masters thesis, University of California, Santa Barbara.
Jerome, D. (1984) 'Good company: the sociological implications of friendship', *Sociological Review* 32 (4): 696–718.
Johnston, J. (1973) *Lesbian Nation*, New York: Simon & Schuster/Touchstone.
Jones, C. (1985) 'Motherlines', *Coming Up* 7 November.
Kağıtçıbaşı, C. (1982) 'Sex roles, value of children and fertility', in C. Kağıtçıbaşi (ed.) *Sex Roles, Family and Community in Turkey*, Bloomington, IN: Indiana University Press.
Kandiyoti, D. (1977) 'Sex roles and social change: comparative appraisal of Turkey's women', *Signs* 3 (1).
Kandiyoti, D. (1982) 'Urban changtes and women's roles in Turkey: an overview and evaluation', in C. Kağitçibaşi (ed.) *Sex Roles, Family and Community in Turkey*, Bloomington, IN: Indiana University Press.
Karmen, A. (1990) *Crime Victims*, Pacific Grove, CA: Brooks/Cole.
Katz, J. (1976) *Gay American History*, New York: Thomas Y. Crowell.
Katz, J. (1983) *Gay/Lesbian Almanac: A New Documentary*, New York: Harper & Row.
Katz, J. (1990) 'The invention of heterosexuality', *Socialist Review* 21: 1.
Khan, B. (1990) 'Not-so-gay life in Karachi', *SOLGA Newsletter* 12 (1): 10–19.
Kiecolt-Glaser, J. and Glaser, R. (1988) 'Psychological influences on immunity: implications for AIDS', *American Psychologist* 43 (11): 892–8.
Kinsey, A.C., Pomeroy, W.B., and Martin, C.E. (1948) *Sexual Behaviour in the Human Male*, Philadelphia, PA: Saunders.
Kinsey, A.C., Pomeroy, W.D., Martin, C.E., and Gebhard, P.H. (1953) *Sexual*

Behaviour in the Human Female, Philadelphia, PA: Saunders

Kiray, M. (1976) 'Changing roles of mothers: changing intra-family relations in a Turkish town', in J. Peristiany (ed.) *Mediterranean Family Structures*, Cambridge: Cambridge University Press.

Kirk, C. and Madsen, D. (1989) *After the Ball*, New York: Doubleday.

Kitzinger, C. (1987) *The Social Construction of Lesbianism*, London: Sage.

Kitzinger, S. (1985) *Woman's Experience of Sex*, London: Penguin.

Klein, F. and Wolf, T.J. (eds) (1985) *Bisexualities: Theory and Research*, New York: Haworth Press.

Klein, M. (ed.) (1989) *Poets for Life*, New York: Crown.

Kleinberg, S. (1980) *Alienated Affections: Being Gay in America*, New York: Warner Books.

Koedt, A. (1974) 'The myth of the vaginal orgasm', in the Radical Therapist Collective (eds) *The Radical Therapist*, London: Penguin.

Kokula, I. (1983) *Formen Lesbischer Subkulture*, Berlin: Rosa Winkel Verlag.

Komin, S. (1988) 'Thai value system and its implication for development in Thailand', in D. Sinha and H. Kao (eds) *Social Values and Development: Asian Perspectives*, London: Sage.

Krieger, S. (1982) 'Lesbian identity and community: recent social science literature', *Signs* 8 (1): 91–108.

Krieger, S. (1983) *The Mirror Dance: Identity in a Women's Community*, Philadelphia, PA: Temple University Press.

Kurdek, L. and Schmitt, J.P. (1987) 'Perceived emotional support from families and friends in members of homosexual, married, and heterosexual cohabiting couples', *Journal of Homosexuality* 14 (3/4): 57–68.

Kutchinsky, B. (forthcoming) *Law, Pornography and Crime: The Danish Experience*, New Haven, CT: Yale University Press.

Laclau, E. and Mouffe, C. (1985) *Hegemony and Socialist Strategy*, London: Verso.

Lady, W. (ed.) (1987) *The Leading Edge: An Anthology of Lesbian Sexual Fiction*, Denver, CO: Lace.

Lang, T. (1940) 'Studies on the genetic determination of homosexuality', *Journal of Nervous and Mental Disease* 92: 55–64.

Lauritsen, J. and Thorstad, D. (1974) *The Early Homosexual Rights Movement (1864–1935)*, New York: Times Change Press.

Lee, J.A. (1987) 'What can homosexual ageing studies contribute to theories of ageing?', *Journal of Homosexuality* 13 (4): 43–71.

Leeds Revolutionary Feminist Group (1981) 'Political lesbianism: the case against heterosexuality', in Onlywomen Press (eds) *Love Thy Enemy?*, London: Onlywomen Press.

Lehne, G. (1989 [1980] 'Homophobia among men: supporting and defining the male role', in M. Kimmel and M. Messner (eds) *Men's Lives*, New York: Macmillan, pp. 416–29.

Lesbian History Group (1989) *Not a Passing Phase: Reclaiming Lesbians in History 1840–1985*, London: The Women's Press.

Lesbian Action for Parenting and Reproductive Rights (1991) Letter to the Editor, *The Pink Paper* 8: 9 February.

Lewis, S.G. (1979) *Sunday's Women! A Report of Lesbian Life Today*, Boston, MA: Beacon.

Leznoff, M. and Westley, W.A. (1955) 'The homosexual community', *Social Problems* 3: 257–63.

Liebman, R. and Wuthnow, R. (eds) (1983) *The New Christian Right*, New York: Aldine.

263

Linden, R. *et al.* (eds) (1982) *Against Sadomasochism: A Radical Feminist Analysis*, Palo Alto, CA: Frog in the Wall Press.

Little, G. (1989) 'Freud, friendship. and politics', in R. Porter and S. Tomaselli (eds) *The Dialectics of Friendship*, London: Routledge, pp. 143–58.

Litwak, E. and Szelenyi, I. (1969) 'Primary group structures and their functions: kin, neighbours, and friends', *American Sociological Review* 34 (4): 465–81.

Lockard, D. (1985) 'The lesbian community: an anthropological approach', in *Journal of Homosexuality* 11: 83–96.

Lofland, L.H. (1973) *A World of Strangers: Order and Action in Urban Public Space*, New York: Basic.

Loulan, J. (1984) *Lesbian Sex*, San Francisco: Spinsters Ink.

Lumsden, I. (1991) *Homosexuality, Society and State in México*, Toronto: Canadian Gay Archives.

Lunde, H. (1988) 'De kommunefarvede danskere – en nation af mindretal' ('The average Danes – a nation of minorities'), *Grus* (Denmark) 9 (26): 23–42.

Lundy, S.E. (1986) '"I do" but I can't: immigration policy and gay domestic relationships', *Yale Law and Policy Review* 5 (157): 13–42.

Lützen, K. (1988) *At prÿve lykken: 25 lesbiske livshistorier (Try your Luck: 25 Lesbian Life Stories)*, Copenhagen: Tiderne Skifter.

Lynch, L. (1990) 'Cruising the libraries', in K. Jay and J. Glasgow (eds) *Lesbian Texts and Contexts: Radical Revisions*, New York: New York University Press.

McIntosh, M. (1968) 'The homosexual role', *Social Problems* 16 (2): 182–92. (Reprinted with a 'Postscript' in K. Plummer (ed.) (1981) *The Making of the Modern Homosexual*, London: Hutchinson, pp. 30–49.)

MacIntyre, S. (1976) 'Who wants babies? The social construction of instincts', in D. Barker and S. Allen (eds) *Sexual Divisions in Society*, Britain: Tavistock, pp. 150–73.

MacKinnon, C. (1982) 'Feminism, Marxism, method and the state: an agenda for theory', *Signs* 7 (3): 515–44.

MacKinnon, C. (1987) *Feminism Unmodified: Discourses on Life and Law*, Cambridge, MA: Harvard University Press.

Macourt, M.P.A. (1989) *How Can We Help You?*, London: Bedford Square Press.

McWhirter, D.P. and Mattison, A.M. (1984) *The Male Couple*, Englewood Cliffs, NJ: Prentice-Hall.

McWhirter, D.P., Sanders, S.A., and Reinisch J.M. (eds) (1990) *Homosexuality/Heterosexuality: Concepts of Sexual Orientation*, Oxford: Oxford University Press.

Maggenti, M. (1990) 'A round table discussion: AIDS and democracy', in B. Wallis (ed.) *Democracy: A Project by Group Material*, Seattle, WA: Bay Press.

Maggenti, M. (1991) 'Women as Queer Nationals', *Out/Look* 11, Winter: 20.

Magneralla, P.J. (1974) *Tradition and Change in a Turkish Town*, New York: Wiley.

Mansfield, P. and Collard, J. (1988) *The Beginning of the Rest of Your Life? A Portrait of Newly-Wed Marriage*, Basingstoke, Hants: Macmillan.

Marotta, T. (1981) *The Politics of Homosexuality*, Boston, MA: Houghton Mifflin.

Marshall, J. (1981) 'Pansies, perverts and macho men: changing conceptions of male homosexuality', in K. Plummer (ed.) *The Making of the Modern Homosexual*, London: Hutchinson.

Martin, D. and Lyon, P. (1972) *Lesbian/Woman*, New York: Bantam.

Masters, W.H. and Johnson, V.E. (1966) *Human Sexual Response*, Boston: Little, Brown & Co.

Meer, T. van der (1988) 'The persecution of sodomites in eighteenth-century Amsterdam', *Journal of Homosexuality* 16 (1/2): 263–307.

Melker, M.E. (1976) 'Meaning and society in the Near East', *International Journal of Middle Eastern Studies* 7 (2/3).

Mieli, M. (1980) *Homosexuality and Liberation: Elements of a Gay Critique*, London: Gay Men's Press.'

Mikkelsen, H. (1984) *Bundfald: Om den 'homoseksuelle fare' i 50'ernes Danmark (Dregs: On the 'Homosexual Danger' in Denmark in the 50s)*, duplicate, Roskilde University Center (Denmark).

Mohr, R.D. (1988) *Gays/Justice: A Study of Ethics, Society and Law*, New York: Columbia University Press.

Moraga, C., Anzaldua, G., Lorde, M., *et al.* (1983) *This Bridge Called My Back*, Massachusetts: Persephone Press.

Mordden, E. (1986) *Buddies*, New York: St Martin's Press.

Moses, A. (1978) *Identity Management in Lesbian Women*, New York: Praeger.

Mulder, N. (1985) *Everyday Life in Thailand*, Bangkok: Duang Kamol.

Murray, S.O. (1984) *Social Theory, Homosexual Realities*, New York: Gay Academic Union.

Murray, S.O. (1987) *Male Homosexuality in Central and South America*, New York: Gay Academic Union.

Murray, S.O. (1988) 'What does "gay community" mean?', in G. Herdt (ed.) *The Ethnography of Gay American Men*, Boston, MA: Beacon.

Nardi, P.M. (1992) 'Sex, friendship and gender roles amongst gay men', in P.M. Nardi (ed.) *Men's Friendships*, Newbury Park, CA: Sage, pp. 173–85.

Nestle, J. (1988) *A Restricted Country: Essays and Short Stories*, London: Sheba.

Nestle, J. and Edel, D. (1981) 'Butch-fem relationships: sexual courage in the 1950s', *Heresies* 12: 22–5.

Newton, E. (1984) 'The mythic mannish lesbian: Radclyffe Hall and the new woman', *Signs* 9 (4): 557–75.

Nichols, M. (1987) 'Lesbian sexuality: issues and developing theory', in Boston Lesbian Psychologies Collective (eds) *Lesbian Psychologies*, Chicago: University of Illinois Press.

Nordic Council of Ministers (1988) *Kvinnor och mn i Norden: Fakta om jmstlldheten 1988 (Men and Women in Nordic Countries: Facts on Equal Opportunities 1988)*, Copenhagen: Nordic Council of Ministers.

Oakley, A. (1979) *Becoming a Mother*, Oxford: Martin Robertson.

O'Brien, S. (1984) '"The thing not named": Willa Cather as a lesbian writer', *Signs* 9: 576–99.

Olson, E.A. (1982) 'Duofocal family structure and an alternative model of husband–wife relationship', in C. Kağıtçıbaşı (ed.) *Sex Roles, Family and Community in Turkey*, Bloomington, IN: Indiana University Press.

O'Meara, J.D. (1989) 'Cross-sex friendship: four basic challenges of an ignored relationship', *Sex Roles* 21 (7/8): 523–43.

Onlywomen Press (eds) (1981) *Love Thy Enemy?*, London: Onlywomen Press.

Østergaard, U. (1989) 'Findes der en dansk politisk kulture?' ('Is there a Danish political culture?'), in A. Holan and J. Normann Jorgensen (eds) *Enhedskultur – helhedskultur*, Copenhagen: Danmarks Laererhojskole.

Özbay, F. (1988) *Turkiy'de Aile ve Ev Halki Yapisi Degisimi*, Istanbul: Institute of Social Sciences, Bogazici University.

Panos Institute, The (1990) *The Third Epidemic: Repercussions of the Fear of AIDS*, London: Panos Publications.

Parker, R. (1985) 'Masculinity, femininity and homosexuality: on the anthropological interpretation of sexual meaning in Brazil', *Journal of Homosexuality* 11 (3/4).

Patten, J. (1991) Letter to Robin Squire, MP, 8 February.

Patton, C. (1985) *Sex and Germs*, London: South End Press.

Paz, O. (1961) *The Labyrinth of Solitude*, New York: Grove Press.

Peplau, L.A. (1988) 'Research on homosexual couples: an overview', in J.P. De Cecco (ed.) *Gay Relationships*, New York: Haworth Press.

Phelan, S. (1989) *Identity Politics: Lesbian Feminism and the Limits of Community*, Philadelphia, PA: Temple University Press.

Pies, C. (1985) *Considering Parenthood*, San Francisco: Spinsters/Aunt Lute (2nd edition 1988).

Pink Book Editing Team (1988) *The Second ILGA Pink Book*, Utrecht: Inferfacultaire Werkgroep Homostudies.

Plummer, K. (1975) *Sexual Stigma: An Interactionist Account*, London: Routledge & Kegan Paul.

Plummer, K. (1978) 'Men in love: observations on male homosexual couples', in M. Corbin (ed.) *The Couple*, Harmondsworth, Middx: Penguin.

Plummer, K. (ed.) (1981a) *The Making of the Modern Homosexual*, London: Hutchinson.

Plummer, K. (1981b) 'Homosexual categories: some research problems in the labelling perspective of homosexuality', in K. Plummer (ed.) *The Making of the Modern Homosexual*, London: Hutchinson.

Plummer, K. (1988) 'Organizing AIDS', in P. Aggleton and H. Homans (eds) *Social Aspects of AIDS*, London: Falmer, pp. 20–52.

Plummer, K. (1989) 'Lesbian and gay youth in England', in G. Herdt (ed.) (1989) *Gay and Lesbian Youth*, New York: Haworth Press, pp. 195–216.

Plummer, K. (1990) 'Herbert Blumer and the life history tradition', *Symbolic Interactionism* 13 (2): 125–44.

Ponse, B. (1978) *Identities in the Lesbian World: the Social Construction of Self*, Westport, CT: Greenwood.

Porter, K. and Weeks, J. (1990) *Between the Acts*, London: Routledge.

Porter, V. (1988) 'Letter to the editor', *Gay Community News* 16 (9): 4.

Poster, M. (1990) *The Mode of Information*, Oxford: Polity Press.

Pritchard, C. and Thompson, B. (1987) Southampton City Council Minority Rights Study.

Prondzynski, I. (1989) 'Women in statistics', *Women of Europe (Supplement)* 30, Brussels: European Communities.

Rabinowitz, D. (1990) 'From the mouths of babes to a jail cell: child abuse and the abuse of justice', *Harpers Magazine* May.

Radicalesbians (1973) 'The woman-identified woman', in A. Koedt, E. Levine and A. Rapone (eds) *Radical Feminism*, New York: Quadrangle Books.

Raymond, J. (1986) *A Passion for Friends: Toward a Philosophy of Female Affection*, Boston, MA: Beacon.

Rich, A., (1976) *Of Woman Born*, New York: Norton.

Rich, A. (1980/1984) 'Compulsory heterosexuality and lesbian existence' *Signs* 5 (4) Summer, and reprinted in A. Snitow, C. Stansell, and S. Thompson (eds) *Desire: The Politics of Sexuality*, London: Virago.

Richards, J. (1987) 'Passing the love of women: manly love and Victorian society', in J.A. Mangan and J. Walvin (eds) *Manliness and Morality: Middle-Class Masculinity in Britain and America 1800–1940*, Manchester: Manchester University Press, pp. 92–122.

Richardson, D. (1987) *Women and AIDS*, Boston, MA: Routledge & Kegan Paul.

Richardson, D. (1989) *Women and the AIDS Crisis*, London: Pandora (2nd edition).

Richardson, D. (1990) *Safer Sex*, London: Pandora.

Richmond, L. and Noguera, G. (1973) (eds) *The Gay Liberation Book*, San Francisco: Ramparts Press.

Rights of Women (1990) 'Backlash against lesbian parenting', *Lesbian Custody*

Project Rights of Women Briefing Paper, London: Rights of Women.

Risman, B. and Schwartz, P. (1988) 'Sociological research on male and female homosexuality', *Annual Review of Sociology* 14: 125–47.

Rorty, R. (1989) *Irony, Contingency and Solidarity*, Cambridge: Cambridge University Press.

Roscoe, W. (1988) 'Making history: the challenge of gay and lesbian studies', *Journal of Homosexuality* 15 (3/4): 1–40.

Ross, M.W. (1988) *The Married Homosexual Man: A Psychological Study*, London: Routledge & Kegan Paul.

Rothblum, E.D. and Cole, E. (1989) (eds) *Lesbianism: Affirming Nontraditional Roles*, New York: Haworth Press.

Rotundo, A. (1989) 'Romantic friendships: male intimacy and middle-class youth in the northern United States, 1800–1900', *Journal of Social History* 23 (1): 1–25.

Rubin, G. (1984) 'Thinking sex', in C. Vance (ed.) (1984) *Pleasure and Danger*, London: Routledge.

Rubin, L. (1985) *Just Friends: The Role of Friendship in Our Lives*, New York: Harper & Row.

Ruehl, S. (1983) 'Sexual theory and practice: another double standard', in S. Cartledge and J. Ryan (eds) *Sex and Love*, London: The Women's Press.

Rupp, L.J. (1989) '"Imagine my surprise": women's relationships in mid-twentieth century America', in M.B. Duberman and M. Vicinus (eds) *Hidden from History*, New York: New American Library, pp. 395–410.

Ruskin, C. (1988) *The Quilt*, New York: Simon & Schuster.

San Francisco AIDS Foundation (1986) 'Lesbians and AIDS: what's the connection?' (July) *Women's AIDS Network*, 4-page brochure.

Sabatier, R. (1988) *Blaming Others: Prejudice, Race and Worldwide AIDS*, London: New Society Publications.

Sabbah, A.F. (1981) *Women in the Muslim Unconscious*, New York: Pergamon Press.

Sandel, M.J. (ed.) (1984) *Liberalism and its Critics*, New York: New York University Press.

Sandoval, C. (1984) 'Comment on Krieger's "Lesbian identity and community: recent social science literature"', in *Signs* 9 (4): 725–9.

Sapadin, L. (1988) 'Friendship and gender: perspectives of professional men and women', *Journal of Social and Personal Relationships* 5 (4): 387–403.

Sartre, J.-P. (1963) *Saint Genet: Actor and Martyr* (trans. B. Frechtman), New York: Braziller.

Schifter Sikora, J. (1989) *La formación de una contracultura*, San José: Costa Rica.

Schneider, B. (1984) 'Peril and promise: lesbian workplace participation', in T. Darty and S. Potter (eds) *Women-Identified Women*, Palo Alto, CA: Mayfield.

Schneider, B. (1992) 'AIDS and class, gender and race relations', in J. Huber and B. Schneider (eds) *The Social Context of AIDS*, California: Sage.

Schreurs, K. (1985) *Het is maarhoeje het bekijkt*, Utrecht: Homostudiesreeks.

Schur, E. (1984) *Labelling Women Deviant: Gender, Stigma, and Social Control*, Philadelphia, PA: Temple University Press.

Schuyf, J. (forthcoming) *Een stilzwijgende samenzwering*, Utrecht: Rijksuniversiteit.

Scruton, R. (1986) *Sexual Desire*, London: Weidenfeld & Nicolson.

Sedgwick, E.K. (1985) *Between Men: English Literature and Male Homosocial Desire*, New York: Columbia University Press.

Sedgwick, E.K. (1991) *Epistemology of the Closet*, London: Harvester Wheatsheaf.

Segal, L. (1990) *Slow Motion: Changing Masculinities, Changing Men*, London: Virago.

Segrest, M. (1989) 'Southern reflections', *Out/Look* Winter: 10–15.

Seiden, A. and Bart, P.(1975) 'Woman to woman: is sisterhood powerful?', in N. Glazer-Malbin (ed.) *Old Family/New Family*, New York: Van Nostrand, pp. 189–228.

Sengers, W.J. (1968) *Gewoon hetzelfde? Een visie op vragen rond de homofilie*, Bussum: Paul Brand.

Shaw, N. and Paleo, L. (1986) 'Women and AIDS', in L. McKusick (ed.) *What to do about AIDS?*, Berkeley, CA: University of California Press.

Sheba Collective (1989) *Serious Pleasure: Lesbian Erotic Stories and Poetry*, London: Sheba.

Sheba Collective (1990) *More Serious Pleasure*, London: Sheba.

Shepherd, S. and Wallis, M. (eds) (1989) *Coming on Strong: Gay Politics and Culture*, London: Unwin Hyman.

Sherrod, D. (1987) 'The bonds of men: problems and possibilities in close male relationships', in H. Brod (ed.) *The Making of Masculinities: The New Men's Studies*, Boston, MA: Allen & Unwin.

Sherrod, D. and Nardi, P.M. (1988) 'The nature and function of friendship in the lives of gay men and lesbians', paper presented at ASA, Atlanta.

Shibutani, T. (1961) *Society and Personality*, Englewood Cliffs, NJ: Prentice-Hall.

Shibutani, T.(1966) *Improvised News: A Sociological Study of Rumor*, Indianapolis: The Bobbs-Merril Company.

Shotter, J. (1984) *Social Accountability and Selfhood*, Oxford: Basil Blackwell.

Showalter, E. (1991) *Sexual Anarchy: Gender and Culture at the Fin de Siècle*, London: Bloomsbury.

Shulman, S. (1983) 'When lesbians came out in the movement', *Trouble and Strife* 1: 51–6.

Shulman, S. (1986) 'Lesbian feminists and the great baby con', *Gossip - Journal of Lesbian Feminist Ethics* 1: 68–90.

Simmel, G. (1971) 'The metropolis and mental life', in *On Individuality and Social Forms*, Chicago: University of Chicago Press. (German original published 1903.)

Simon, W. (1989) 'Commentary on the status of sex research: the postmodernization of sex', *Journal of Psychology and Human Sexuality* 2 (1): 9–37.

Simon, W. and Gagnon, J.H. (1967a) 'Homosexuality: the formulation of a sociological perspective', *Journal of Health and Social Behaviour* 8: 177–85.

Simon, W. and Gagnon, J.H. (1967b) 'Femininity in the lesbian community', *Social Problems* 15: 212–21.

Sirman, N. (1990) 'Koy halkinin aile ve evlilikte guclenme mucadelesi', in S. Tekeli (ed.) *Kadin Bakis Acisindan 1980' ler Turkiye' sinde Kadin*, Istanbul: Iletisim Yayincilik.

Sisley, E.L. and Harris, B. (1977) *The Joy of Lesbian Sex*, New York: Firestone/Simon & Schuster.

Smalley, S. (1987) 'Dependency issues in lesbian relationships', *Journal of Homosexuality* 14 (1/2): 125–35.

Smit, A.M. (1987) *Lesbiese identiteiten binnnen en buiten de vrouwenbeweging*, (unpublished) MA thesis, Tilburg, Katholieke Universiteit Brabant.

Smith-Rosenberg, C. (1975) 'The female world of love and ritual: relations between women in nineteenth-century America', *Signs* (9 (1): 1–29.

Smyth, C. (1990) 'The pleasure threshold: looking at lesbian pornography on film', *Feminist Review* 34: 152–9.

Smyth, C. (1991) 'Get out! Get angry?', *City Limits* 64: 14–21 February.

Snitow, A. (1985) 'Retrenchment versus transformation: the politics of the Anti-pornography Movement', in V. Burstyn (ed.) *Women against Censorship*, Vancouver: Douglas & McIntyre.

Snitow, A. *et al.* (eds) (1983) *Powers of Desire: The Politics of Sexuality*, New York: Monthly Review Press.

Socarides, C.W. (1979) 'The psychoanalytic theory of homosexuality with special reference to therapy', in I. Rosen (ed.) *Sexual Deviation*, Oxford: Oxford University Press (2nd edition).

Social & Community Planning Research (1988/9) *British Social Attitudes*, London: Gower.

Social Trends 21 (1991) London: HMSO.

Sonenschein, D. (1968) 'The ethnography of male homosexual relationships', *Journal of Sex Research* 4 (2): 69–83.

Sontag, S. (1966) 'Notes on "camp"', in *Against Interpretation*, New York: Farrar, Straus & Giroux.

Sontag, S. (1977) *On Photography*, Harmondsworth, Middx: Penguin.

Southern California Women for Understanding (1986) 'Lesbians: low risks for AIDS, high risks for discrimination', (Spring) SCWU Central Educational Committee, West Hollywood. Brochure.

Stanley, L. (1982) '"Male needs": the problems of working with gay men', in S. Friedman and E. Sarah (eds) *The Problem of Men: Two Feminist Conferences*, London: The Women's Press.

Stein, E. (ed.) (1990) *Forms of Desire: Sexual Orientation and the Social Constructionist Controversy*, New York: Garland.

Stimpson, C.R. (1990) 'Afterward: lesbian studies', in K. Jay and J. Glasgow (eds) *Lesbian Texts and Contexts: Radical Revisions*, New York: New York University Press, pp. 37–82.

Stokvis, B. (1939) *De Homo-sexueelen*, Lochem: De Tijkstroom.

Storr, A. (1964) *Sexual Deviation*, London: Penguin.

Sundahl, D. (1985) 'Lesbian Sex-Part 11', *The Advocate* October.

Suttles, G. (1970) 'Friendship as a social institution', in G. McCall, M. McCall, N. Denzin, G. Suttles, and S. Kurth *Social Relationships*, Chicago: Aldine, pp. 95–135.

Tanner, D. (1978) *The Lesbian Couple*, Lexington, MA: Lexington Books.

Task Force on Family Diversity (1987) *Strengthening Families: A Model for Community Action*, City of Los Angeles.

Tatchell, P. (1987) *Aids: A Guide to Survival*, London: Gay Men's Press.

Tatchell, P. (1991) 'Criminal injustice', *The Pink Paper*, 26 October.

Tatchell, P. (1992) *Europe in the Pink: Lesbian and Gay Equality in the New Europe*, London: Gay Men's Press.

Thayer, H.S. (1982) *Pragmatism: The Classic Writings*, Indianapolis: Harlett Publishing.

Thomas, P. and Costigan, R. (1990) 'Promoting homosexuality: Section 28 of the Local Government Act 1988', Cardiff: Cardiff Law School, PO Box 427.

Thompson, B. (1987) Southampton City Council Minority Rights Study.

Thompson, B. (1989) *Pornwars: Moral Panics, Pornography and Social Policy*, paper presented at the American Society of Criminology, Reno.

Thompson, B. (1992) 'Britain's Moral Majority: a socio-historical study', in B. Wilson (ed.) *Religion: Contemporary Issues*, London: Bellew (forthcoming).

Thompson, B. and Annetts, J. (1990) *Soft-Core*, London: GJW.

Thompson, M. (1987) *Gay Spirit: Myth and Meaning*, New York: St Martin's Press.

Tielman, R. (1988) 'Dutch gay emancipation history', *Journal of Homosexuality* 13 (2/3): 9–18.

Timur, S. (1972) *Turkiye'de Aile Yapisi*, Ankara: Hacettepe University.

Tobin, A. (1990) 'Lesbianism and the Labour Party: the GLC experience', *Feminist Review* 34, Spring.

Toch, H. (1971) *The Social Psychology of Social Problems*, London: Methuen.

Touraine, A. (1988) *Return of the Actor: Social Theory in Postindustrial Society*, Minneapolis: University of Minnesota Press.

Troiden, R.R. (1988a) 'Homosexual identity development', *Journal of Adolescent Health Care* 9: 105–13.

Troiden, R.R. (1988b) *Gay and Lesbian Identity*, New York: General Hall.

Trumbach, R. (1977) 'London's sodomites: homosexual behaviour and western culture in the eighteenth century', *Journal of Social History* 11: 1–33.

Turner, B. (1990) 'Outline of a theory of citizenship', *Sociology* 24 (2) 189–217.

Tüsiad (1986) *Turkiye'de Sosyo-ekonomik Onceliker, Hane Gelirleri, Harcamalari Ve Sosyo-ekonomik Ihtiyaclar Uzerine Arastirma Dizisi*, Ankara: Tüsiad.

Vance, C. (ed.) (1984) *Pleasure and Danger*, London: Routledge.

Vicinus, M. (1984) 'Distance and desire: English boarding school friendships', *Signs* 9: 600–22.

Vicinus, M. (1988) '"They wonder to which sex I belong": the historical roots of the modern lesbian identity', in *Homosexuality, Which Homosexuality?*, Amsterdam: An Dekker/Schorer, pp. 171–98.

Warmerdam, H. and Koenders, P. (1987) *Cultuur en ontspanning*, Utrecht: Homostudies.

Warner, M. (1991) 'Fear of a queer planet', *Social Text* 29: 3–17.

Warren, C.A.B. (1974) *Identity and Community in the Gay World*, New York: Wiley.

Warren, C. (1980) 'Homosexuality and stigma', in J. Marmor (ed.) *Homosexual Behavior*, New York: Basic, pp. 123–41.

Watney, S. (1987) *Policing Desires; Pornography, Aids and the Media*, London: Methuen.

Watney, S. and Carter, E. (eds) (1989) *Taking Liberties: AIDS and Cultural Politics*, London: Serpent's Tail.

Weeks, J. (1977) *Coming Out: Homosexual Politics in Britain from the Nineteenth Century to the Present*, London: Quartet (2nd edition 1990).

Weeks, J. (1981a) 'Discourse, desire and sexual deviance: some problems in a history of homosexuality', in K. Plummer (ed.) *The Making of the Modern Homosexual*, London: Hutchinson.

Weeks, J. (1981b) *Sex, Politics and Society: The Regulation of Sexuality since 1800*, London: Longman.

Weeks, J. (1985) *Sexuality and its Discontents: Meanings, Myths and Modern Sexualities*, London: Routledge & Kegan Paul.

Weeks, J. (1989a) 'Decades of desire', *Gay Times* 135.

Weeks, J. (1989b) 'Altruism and the New Right', in S. Watney and E. Carter (eds) *Taking Liberties: AIDS and Cultural Politics*, London: Serpent's Tail.

Weeks, J. (1989c) *Sex, Politics and Society* (2nd edition), London: Longman.

Weeks, J. (1991) *Against Nature: Essays on History, Sexuality and Identity*, London: Rivers Oram Press.

Weinberg, G. (1973) *Society and the Healthy Homosexual*, New York: Doubleday.

Weinberg, T. (1978) 'On doing and being gay: sexual behaviour and homosexual male self-identity', *Journal of Homosexuality* 4: 143–56.

Weitz, R. (1984) 'From accommodation to rebellion: the politicalization of lesbianism', in T. Darty and S. Potter (eds) *Women-Identified Women*, Palo Alto, CA: Mayfield, Ch. 15.

Weston, K. (1991) *Families We Choose: Gays, Lesbians, and Kinship*, New York: Columbia University Press.

Whitam, F.L. and Mathy, R.M. (1986) *Male Homosexuality in Four Societies: A Cross-cultural Study of the US, Guatemala, Brazil, the Philippines*, London: Praeger.

White, E. (1983) 'Paradise found: gay men have discovered that there is friendship after sex', *Mother Jones* June: 10–16.

White, M. (1987) *Aids and the Positive Alternatives*, London: Marshall Pickering.

Wikan, U. (1984) 'Shame and honour; a contestable pair', *Man* 19: 635–52.

Winnow, J. (1989) 'Lesbians working on AIDS', *Out/Look* 5, Summer: 10–18.

Witte, B. (1969) 'Homoseksualiteit', in *Sex in Nederland*, Utrecht: het Spectrum, pp. 127–47.

Wolf, D.G. (1979) *The Lesbian Community*, Berkeley and Los Angeles, CA: University of California Press.

Wolf, D.G. (1984) 'Lesbian childbirth and women-controlled conception', in T. Darty and S. Potter (eds) *Women-Identified Women*, Palo Alto, CA: Mayfield.'

Women's AIDS Project (1986) 'Women address AIDS', 4-page brochure, West Hollywood, CA: Mayfield.

Young, I. (1990) *Justice and the Politics of Difference*, Princeton, NJ: Princeton University Press.

Zahava, I. (ed.) (1989) *Lesbian Lovestories*, California: The Crossing Press.

Zimmerman, B. (1984) 'The politics of transliteration: lesbian personal narratives', *Signs* 9: 663–82.

Zimmerman, B. (1990) *The Safe Sea of Women: Lesbian Fiction 1969–1989*, Boston, MA: Beacon.

NAME INDEX

Adair, N. 68, 70
Adam, Barry 23, 176, 177, 178, 180, 182, 218
Alcorn, Keith 209
Allan, Graham 110, 111, 112, 113
Allyn, E. 30, 31, 32, 35
Altman, Dennis 6, 7, 10, 11, 16, 17, 110, 170, 176, 178, 217, 227, 228, 232, 235
Andrews, Geoff 22
Atkinson, Ti-Grace 6, 187, 194

Baetz, J. 68, 71
Banks, Olive 233
Bart, Pauline 115
Bech, Henning 10, 21, 138, 139, 142
Bell, A.P. 125
Ben-Yehuda, N. 228
Berman, Marshall 13
Berube, Alan 224
Beshstain, J. 7
Bittner, Egon 69
Blackwood, Evelyn 8
Blumstein, P. 113
Boffin, T. 156
Bolak, H. 44
Boston Lesbian Psychologies Collective 8
Bouchier, David 233
Bouhdiba, A. 45
Bowles, G. 12
Bozzett, F. 20
Bradbury, Malcolm 13
Briggs, Senator 217–18
Bright, Suzie 195, 196
Brittan, Arthur 19
Bronski, Michael 7, 16
Butler, Judith 9

Butters, R. 9

Caithness, Earl of 202, 203
Califia, Pat 164, 195, 196, 197
Campbell, Bea 195
Campbell, Lord 203
Carr, A. 125
Carrier, J. 30, 48
Carro, J.L. 123
Carter, E. 156, 178
Cashman, Michael 220, 224
Cass, Vivienne 66, 75
Castells, Manuel 10
Chester, G. 233
Chirimuuta, R. 152
Cohen, J. 22
Collard, J. 88
Collier, C. 231
Collins, J. 30, 31, 32, 35
Connolly, W. 22
Cook, B. 72
Cory, Donald Webster 56
Costigan, R. 222
Coveney, Lal 189
Covina, G. 6
Coyle, A.C. 75
Crimp, Douglas 10, 156
Cruikshank, Margaret 68, 71

Daly, Mary 6, 16
Dank, Barry 66, 75
Darty, T. 100
Davis, M. 55
De Lauretis, Teresa 7, 15
D'Emilio, John 5, 67, 119
Desart, Lord 207, 210
Dewey, John 69
Dickey, J. 233

SUBJECT INDEX

texts 9
Thailand 29, 30, 31, 32, 34, 35, 36,
    128, 129, 130
Thatcherism 201, 228
Turkey, homosexuality in Ch. 3; and
    family 44–6; and gay movement
    46–8; and traditional gender roles
    40–6
turning-points: in coming out 154–5;
    in gay marriages 88

United Kingdom Chs 6, 7, 8, 16, 17,
    18, 19
United States of America Chs 5, 9,
    13, 14

victims 227, 229–33

Well of Loneliness, The 5
West Hollywood 16
Wolfenden Report 203
women of colour 6, 223; *see also* black
    communities, black lesbian
    groups, Chicano community
women of desire 6, 194, 233
women-identified women 6, 194–7
women's movement 6, 10, 11, 116,
    233; *see also* lesbian and gay
    movement, lesbian politics
women's studies 3, 6, 10; *see also*
    lesbian and gay studies

youth 180